# Police Aesthetics

# POLICE AESTHETICS

*Literature, Film, and the Secret Police
in Soviet Times*

*Cristina Vatulescu*

STANFORD UNIVERSITY PRESS

STANFORD, CALIFORNIA

Stanford University Press,
Stanford, California
© 2010 by the Board of Trustees of the
Leland Stanford Junior University
All rights reserved

Library of Congress Cataloging-in-Publication Data

Vatulescu, Cristina.

 Police aesthetics : literature, film, and the secret police in Soviet times /
Cristina Vatulescu.
      p. cm.
 Includes bibliographical references and index.
  ISBN 978-0-8047-6080-5 (cloth : alk. paper) —
  ISBN 978-0-8047-8692-8 (pbk. : alk. paper)
  1. Russian literature—20th century—History and criticism. 2. Russian
literature—Political aspects. 3. Romanian literature—20th century—History and
criticism. 4. Romanian literature—Political aspects. 5. Secret police—Soviet
Union—History. 6. Secret police—Romania—History. 7. Literature and
state—Soviet Union. 8. Motion pictures—Political aspects—Soviet Union.
I. Title.

PG3026.P64.V37   2010
791.43'6556—dc22                                            2009044481

Typeset at Stanford University Press in 10.5/13 Garamond

*For Kiki*

# Contents

4 Secret Police Shots at Filmmaking: The Gulag and Cinema        123

5 Literary Theory and the Secret Police: Writing and
Estranging the Self                                            161

Concluding Thoughts                                            187

# Acknowledgments

This project, like many others, has its beginnings scattered in different places. Part of it probably sprouted, together with my grandmother's tomato seedlings, in her kitchen, as she instructed me in the first household task I can remember. Long before I was trusted with dusting, my grandparents taught me how to turn the radio dial from the static-covered sounds of *Radio Free Europe* to the official Romanian radio station *Programul 1*; I was to do this every time the doorbell rang and they hurried to the door to welcome visitors. From those forbidden radio shows and from countless more or less oblique references I learned that people's lives were recorded in secret police files whose words came back to haunt them. This awareness that our lives were continuously written somewhere, as we talked, slept, or listened to the radio, webbed in and out, often muted by the louder events of one's private life but sometimes stridently brought back by a slip of a tongue: my husband still remembers the panicked tears he cried at the age of four while confessing to his parents that he had somehow slipped to his friend Larsi, also four, the forbidden news of Russia's invasion of Afghanistan. For those given to worrying about the denouement, let me say that it was a happy ending, of sorts: nothing happened. Larsi was a good friend, too busy going about his four year old business to do much with this piece of Afghanistan news. Others, however, spent considerable energy trying to influence the secret police account of their lives and the lives of others. Who knew? If this or that fact got noted in a file, maybe one would finally get that promotion or at least put an end to a grueling commute. Most people I knew seemed intent on keeping themselves just below the radar, making themselves invisible and inaudible, with the ultimate hope of passing *unwritten*. I feared these secret police texts long before I knew that people's lives could also be written as autobiographies, or memoirs, or novels, indeed long before I had any real concept of literature. But when, in 2000, I finally got to read the secret police files of the Romanian Securitate, these texts already belonged to the previous century, and I had a hard time deciphering them other than through analogy with the literary texts that I now read for a living in a different part of the world. It might seem like the reading of literature and the reading of police files would run on different tracks, or air on different wavelengths. But even *Radio Free Europe* and the state-sponsored radio sometimes crossed, and as Vladimir Nabokov quipped, "if parallel lines do not meet, it is not because they cannot, but because they have other things to do."[1] For this book, I convoked literature, film, and policing for a series of encounters, and I luckily caught them a few times when they did not have other things to do. In fact, it turned out that the three of them had a long history together.

Before we get to that history, here are my thanks to those who made this book's writing possible. I'll start with Svetlana Boym, who acquainted me with this liberating line from Nabokov, among many other lines of great literature, and who inspired me to venture out of old intellectual haunts about as far as I could dare, and then some. Indeed, I cannot imagine a more inspiring mentor than Svetlana: her creativity and verve are contagious, and her readings have an uncanny way of cutting right to the heart of the matter. Also at Harvard, William Mills Todd III's expert advice and unsparing support have reassuringly guided me through many twists and turns of research and writing. Julie Buckler's lucid readings, sheer grace, and precious friendship mixed into a unique blend of intellectual and personal support. Amy Powell asked the first question when I presented the first ten pages of this project and went over each and every image when the book was almost done: in the long time that passed between those two moments, she has done a lot more for this book and stayed a true friend. I also owe thanks to Giuliana Bruno, Julie Cassiday, Julia Chadaga, Marina Goldovskaya, John Henriksen, Barbara Johnson, Esther Lieberman, John Mackay, Jann Matlock, Robb Moss, Monica Onojescu, Natalia Pokrovsky, Cathy Popkin, Eric Rentschler, Yuri Tsivian, and Julia Vaingurt.

The Harvard Society of Fellows has been a true haven for writing, offering the best of teas and colleagues. This book has hugely benefited from the greatest luxury the Society gives its fellows—time—as well as from the readings, discussions, and all sorts of wonderful support offered by Edyta Bojanowska, Jonathan Bolton, Manduhai Buyandelgeriyn, Deborah Coen, Donald Fanger, Anna Henchman, Barry Mazur, Diana Morse, Ben Olken, Elaine Scarry, Amartya Sen, Benjamin Spector, Jurij Striedter, Seth Sullivant, and last but certainly not least, Tara Zahra.

Becoming part of the Department of Comparative Literature and a close affiliate of the Department of Russian and Slavic Studies at New York University has given a new impetus to this book, as I found fresh inspiration in my colleagues' intellectually stimulating company as well as in my students' unparalleled drive to share opinions and test ideas. For invaluable readings and comments I am particularly thankful to Mikhail Iampolski, Jacques Lezra, Nancy

Ruttenburg, and Mark Sanders. To them, as well as to Gabriela Basterra, Eliot Borenstein, Ana Dopico, Yanni Kotsonis, Anne Lounsbery, Tim Reiss, Avital Ronnell, Richard Sieburth, and Xudong Zhang, I am also grateful for being so welcoming at first and supportive throughout. My research assistants, Diana Hamilton, Mihaela Păcurar, Jennifer Furman, Sarah O'Hare, and Dina Moyal, have greatly helped me through their resourcefulness and dedication.

I would also like to thank Consiliul Național pentru Studierea Arhivelor Securității, in particular Csendes Ladislau, Ancuţa and Valeriu Median, as well as Cristina Anisescu, Alina Ilinca, Silviu Moldovan, Gheorghe Onişoru, Dragoş Petrescu, Liviu Pleşa, and Claudiu Secaşiu, for granting and facilitating my access to materials from the former Securitate archives. I am also very grateful to Irene Lusztig for sharing the secret police files and film concerning her grandmother, Monica Sevianu. The Davis Center for Russian Studies at Harvard has generously supported my fieldwork in Russia and Eastern Europe for five years, and also granted me a yearlong Writing Fellowship for 2003–2004. I have also benefited from the support of the Kokkalis Foundation Summer Research Grant in 2000, the Open Society Archives (Budapest) Summer Research Grant in 2002, the John Thornton Kirkland Fund Term-Time Research Fellowship in the spring of 2003, the generous support of the Harvard University Milton Fund, 2007–2008, and the NYU Humanities Initiative, 2010.

The existence of this book owes greatly to Emily-Jane Cohen, my editor at Stanford University Press. Not only has her sustaining enthusiasm, which welcomed the book submission, never wavered, but it was buttressed with the insight, tact, and responsiveness that made sure this book happened. I thank her and her editorial assistant, Sarah Crane Newman, whose always prompt help has ensured that the book will read and look better. As in-house editor, John Feneron sensitively guided the manuscript through the various editorial and production stages. Jeff Wyneken copyedited the manuscript with much care and understanding. I am also deeply indebted to my readers for getting involved with the project and offering invaluable advice for its revision. Now knowing that the first reading came from Catharine Nepomnyashchy, I am greatly pleased to be able to thank her for her judicious readings and precious support.

My friends and family have offered great readings, stiff drinks, warm meals, and the best perspective on my work. I first thank my beloved grandparents, Maria and Toader Marian, Ana and Pantelie Vatulescu, as well as my sister Simina and her bustling family, Laura, Paul, and Vlad Bodea. I also thank Jenny Barber, Mihaela Bojin, Peter Brown, Frank Buffone, Tom Craveiro, Jacobia Dahm, Alan Dee, Sarah Demeuse, Lia and Rica Eleches-Lipsitz, James Habyarimana, Macartan Humphreys, Clementine Igou, Janet Irons, Sidney Kwiram, Keena

Lipsitz, Dave and Michelle Merrill, Svetlana Mudrik, Bia Pandrea, Grigo, Renate, and Grigore Pop-Eleches, Susan Protheroe, Nazy Roth, Bogdan Vasi, Balint and Curie Virag, and Owen Wozniak. Howard Wishnie's wisdom and deep care have made him a life-changing interlocutor; this book, and much else, has benefited greatly from our dialogue. One of the best things about writing a book is that you get to thank, in beautiful typeset letters, those who deserve more gratitude than one ever manages to adequately express. No one fits that description better than my parents, so it gives me deep pleasure to give this printed hug to Rodica and Dan Vatulescu, who still find new ways to love and support me, such as crossing an ocean to help care for my newborn. Finally, I thank my daughter, Veronica Vatulescu-Eleches, for making her wondrous appearance, and for learning to sleep through the night just in time for the revisions.

The dedication goes to Kiki Pop-Eleches, who accompanied me every step of the way, getting farther than Solovki and closer than I thought possible.

# Police Aesthetics

# Introduction

The history of Russia ... could be considered from two
points of view: first, as the evolution of the police ... and
second, as the development of a marvelous culture.
—Vladimir Nabokov, *Speak, Memory!*[1]

## Zones of Contact: Literature, Film, and the Secret Police

Broadly defined, the two subjects of this book—twentieth-century Eastern European culture and the secret police—largely fit the plan of study that
Nabokov suggests in my epigraph. However, while Nabokov emphasizes the
unbridgeable chasm between the "marvelous culture" and "the police," this
book explores their entangled intersections. Indeed, I am intent on mapping
a wide range of relationships between culture and policing, and probing their
still unfathomed depth. Not only did the secret police shape many an artist's
biography; its personal files redefined the way a life, and thus biography itself,
was to be written in Soviet times. How did the secret police write about its
subjects in the infamous personal file? What impact did this powerful new
genre of writing have on the literature of its times? How did the secret police's
penchant for confiscating diaries and extracting confessions influence writing
in the first person? What uses did the secret police have for the cinema? And
what fantasies did cinema harbor about policing? What role did cinema play
in the first Soviet show trial? Why were avant-garde filmmakers mounting
their cameras on top of machine guns? What were film cameras doing in the
Gulag? And how was the moving image affected by its excursion through
the camps? How did vision, visual technologies, and policing intersect in the
foundational decades of the Soviet regime?

Before setting out in search of answers to these questions, I will address
the first query that usually greets this project: How could the secret police,
and its key artifacts, such as personal files and films, play a role in the culture
of its times if it was indeed *secret?* The following anecdotes should give a

preliminary sense of the degree of awareness of the secret police in contemporary writers' circles. Two of the protagonists of my study, Isaac Babel and Mikhail Bulgakov, crossed paths early in their careers when they were asked to polish the prose of a top secret-police agent, Fedor Martinov, whose short stories were closely based on investigation files.[2] Bulgakov edited Martinov's story on Saban, self-defined as "universal criminal and fighter for freedom."[3] At the time, Bulgakov's work was showing a growing interest in criminality; he was "in the process of writing *Zoika's Apartment (Zoikina kvartira)*, a play whose characters came out of criminal investigations. (In the first version of the play, an epidiascope was supposed to show the audience mug shots from actual files)."[4] Babel edited and wrote an introduction to Martinov's "The Bandits," a story based on the Cheka investigation of a holdup of Lenin's car.[5] Even before this incident, Babel was deemed well qualified to assist the secret police in its dealings with language. In his youth, he had worked as a translator for the Cheka. His interest in the secret police lasted until the tragic end of his life: before he was shot in the secret police headquarters, he was researching a book about the secret police using his strong personal connections with some of its leaders. Viktor Shklovsky, another strong presence in my study, traced his own infamous turn toward the establishment (a critical moment not only for his own oeuvre but for the Formalist movement in general) to the experience of reading a secret police file on himself. "Just before 1937. An acquaintance of mine who worked in the Cheka brought me a file he wanted to show me, with documents against me. I saw that they were doing a poor job, that there was a lot that they didn't know about me. But they knew enough to make me a center [of a conspiracy]."[6] Even if they did not have direct access to the files, most writers, indeed most of the population, had a vested interest in knowing what their file contained, and they could make educated guesses.

The word *secret* is then misleading—the police was never interested in hiding its existence, and instead put up a highly visible spectacle of secrecy. Indeed, the Soviet secret police was the subject of a carefully orchestrated public cult, in full force at the peak of the 1937 purges, when "the publicity for the NKVD flood[ing] the national press included poems about Ezhov [the head of the NKVD] and the police, articles about espionage techniques, photographs of police officials" and a grand gala celebration of the twenty-year anniversary of the secret police held in the Bol'shoi Theater and heavily covered in both print and film.[7] One of the models of socialist realist art, *Belomor (Belomorsko-Baltiiskii kanal imeni Stalina)*, a book written as celebration of a labor camp, was coedited by the OGPU camp chief together with two leading Soviet writers, Maxim Gorky and Leopold Averbakh.[8] The conversion stories of the various criminals are explicitly based on their secret police files and illustrated with original mug shots, so that the OGPU is the most featured author in the bibliography.[9]

Why then use the word *secret*, and in general the name "secret police"? It is certainly not for the lack of names. The dizzying succession of acronyms that have stood for the Soviet secret police (Cheka, GPU, OGPU, NKVD, NKGB, MGB, MVD, KGB) speaks of the institution's attempts at creating a new language that does not reveal its referent but rather mystifies it. Even for Russian speakers, it takes a dictionary to remember what "OGPU" stands for, and when one sees that it is the "United Governmental Political Administration," one is not much the wiser. In any case, the more the names changed, the more the fetishism of the secrecy-enshrouded acronyms stayed the same. The Romanian secret police, the other subject of this study, has displayed a similar inclination for frequent name changes, preserving however the key term that has become its standard abbreviation: the Securitate.[10] I use these particular names or acronyms when I refer to a specific period, but while writing a book that often refers to these institutions in synchronic and comparative ways, I needed one general appellation. Recent scholarly literature uses "political police," "secret police," and "security services," often interchangeably.[11] No matter how much the secret police itself might bristle at this appellation, I do believe that *police* is a more accurately descriptive term than *organ*, *agency*, *commission*, *service*, or *administration*—the terms most often featured in the acronyms. Starting with the Cheka and ending with the KGB or Securitate, all of these "organs" engaged in policing activities—surveillance, investigation, arrest, detention—and in fact went beyond regular policing in ways that are usually associated with a secret police. In terms of their goals and their means, they were certainly policing the population more than they were doing it a service, or assuring its security, as "security services" suggests.[12] "Political police," which calls the police by its name, has the advantage that both the secret police and its critics have used the word "political." However, its common use by different parties usually bespeaks misunderstandings rather than dialogue—the regime meant it as a compliment to its security organs, while its critics use it from the perspective of a human rights discourse that sharply distinguishes between penal and political crimes. "Secret police" also creates its own misunderstandings, particularly the idea that the existence of the police was hidden, which was manifestly untrue. I keep the appellation, however, because I think that the histrionic show of secrecy and the actual investment in policing the population did define these institutions.

Such histrionic secrecy is aptly illustrated by a well-known Stalinist icon: the windows of the secret police headquarters (Lubianka), brightly lit throughout

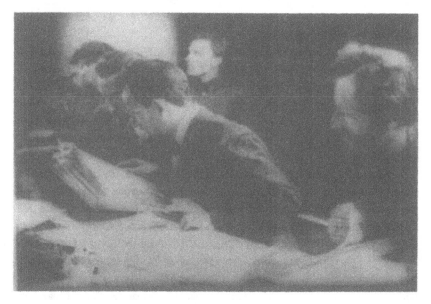

Court secretaries reading a file. *Kino-Pravda 7,* 1922, frame enlargement.

the night. Lubianka's windows correspond to a historical truth, since interrogations were often conducted at night. At the same time, they are a fitting
symbol for the Stalinist spectacle of secrecy. While the brightly illuminated
windows exposed nothing, the terror within was not eclipsed; instead, it was
carefully framed in secrecy and exhibited as the monopoly spectacle of the
Stalinist night. Although the details of the spectacle were impossible to make
out, the lights alone were arresting enough. Lubianka's windows invite comparison with the window that Ortega y Gasset made into a powerful metaphor for different modes of signification.[13] Realism invites the viewer to look
straight through its signifiers—whether words or images—like through a window giving into a beautiful garden. Modernism invites the viewer to focus on
the surface of the window, on the signifier itself. The Stalinist window stands
for yet another regime of signification, where the shiny signifier captures the
gaze only to refract it right back to the viewer. There is no garden in sight; and
the light behind the shiny window can always turn into a searchlight, another
stock image of the times.

The files were at the heart of this spectacle of secrecy. Like the secret
police itself, the files were routinely paraded in front of the public. A sequence
from Dziga Vertov's newsreel coverage of the 1924 trial of the Socialist Revolutionaries, usually considered the earliest model of the Soviet show trial,
showcases the secret police files as tantalizing visual spectacle. In another

Close-up perusal of a secret police file. *Solovki,* 1928, frame enlargements.

documentary film of the period, *Solovki* (1928), we see close-ups of police file covers, and hands browsing them at leisure, sometimes stopping to allow for a quick close-up of a particular page. This dramatic presentation of the file draws our attention to it but makes sure that we do not get close enough to actually read its contents.

Even if one did get close enough to read the files, secrecy still jealously shrouded their contents from prying eyes. Pseudonyms replaced names, and fictitious addresses obscured the secret meeting places, which were also the subject of "house files."[14] The proliferation of nicknames, abbreviations, acronyms, and euphemisms actually makes the files largely illegible to lay-people, to the point that one needs a dictionary. In fact, the present-day cus-todians of the Romanian Securitate archives wisely posted on their website a dictionary of terms and abbreviations used in Securitate documents.[15] Some of the abbreviations and code words follow common logic, but many do not. Among my favorites is the baptism of the aural surveillance technology with the biblical-sounding name Teofil.[16] The code names for Soviet surveillance technology makes one think of reading the adventures of a *ménage à trois,* as Tat'iana, Sergei, and Ol'ga stand in for radio, telephone, and visual sur-veillance.[17] The ubiquitous "top secret" seal ritually showcases this brand of secrecy. In a dramatic illustration of Hannah Arendt's theory that in totalitar-ian societies the spectacle of secrecy was necessary to camouflage the absence of a secret, this spectacle of secrecy was, at its height, meant to frame the uncovering of the (fabricated) anti-Stalinist plots.[18] In the absence of actual plots, the spectacle of secrecy remains like a highly wrought frame around an image that has long crumbled.

The secrecy that kept the Soviet-era file away from critical readings also knowingly framed it as the center of obsessive fascination. As a result of the carefully orchestrated presentation of the files, their number and reach was not only constantly guessed at but often overestimated. In *The Origins of Totalitarianism*, Hannah Arendt wrote that each Soviet citizen was believed to have a file.[19] The belief was widespread: the opening of the archives was a disappointment to many who found out that they did not have files, given the general perception that "everyone who was anyone had their own lengthy file."[20] But chances were, even if not the subject of a lengthy file, a significant portion of the population was at least entered in a secret police registry. Approximately seven million people, or one third of the total adult population, appeared in the Securitate's general registry already in 1965.[21] Writers and artists in general were singled out as subjects of files. Already in 1919, a Cheka document establishing categories of people to be put under surveillance places artists at the very top of the list, sandwiched between "specialists" and "speculators."[22] Vitaly Shentalinsky put the point bluntly: "Lubianka did not neglect a single major writer."[23] Romanian bard Alexandru Andrieş sang wryly, "I am a bit of an artist, so I have a guardian angel . . . securist."[24]

The files were the objects of intense preoccupation and fascination, and I think it is fair to say that they exerted a stronger impact on the public and literary imagination than many books in the state libraries. As is well known, the secret police had a keen interest in and incommensurable power over men and women of letters. Writers, publishers, censors, or anyone having much to do with the written word were deeply affected by the words written about them within the gray binders. Furthermore, the police file sometimes grew precisely by devouring literary texts. It routinely incorporated manuscripts and turned them into incriminating evidence. Whole books or just isolated sentences perversely severed out of their context lived a second life within these binders, too often burying their authors. Personal letters, manuscripts, and published work acquired strange new configurations within the files. Sometimes all that is left of a lifetime's collection of books are the lonely dedication pages, hastily ripped out during house searches and meticulously sewn together in the file. Dedication pages were high on the wanted list, as they unwittingly divulged, at a glance, connections that were (too) often deemed incriminating. (The police of that time eyed them as greedily as the present-day police eyes suspect cell phones.) However, the crossing of boundaries between files and literature was much more extensive and complex than this literal incorporation, and as such it deserves closer analysis than it has been hitherto given. The secret police file competed with propaganda as the largest area of state textual production, filling thousands of miles of archives. The file won the battle over propaganda in the fascination it exerted on the public. But propaganda certainly won the competition for the attention of literary critics, who unlike historians have largely overlooked the opening of the former secret police archives.[25]

This has not always been true. Contemporary literary critics were keenly interested in the relationship between literature and extra-artistic genres, including the secret police file. Leading Formalist critic Boris Tomashevskii cautioned against a kind of literary biography that could turn into a denunciation, and found it necessary to remind literary historians that "the biography they need was neither the curriculum vitae nor the investigation file [*sledstvennoe delo*]" of the writer.[26] Andrei Bely wrote to the GPU asking them to move his diary from the box of confiscated manuscripts to his file, so that it could be used for "the study of his literary and ideological character in its full complexity."[27] To his satisfaction, the GPU agreed that the diary belonged in the file.[28] Tomashevskii's and Bely's comments are rooted in a keen awareness of their times and in a deep interest in the porosity between literature and nonliterary writing, an interest that defined contemporary literary theory and practice.

The secret police file emerged and acquired its overwhelming authority precisely at a time when the authority of literary texts was in deep crisis.[29] A wide-ranging modernist phenomenon, this crisis in the authority of the text was in the Soviet Union exacerbated and fundamentally shaped by a distinct political course. As contemporary writers were deeply aware, the authority of the text as well as of its author was radically undermined by censorship and political persecution. In 1929, shortly before his one-man journal was closed down, Boris Eikhenbaum wrote:

> A writer cuts today a grotesque figure. He is by definition inferior to the average reader, since the latter, as a professional citizen, is assumed to have a consistent, stable and clear-cut ideology. As for our reviewers—critics we do not have anymore, since no differences of opinions are permissible—they are certain to be infinitely superior to, and more important than, the writer in the same way in which the judge is always superior to, and more important than, the defendant.[30]

Responding to the politicized crisis in the authority of the literary texts, another Formalist, Iurii Tynianov, expressed a popular new idea when he argued, "The novel finds itself in an impasse: what is needed today is a sense of a new genre, i.e., a sense of decisive novelty in literature."[31] According to Formalist theory, when a literary genre finds itself in an impasse, the way is paved for subliterary or extraliterary genres to infiltrate it and infuse new life into it. The Formalists believed that the way out of the contemporary impasse of the novel was through factography (*literatura fakta*), "a mixture of half-fictional, half-documentary genres" which emphasized the use of reportage, documents, statistics, and diaries.[32]

In literary practice as in theory, the 1920s were a time when the boundaries between literature and nonliterature appeared manifestly fluid. Influential

members of the avant-garde dramatically proclaimed the end of the separation between art and life. Nikolai Evreinov theorized the breaking of the
fourth wall in theater, arguing that "to make life theatrical, this will be the duty
of every artist. A new breed of directors will appear—directors of life."[33] His
famous 1920 in situ reconstruction of the Revolution's iconic moment—*The
Storming of the Winter Palace*—put some of these ideas into practice. Another
intriguing application of his theories was suggested in an article advertising
theater's uses for policemen and secret investigators.[34] It is significant that
even the Formalists, long criticized for their defense of the autonomy of art,
came to argue that "there is no unbridgeable chasm, indeed, no fixed boundary, between the esthetic and the non-esthetic."[35] While the Formalists maintained their critique of the mimetic function of art, they became avidly interested in the shifting boundaries between literature and nonliterature: "The
notion of literature changes all the time. . . . Literature never mirrors life, but
it often overlaps with it."[36] According to Tynianov, it was precisely when the
literary system was in crisis that it tended to shift its boundaries by overlapping with other "systems" that dominated society at a particular time. Some
favorite Formalist examples from literary history include the influence of the
"system of polite society" and its textual practices—such as album and letter
writing—on Pushkin's lyrics; and the influence of "the system of popular
culture," with its feuilletons, on Chekhov's short stories and on Dostoevsky's
novels. Following in their footsteps, I will attempt to understand how a defining "system" of Soviet society—the secret police—and its main textual and
visual practices overlapped with the dramatically shifting boundaries of contemporary literature and film.

Building from Russian Formalist as well as Bakhtinian theories about the
intersection of aesthetic and extra-aesthetic genres, part of this study traces
the relationship between the personal file and key representatives of two literary genres: the novel and autobiography.[37] The personal file brought together
some of Bakhtin's favorite examples of extra-artistic genres, "the confession,
the diary, travel notes, biography, the personal letter," "the shopping list, telephone conversations," "public rumor, gossip, [and] slander,"[38] and became
the most widespread and authoritative account of an individual life in Soviet
times. It did so at a time when, as we have seen, the novel was undergoing a major crisis of authority, while first-person narratives proliferated in
myriad attempts to come to terms with the radical transformations of the self
and its position in a society undergoing profound changes.[39] I trace the ways
in which selected literary authors came to terms with this powerful genre,
whether through strategies of appropriation, adaptation, parody, exorcism, or
exposure. I have tried to go beyond a catalogue of explicit secret police file

cameos in literature toward close readings aimed to identify the files' influence not only on what was or was not written but also on *how* literary texts were written. Since I am interested in showing just how deep-seated this "zone of contact" between the files and literature was, I have tried to go beyond the most obvious choices of texts that famously feature the secret police. There will be relatively few references to Alexander Solzhenitsyn and other famous Gulag memoirists; instead, I have chosen to focus on writers whose relationship to the secret police and to politics in general was more ambiguous, such as Isaac Babel, Mikhail Bulgakov, Maxim Gorky, and Viktor Shklovsky.

In Russia literature has traditionally epitomized the arts' relationship to power, with Alexander Solzhenitsyn famously commenting that major writers served as a second government.[40] My focus on literature then almost goes without saying. Additionally, given my twentieth-century time line, it seemed important to understand how cinema—the new "most important of all arts," according to Lenin—also fared in relationship to power and its police. It turns out that after a short period of hesitation between treating cinema as a potential suspect or seeing it as a precious propagandist, the secret police arrived at an appreciation for the importance of this "ideological weapon," founding the popular association the Society of Friends of Soviet Cinema (Obshchestvo druzei sovetskogo kino, or ODSK), which was led by none other than the first head of the Cheka, Felix Dzerzhinsky. A strong presence in the first decades of Soviet cinema, ODSK was particularly interested in monitoring cinema reception, to the point where it even pioneered scientific audience surveys.[41] And as "all cinemas and theaters" had, by law, "to put at the disposal of the 'political control department' of the OGPU permanent seats (no further than the fourth row)," few film critics can rival secret police data on early cinema reception.[42]

The legendary beginnings of director Fridrikh Ermler show that a Chekist could not only get free admission to the cinema but also had a good shot at film school.[43] In 1915, as a seventeen-year-old "almost illiterate" errand-boy, Vladimir Markovich Breslav traveled to Moscow in the hopes of becoming a film star.[44] Quickly disappointed, in 1918 he was already working as a spy under the name "Fridrikh Ermler" in German-occupied territories. By 1920 Ermler transferred to the Petrograd Cheka, keeping his spy name to the end of his life.[45] Still dreaming of becoming a movie actor, in 1923 the now seasoned Chekist walked up to the Institute of the Screen Arts, where the student-policeman informed him that he had to apply and be selected to matriculate. Ermler pulled out his Browning pistol and walked right in saying, "*This* has selected me." As Ermler proudly recounted, his job at the Cheka continued to help him in his cinema career.[46] So he held on to his revolver and even pulled it out again while directing *Fragment of an Empire* (1929), when he threatened to shoot his star, Fedor Nikitin, for "insubordination on the set."[47] To the surprise of Ermler aficionados, it has transpired from Lenfil'm production papers that Ermler's last film, *Judged by History* (*Pered sudom istorii*, 1965), was also "made with the active assistance of the KGB [*pri aktivnom sodeistvii KGB*]."[48] Indeed, a letter written by Ermler to the KGB on May 9, 1965, expresses his "pride for being creatively linked to the KGB," and his belief that "without you, Chekists, it wouldn't have been possible to realize my last film, *Judged by History*."[49] While Ermler's career is certainly not typical, it vividly shows that the secret police's influence on cinema went far beyond censorship. My study traces the various roles that the secret police played in the foundational decades of Soviet cinema, from censor, to self-styled model spectator, audience watchdog, sponsor, protagonist, and auteur.

The secret police openly or covertly supported, commissioned, or authored films that ranged from short newsreels to full-length documentaries and feature films. Some training films, such as demonstrations of how to conduct an apartment search, an arrest, or a surveillance assignment, were meant only for internal circulation. While we know about the existence of these films from secret police documents or criminology manuals, they remain even more inaccessible than the files. Even when the law specifies that all the collections of the former secret police have to be passed into the public domain, the visual materials are the last to surface. I spent years searching for such films with only limited success. For example, while working in the Open Society Archives in Budapest, I came across a collection of training films made by the Hungarian Interior Ministry.[50] But I soon realized that arguably the most important secret police films, like the purloined letter, were not in closed archives but out in the open. For example, the secret police ordered the first feature-length Russian sound film, *Road to Life (Putevka v zhizn')*. Openly dedicated to the founding head of the secret police, Felix Dzerzhinsky, *Road to Life* not only made more money at the box office than any other Soviet film before but also won accolades at the first Venice Film Festival and is still shown in art houses as a vintage treat. *Road to Life* was part of a series of early films about the Gulag that the secret police supported in order to mold popular opinion about the camps. My analysis of this fascinating, if largely forgotten, cinematic corpus follows its ever-shifting representation of the Soviet antihero—whether petty criminal or state enemy—and the crafty manipulation of the audience. Furthermore, it reveals highly influential contemporary positions toward vision and visual technologies, such as the promotion of the most fashionable way to look in the Stalinist 1930s; watchfulness or vigilance (*bditel'nost'*); the cultivated suspicion toward empirical vision; and the gradual privileging of fiction film, especially melodrama, over documentaries.

It was not the secret police, however, that first discovered cinema's potential for policing but some of the most resourceful young Soviet filmmakers. As Boris Groys has influentially shown, despite their many glaring differences, Soviet avant-garde and socialist realist artists shared a passionate rejection of the autonomy of art: artists, freed from the burden of slavishly representing reality, were to play a great role in the construction of the new society.[51] What this role would be, exactly, was up for heated debate, and various models were proposed. While Stalin later famously granted artists the role of "engineers of the human soul," the three Soviet filmmakers featured in Chapter 3—Dziga Vertov, Alexander Medvekin, and Ivan Pyr'ev—sometimes chose the secret police agent, state prosecutor, and criminologist as their role models. This study, then, sheds light on one particular way in which early Soviet cinema engaged with contemporary reality—by aiming to police it. This was certainly not a monolithic or even coherent movement: Ivan Pyr'ev is remembered as a prolific socialist realist director, while Dziga Vertov and Alexander Medved-kin have been repeatedly appropriated as pioneers of avant-garde, modernist, experimental, and cinema verité movements. While Vertov and Medvedkin's mythology has continuously developed, it has persistently ignored some of the artistic personae that they themselves carefully cultivated. In exploring the policing fantasies entertained by these filmmakers, I do not aim to paint over their now canonical portraits as cinematic visionaries who suffered censor-ship and even persecution. Instead, I aim to add another layer of complexity to that portrait, carefully foregrounding the differences between their various cinematic fantasies, theories, and practices. For indeed, while some of these early Soviet filmmakers' experiments in "kino policing" were complicit with the secret police, others exposed or parodied the work of policing. It is precisely because of these differences that the story of cinema's fantasies about policing deserves to be told along with the story of the secret police's fantasies about cinema.

## Reading a Secret Police File

My project is rooted in a reading dilemma. It took four often-frustrating years since I first started my search for access to secret police materials until I finally sat down in front of a desk overflowing with gray binders—the files of some of my favorite Romanian writers. The suspense was long in the making, and this was no doubt one of the most exhilarating moments of my life; but soon after opening the binders, I realized that I had no idea how to read the thousands of pages of wiretapping logs, mangled literary manuscripts, love letters, newspaper clippings, informers' reports, and scalloped-edged photographs. I had not been at such a loss in front of a written text since the age of fourteen, when in the wake of the 1989 Romanian revolution a new literature teacher led a class, whose students had been raised on socialist realism, in analyzing the stories of Jorge Luis Borges.

I soon discovered that I was the second reader for most of these files. My predecessor, either a supervising investigator or a secret police archivist, had left thick red pencil marks, which had survived the decades. I could thus easily trace the trajectory of that first reading, with its narrow emphasis on the main narrative and the conclusive evidence, names, and court decisions. The red thread rushed to the inexorable closing of the files, intent on quelling any questions along the way. Following it, I gradually learned to decode acronyms and pseudonyms, and to read for the plot. However, I soon lost my place in this tedious, complicit reading, which might have helped make some preliminary sense of these puzzling texts but was far from doing them justice. Devising a way of reading the files, and later watching secret police films, turned out to be no less exacting, if more intellectually absorbing, a challenge than getting access to the archives had been. In this process, I came to rely on insights and approaches from a variety of disciplines. I delved into criminology and history to understand how police records have been structured and altered through time. Following the changing narrative of the files also required an excursion into Soviet psychology, whose shifting views of human nature are closely reflected in the files. Most often, however, I rallied reading strategies I had gleaned from my own field, literary studies, building particularly on work that broaches the question: "Do we have a way of thinking reading as other than an encounter with a book?" How can we responsibly read what urgently presents itself to us—whether the testimonies of apartheid victims or secret police files? Far from a mechanical application of existent reading tools, the interpretation of these challenging texts tests both the potentials and the limits of literary studies, "alter[ing] our very concept of reading."[52]

A few pages into his fascinating essay on prerevolutionary French police files, Robert Darnton notes that his analysis would have ended right there had not "literary historians taught historians to beware of texts, which can be dissolved into 'discourse' by critical reading, no matter how solid they may seem. So the historian should hesitate before treating police reports as hard nuggets of irreducible reality, which he has only to mine out of the archives, sift, and piece together in order to create a solid reconstruction of the past."[53] My readings of the secret police files draw on the rich corpus of scholarship which both theorizes and demonstrates the uses of literarily informed readings that focus on the rhetoric of historical and legal documents, while also questioning the clear-cut distinction between rhetoric and those "hard nuggets of irreducible reality."[54]

There are few archives where these "nuggets" have proved harder to find than in the archives of Eastern European secret services, which house the records of millions of fabricated crimes and hush the traces of countless criminal punishments. It's not that this has not been tried. The opening of the archives has been dominated by an avid search for the truth about the past, which betrays an enduring belief in the authority of their holdings even on the part of the staunchest critics or victims of the secret police. Lustration laws rely on the secret police archives for information on the eligibility of present-day politicians for public office. However, looking for reliable answers in the archives of an institution famous for its misinformation departments has proved to be a difficult task. I will approach the archives from a complementary angle by focusing precisely on the files' rhetoric, which one is too often tempted to sift right through in search of the "nuggets" of true information. My belief is that if we are going to get anywhere in the study of these archives, not least to the famous nuggets, we have to patiently (re)learn to read. Sometimes wildly or craftily skewed records of historical fact, the files are at the same time priceless representations of the values, apprehensions, and fantasies entertained by the secret police. While a personal file can mislead about the particulars of a victim's fate, its close reading can be abundantly revealing about what the secret police understood by evidence, record, writing, human nature, and criminality.

This approach is certainly not to be applied en masse to all the holdings of the secret police archives. The activity of the secret police overstepped any reasonable borders: at various periods of its history the secret police supervised the production of all maps, the registration of marriages and divorces, and the running of optics factories. Its busy statistics departments collected the most random information and processed it into kilometers of reports. Many of its collections, from the endless statistics on the production of steel to cloth odor samples carefully bottled and arranged like colorful pickles, would likely blunt the analytical tools sharpened by literary studies before yielding to them. Instead, I have chosen to focus on the archives' most infamous holdings, the personal files, as well as on their little-known film collections.

I will argue that while a typical police file is usually limited to recording one crime, the Soviet-style personal file is defined by its attempt to cover the extensive biography of the suspect. Like any biography, a personal file tells the story of a life; unlike most biographies, the secret police file also had enormous power to radically alter the course of that life, and even to put a full stop to it. How does the secret police go about translating a life into a text? The investigation material collates glimpses of the subject, like blurred photographs taken from the strange angles of hidden cameras. How are they morphed into an authoritative portrait of the subject, as unwavering as a mug shot? How is the hodgepodge of informer reports, confiscated manuscripts, denunciations, intercepted letters, and wiretap logs molded into a conclusive case presented by the prosecution to a judge? What endows this story with authority and persuasiveness? How does this story then culminate in one judicial sentence—to death, to a labor camp, to exile? The secret police has its own ways of doing things with words. The first challenge of this study is to identify the poetics of the personal file, its narrative devices, its rhetorical figures, as well as the shifting contexts of its production and reception.

Who authored the file, and who were its intended and actual readers? Few texts of the period put into practice the much-extolled communist ideal of communal authorship as thoroughly as the personal file.[55] I deliberated at length about the authorship rubric of my reference list: who should go first, the secret police as an institution, the loquacious informer who contributed the most pages to the file, the investigator who synthesized the surveillance reports into an incriminating story, or the archivist who cut all "extraneous material" and sewed the file in its final form? And how do you give credit to the subject of the file, to her testimony or confession, sometimes overlooked, written over or out of the master narrative, and sometimes its climax? The list of authors grew and grew, and then came the question, ridden with uncertainties and ethical conundrums, about who should go first and last. Unwilling to straighten out the complicated web of authors and questions into a linear reference, I finally listed the files by title only, and addressed the question of authorship and readership in my analysis of the files.

Like the authors of the file, its readers were also arranged in a complex and deeply hierarchical web. On the whole, the balance of power was strongly tilted toward readers over writers. In the case of a writer's file, informers and solicited reviewers read the writer's work without the latter being able to access their writing about it. Next in the chain came the investigator, who was able to read the informers' reports while normally denying them access to one another's reports. His reviews could then be read over by a superior, who had the power to overwrite, or rather "overread," previous decisions. Reader and writer were thus bound in a nonreciprocal relationship of authority. The reader's expectations, exigencies, and whims shaped the text more powerfully than the work of any writer. On the lowest step of this reading hierarchy was the subject of the investigation, who had the most interest in reading his file and the least power to do so. Constitutive of the making of each file, this power structure also defined the overall relationship between each citizen (whose vested interest in reading his file was further whetted by a carefully designed spectacle of secrecy) and the secret police, who held exclusive reading rights over its archives.

The last reader of the files was the archivist. Behind the scenes, these éminences grises had (and often still have) unsuspected powers. Vitalii Shenta-linskii's description of his interaction with the Soviet secret police archivists testifies to their past and present power over their holdings.[56] One of the top archivists, Colonel Kraiushkin, explained that he was "'the first to begin the present rehabilitation. . . .' Long before the perestroika began, Kraiushkin had been quietly filling a separate card index with materials about writers, actors and artists who had been arrested or shot."[57] A sensational proof of the archivist's power was given by the 1992 defection to the West of Vasilii Mitrokhin, chief archivist for the foreign-intelligence arm of the KGB, who brought with him thousands of pages of notes on top-secret documents.[58]

A long list of internal Securitate memos on its registration and archive department gives us the insider's view of the role of secret police archivists and challenges the little attention formerly paid to them.[59] The comprehensive list of the archivist's "duties and responsibilities" challenges any notions about reader passivity.[60] The archivist's reading of the material had a literal impact on the text, which was definitively shaped by it. Finishing the work of the investigators, archivists ordered, purged, underlined (in color pencil), collated, and then sewed together the contents of the files.[61] Additionally, the archivists were expected to read all files in their charge "in their entirety," checking and correcting the list of names and the identifying characteristics of all individuals mentioned in the file (including informers), and creating individual registration cards for each.[62] In case this reading identified any suspect individual who might have been previously overlooked and who was still "at large," the archivist had the obligation, and extraordinary power, to immediately forward the compromising material for investigation.[63] In fact, the Securitate ranked archival material highly, right next to informer reports and interrogation-derived intelligence, as a source for the creation of new individual files.[64] The archivist's was a performative reading, one that was actively altering and recreating the text; it was also potentially productive, sowing the seeds for new files in a hothouse environment where they were guaranteed to grow. For as opposed to most institutional archives, which house documents outside of current operational use, the police archive is meant to be routinely searched and "exploited" as a source for new files: as such it is both an active and a self-reproducing archive.

With such precursors, it is difficult not to become self-conscious of one's place as a reader in the archives. What would I get out of reading the files as texts, focusing on their rhetoric and narrative structure? Before I came to answer this question in Chapter 1, I worried that this kind of reading would get me into trouble. Pondering over Walter Benjamin's warning about the dangers of rendering politics "aesthetic," I wondered if my reading of these political documents was in any way aestheticizing them.[65] In the meantime, it became clear to me that the files had been "aestheticized" long before I got to see them. While tracing previous readings of the files, I was struck by a widespread tendency to describe police records in literary terms. Isaac Babel's investigators bragged that Lavrentii Beriia praised their files as "real works of art" (*istinnye proizvedeniia isskustva*).[66] A denunciation or confession became, in secret police jargon, "a literary composition."[67] Evgeniia Ginzburg's investigator tried coaxing her into writing a confession by presenting it as an opportunity to show off her literary skills.[68] By presenting these political documents as literary works, representatives of the secret police drew attention away from their problematic content and onto their formal merits. It is significant that Babel's investigators cited Beriia's compliment while they were themselves put on trial in 1956 for their part in past secret police abuses. As their writing became incriminating evidence to be used in a legal judgment, the investigators recalled better days when the files were praised objects of aesthetic judgment. There could hardly be a more classic example than this of the kind of aestheticization of politics that Benjamin warned against in 1936. While Benjamin ended that article with the famous lines, "This is the situation of politics which Fascism is rendering aesthetic. Communism responds by politicizing art," he was hardly prone to conflate the communism performing such feats with the Soviet Union.[69] As his 1926 *Moscow Diary* testifies, Benjamin was one of the first and most perceptive observers of the aestheticization of politics in the Soviet Union, giving detailed descriptions of the emerging cults of Lenin and of the Soviet map in the mid-1920s.

Ten years later, by the time of his famous pronouncement about the aestheticization of politics, the prime example of this phenomenon that dominated the international press was undoubtedly the Moscow "show trials": their theatricality, showcased in their name, was so striking that it became a leitmotif of most contemporary accounts.[70] Benjamin had been fascinated by this phenomenon long before it made it onto the international scene. Indeed, he had been present at its dress rehearsal: a diary entry from December 1926 leaves us a rare description of a Moscow mock trial, the fledgling precursor of the show trial.[71] In the 1920s, workers and peasant clubs staged mock legal proceedings that dealt with particular crimes and social problems, such as theft, prostitution, and abortion. In the 1920s, the principles and rituals of Soviet justice were introduced to the population through shows enjoyed along with many other night entertainments. Benjamin was certainly not the only one of the hundreds of spectators of "the legal proceedings" at the peasants club whose next stop that evening was a "*pivnaia*," an alehouse featuring another "dramatization" (*intsenerovka*) as well as dance variety numbers. But even in the face of such competition, Benjamin notes that the mock trial was playing to a full house, and latecomers were interested enough in the show to concoct shrewd tricks to get in. The audience enjoyed the show, and its representatives asked for the harshest punishment—the death sentence—overriding the jury's sentence of two years' imprisonment. Two sentences that precede and elucidate Benjamin's famous comment about politics being rendered aesthetic could well describe mock and later show-trial audiences: "Mankind, which in Homer's time was an object of contemplation for the Olympian gods, now is one for itself. Its self-alienation has reached such a degree that it can experience its own destruction as an aesthetic pleasure of the first order."[72] It was of course the secret police that orchestrated these unprecedented political spectacles, framing the accused and scripting the audience response.

The fact that the secret police staged its trials like grand theater performances and graced its records with literary pet names is probably not surprising to anyone familiar with Benjamin's warnings about the aestheticization of politics. What might be more surprising is that the victims of the secret police often concurred in calling its show trials and files by literary names; however, they were likely to mean this as abuse rather than praise. Evgeniia Ginzburg declined her investigator's invitation to use her literary talents in writing the file, explaining that this was not "in her line" of writing: "Well, you yourself mentioned the kind of writing I do—articles, translations. But I've never tried my hand at detective novels, and I doubt I could do the kind of fiction you want."[73] By calling the files fictions, Ginzburg exposes their previous aestheticization at the hands of the secret police and denies their legal status. This was a widespread accusation: in common parlance there are at least twelve verbs "which in combination with the word case [file] [*delo*] mean to fabricate a false charge."[74] However, when writers use the word *fiction* as an indictment, more is at stake. By calling the file a detective fiction and opposing it to her line of academic work—articles and translations—Ginzburg also identifies the particular genre practiced by the secret police and disparages it. Mocking the cheap aesthetics of the secret police is a leitmotif in writers' memoirs. The secret police judged their works not on literary grounds but as incriminating evidence. In describing their harrowing experiences at the hands of the secret police, writers retaliate by judging the police on its aesthetics. Their close-up insights into its particular genres and techniques are invaluable for understanding the role played by the secret police in the aestheticization of politics in Soviet times. Judging the aesthetics of the police files offered secret police victims the consolations of poetic justice at a time when no recourse to legal justice was in sight. These days, however, attention to the rhetoric of the files may threaten to unearth carefully buried secrets. The subject of an infamous trial in 1960, Romanian writer Dinu Pillat suggested that a close reading of the files, attentive to sudden shifts in the prisoner's tone, rhetoric, or grammar could detect the otherwise imperceptible traces of torture.[75]

Arnold Mesches, a contemporary American artist, puts a similar point in graphic terms when he subjects his FBI files to close viewing so as to draw attention to what they still hide.[76] On receiving copies of his 1945–72 FBI files through the Freedom of Information Act, Mesches "integrated some of them, together with recent paintings, drawings and other images about those times, into contemporary Illuminated Manuscripts, works on paper and paintings."[77] Mesches literally framed the FBI's shoddy evidence against him and made it into an artifact. Turning a political document into a piece of art is here a subversive political gesture. It blatantly mocks criminology manuals, which routinely address the question of whether the discipline should be categorized as science or art.[78] The orthodox answer is that criminology has more and more incorporated the scientific method, and as such it should, emphatically, be called a science and not an art. After all, the worst insult for a police file is the charge that it is "framed." Framing the files also brings them out of their powerfully guarded secrecy. It exposes them in a way that catches the public's eye and asks for the kind of close attention usually reserved for museum exhibits. Mesches self-consciously chose the file pages that struck him through their "bold, black, slashing strokes" that "look like Franz Kline color sketches, with typewriter words peeking through." Mesches uses what he calls "the sheer aesthetic beauty of these pages" to call attention to the continuing lack of transparency of the FBI, which returned the files with "all the pertinent information—the informers' names, who those close comrades actually were, who you were in bed with . . . black markered-out."[79] In the same vein, the largest international exhibition about artistic responses to surveillance societies spanning the entire twentieth century, *Ctrl (space): The Rhetoric of Surveillance from Bentham to Big Brother*, was based "on the belief that art is a powerful tool for helping people visualize technologies and scenarios that might otherwise remain concealed."[80] The organizer of the exhibit, Thomas Y. Levin, argues that "in the case of surveillance, aestheticization is essential. Without recourse to the senses, data remain invisible."[81]

Calling the files "true works of art" and "detective novels," or incorporating them into a collage as found objects are all ways of aestheticizing them. Some of these aestheticizations deserve Benjamin's famous censure, and some test its limits, so that it is certainly worth looking closely at who performed these aestheticizations, in what ways, and for what purposes. For instance, Svetlana Boym distinguishes between the Wagnerian model of "the grand, total work of art" which "influenced the creation of mass propaganda art in Hitler's

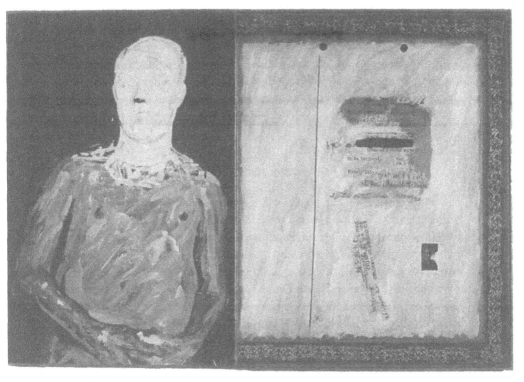

Arnold Mesches. *The FBI Files 35*, 2002, 60" x 87", acrylic and paper on canvas. Collection of the artist. Reprinted from *The FBI Files* ©2004 by Arnold Mesches, by permission of Hanging Loose Press.

Germany and Stalinist Russia," and aesthetic practices such as estrangement that open a space for reflection and freedom.[82] At the same time, Boym cautions that estrangement itself is not a panacea, and that instead "it can function as both poison and cure for the political evils of the age"; for instance, when "estrangement became expropriated by the Soviet state which defamiliarized the everyday perceptions and experiences of ordinary citizens."[83] Following up on her insights, the last chapter of this book zooms in on the encounters between the estranging practices of the secret police and artistic estrangement.

To emphasize the differences between different aestheticizations, the examples above refer mostly to the aestheticization of the files by the secret police and by its victims. Of course, the range of readings of the files defies such easy bad cop/good victim polarizations. At the time when he was no longer a Cheka translator and not yet one of its victims, Isaac Babel told a foreign friend that there are "valuable literary works in the Soviet Union" to be found in the secret police archives.[84] Babel explained that he was referring to the autobiographies and confessions that educated people were asked to compose upon their arrest. His reading of the files as literature places the emphasis on the prisoners' writing over that of the investigators. Babel gives authorship and praise to the file writer with least authority, thus undermining the hierarchy of the secret police in a recuperative and subversive reading.

## "Police Aesthetics"

Standing out from the wealth of relevant contemporary insights, Osip Mandel'shtam's discussion of what he called "police aesthetics" (*politseiskaia estetika*) inspiringly captures and illuminates the complexity of the relationship between aesthetics and the police.[85] Mandel'shtam, one of Russia's greatest twentieth-century poets, died in a camp to which he was probably sentenced for writing a satiric poem about Stalin. Mandel'shtam coined "police aesthetics" in his 1924 *The Noise of Time* (*Shum vremeni*), but he used it, at least ostensibly, to refer not to his own times, ever more dominated by the presence of the Soviet secret police, but rather to the turn-of-the-century Russian empire of his childhood. In *The Noise of Time*, the term "police aesthetics" first takes on meaning through a whole web of associations with drills, medals, emblems, black crêpe, shiny boots, and uniforms that define the child's Saint Petersburg as something "sacred and festive," filled in the imagination with "an unthinkably ideal, universal, military parade."[86] Police aesthetics grounds and permeates the motley elaborate practices and carefully designed image of the imperial police. This aesthetics is not to be found in philosophical treatises about beauty; instead, it emanates from the appearance and movements of young bodies drilled according to its principles, and it infiltrates the sensibility of little boys. For it is not only "the splendid spectacle" that bears the marks of police aesthetics but also its entranced spectator, the young Mandel'shtam:

> I was delirious over the cuirasses of the Royal Horse Guard and the Roman Helmets of the Cavalry Guard, the silver trumpets of the Preobrazhensky band; and after the May Parade, my favorite distraction was the regimental festival at the Royal Horse Guard on Lady Day.. . . . All this mass of militarism and even some sort of police aesthetics [*politseiskoi estetiki*] may well have been proper to some son of a corps commander with the appropriate family traditions, but it was completely out of keeping with the kitchen fumes of a middle-class apartment, with father's study, heavy with the odor of leathers, kidskin and calfskin, or with Jewish conversations about business.[87]

Mandel'shtam's use of the term *aesthetic* recalls its etymology. In his archeology of the term, Terry Eagleton shows that "In its original formulation by the German philosopher Alexander Baumgarten, the term refers not in the first place to art, but, as the Greek *aisthesis* would suggest, to the whole region of human perception and sensation, in contrast to the more rarified domain of conceptual thought."[88] Inasmuch as it inscribes power in the interior of the citizen, modifying perception, aesthetics is, for Eagleton, a form of "policing," a police aesthetics.[89] At the same time, Eagleton emphasizes that "the aesthetic [was] from the beginning a contradictory, double-edged concept," whose subversive and "genuinely emancipatory force" always threatened to exceed its policing potential.[90] Howard Caygill's cogent analysis of the relationship between the emergence of modern aesthetics and the police state in Germany similarly emphasizes the double edge of the aesthetic's relationship to politics.[91] Mandel'shtam's description of the police aesthetics that mesmerized his childhood, on the one hand, and the aesthetics of his own mature prose, on the other, more subtly illustrate just how varied and conflicted the political valences of aesthetics can be.

Having scrutinized the elaborate spectacle of imperial police aesthetics and the fascination it engenders in his younger self, Mandel'shtam's description of this spectacle does not politicize it but rather reframes it through the prism of his adult aesthetics. The descriptions of the police and its aesthetics in *The Noise of Time* bear the marks of Mandel'shtam's unique style. Its fragmentariness, fastidiousness, digressions, and irony introduce the marks of an aesthetic that shows just how far the adult writer has traveled from the child's infatuation with police aesthetics. His adult aesthetics, like his memory, is openly "inimical to this past, laboring not to reproduce but to estrange it [ostraneniem proshlogo]."[92] Privileging the fragment, the miniature, and the contingent, his aesthetics estranges, domesticates, and finally emasculates the police. His magnifying glass gets close enough to the representatives of imperial police aesthetics to reveal and mock the dye on the moustache of "the police officers crawling out onto the street" and into his prose "like red mustachioed cockroaches."[93] As a result, unlike the child, we watch the spectacle he describes in amusement-tempered disgust rather than awe.

Mandel'shtam's irreverence, his poking of the dead body of imperial aesthetics with prickly satire, might seem gratuitous until we realize that police aesthetics is not as dead or as imperial as it might seem. Squeamish or not, anyone familiar with Mandel'shtam's fate will likely get goose bumps from those "red mustachioed cockroaches." Aesthetically repressed in the mocking 1923 passage, the peculiar metaphor returned ten years later in the poem about Stalin that got Mandel'shtam sentenced to the camps where he perished:

His thick fingers, like worms, fat,
And the words, like lead weights, final,
His cockroach moustache laughs,
And his boot tops gleam.[94]

This time neither the poet nor his audience are able to laugh off the unsettling image; instead, it is the moustache that gets the last terrible laugh. But if
the poet no longer breaks into mocking laughter, neither does he swoon with
awe like his younger self. While police aesthetics returns to haunt his fate, it
has been extirpated from his sensibility. This is no small feat. If police aesthetics is not something safely located in a military parade but rather grafted onto
one's very sensibility, exorcising it might take the development of a different
aesthetics.

I place my work under the sign of Mandel'shtam's "police aesthetics" for
several reasons. First, the term illuminates the insidious aestheticization of
policing. Mandel'shtam's police aesthetics refers to the self-presentation of
the police through dress, parades, and the fashioning of the agent's body. I
extend his term to refer to the secret police's self-presentation and representation of its "others" in its practices, such as surveillance, interrogation, or
reeducation, and in textual and visual artifacts—in the files, books, or films
that it sponsored or directly authored. I also follow Mandel'shtam in his belief
that the aesthetics of the police is not easily confined to military parades and
instead seeps in where one might expect it least: among the kitchen fumes
of middle-class apartments, in the psyches of little boys who might or might
not become poets, and in contemporary cultural production. But above all, I
choose police aesthetics because it bespeaks a critical distance from its referent. "Police aesthetics" is not part of police lingo, and neither is it part of the
vocabulary of the young boy enthralled by uniforms and mustaches. Instead,
the term expresses a critical distance enabled by the painstaking creation of a
very different mature aesthetics. Mandel'shtam's "some sort of police aesthetics" is critical to the point of name-calling. I mean to preserve its bite.

The term is both critically descriptive of one side of the project, the aesthetics of the police, as well as representative of the other, the very different
kinds of aesthetics, like Mandel'shtam's, that came into contact with it, left us
unique insights into it, and were sometimes shaped by it, "inimically" or otherwise. "Police aesthetics" thus captures both sides of the picture, Nabokov's
"marvelous culture" and policing, and points to their complex relationship—at
times fascination, repugnance, mimicry, appropriation, parody, or estrangement. Inspired to build on the richness of Mandel'shtam's term, this project attempts to avoid its potentially facile associations—"police aesthetics" is
never used here to suggest that aesthetics is a form of policing or that the work

of the police is beautiful. I also aim to move beyond cold-war binary opposi-
tions between repressive states and subversive artists, while at the same time
leaving behind more recent revisionisms that lump together artists and police
agents in an indiscriminate mass of more or less complicit subjects. Instead, I
try to map a wide range of relationships between aesthetics and policing, of
which the aesthetics of the police represents just one powerful pole.

This range, while wide, is certainly not meant to be exhaustive. There was
so much culture and far too much policing in Soviet times to fit into any one
book. My case studies are thus necessarily idiosyncratic, yet they reflect an
attempt to show just how long and deep a shadow the police cast on contemporary culture, from its major achievements—such as Mikhail Bulgakov's *The
Master and Margarita*, Formalist literary theory, or Dziga Vertov's revolutionary
newsreel—to popular hits, such as the blockbuster *Road to Life*, and to avant-
garde experiments, like Alexander Medvedkin's film trains. In contrast with
arguably the most influential study of the relationship between literature and
policing, D. A. Miller's *The Novel and the Police,* which posited one overarching
thesis—that the novel, long considered "the most free, the most lawless" literary form, in fact took on the work of policing—this book maps out a variety
of relationships between literature and policing as well as the complex changes
in those relationships through time.[95] And since my aim is to show not only
how wide-ranging but especially how deep the intersections between culture
and policing were, shaping artists' lives and subject matter as well as literary
genres, narrative devices, and editing techniques, close attention to a limited
number of artifacts seemed more appropriate than attempting an impossibly
exhaustive coverage.

I then follow up on the invaluable insights of artists like Mandel'shtam,
Babel, Shklovsky, and Steinhardt into the aesthetics of the police while also
trying to understand the major, if largely unrecognized, role that the secret
police played in shaping the literary and visual culture of its times. This criss-
crossing between the secret police and cultural artifacts and practices is based
on the belief that when textual analysis illuminates confounding police documents, the resulting illuminations can also throw light on some dark corners,
and even cornerstones, of literary history. This is not only because writers'
files contain invaluable information but also because this pervasive genre of
writing had a great impact on key issues at the core of literary history, such
as the position of the writer, the authority of the written word, and the status
of (auto)biographical writing. Similarly, the secret police use of visual images
from mug shots to moving pictures played an important role in defining the
status of visual evidence, and vision in general, in Soviet times.

Ultimately, my study of the police aesthetics of Soviet times attempts to understand how the intersections between culture and policing reconfigured what Jacques Rancière has called the "distribution of the sensible" (*partage du sensible*): the (re)configuration of the relationships between words and images, persons and things, speech and writing, foreground and background, the visible and the invisible.[96] For instance, I will argue that the creation and archiving of personal files extensively reconfigured a certain relationship between the subject and the words that claim to represent him, as well as a hierarchy between speaking, writing, and reading, between what counts as a word with political or literary authority and what too often remains an unrecorded cry of pain.[97] I trace the ways in which writers related to these new hierarchies when writing autobiographies and depositions for their files, creating arresting narrative masks or personae, or engaging in various experiments in self-fashioning, self-effacement, and self-estrangement. In the visual realm, I argue that the reform of identity papers and the new practice of fingerprinting instituted new relationships between word, indexical image, and their human referent. Similarly, the rhetoric of unmasking and the new use of depth style in film were instrumental in establishing particular hierarchies between foreground and background, and also between empirical vision and ideological clairvoyance.

## The Road Plan

Chapter 1 attempts an anatomy of the secret police personal file by analyzing its main components, broadly divided in two categories: surveillance and investigation materials. The second part of the chapter traces the overarching trajectory of the personal file, focusing on the differences between Stalinist and post-Stalinist files. My analysis is based on both Soviet and Romanian secret police documents. As Denis Deletant has showed, the Romanian secret police closely followed the Soviet model, with representatives of the Soviet secret police supervising the foundation and expansion of the Securitate.[98] Given that in Romania the transition to socialism started in 1948 and that post-Stalinist Soviet secret police records are largely classified, my analysis places corresponding emphases on the pre-1953 Soviet model for the file and on its post-1948 development in Romania. The central goal of this chapter is to investigate how this genre was structured at different times and in different places, and how it in turn structured its subject, two topics that are as inextricably related as life (*bios*) and writing (*graphike*) are in biography.

Chapter 2 juxtaposes the most popular fictional representation of the Soviet 1930s, Mikhail Bulgakov's *The Master and Margarita* (*Master i Margarita*), with its author's secret police file. Recent studies of Bulgakov's relationship with Stalin have often dwelled on the fateful role of the secret police in Bulgakov's life.[99] This chapter shifts the focus from the impact of Bulgakov's secret police file on his life to its impact on his writing, and more specifically on his use of (auto)biographical personae, narrative masks, and stylistic experimentation. I argue that in search of authority and credibility for his fantastic story, Bulgakov's mysterious narrator deliberately mimics the file written by the novel's secret police investigators, who before him had already "gathered all the infernal stitches of the complicated case/file [*delo*]" of a foreign devil's (or is it just a demonized foreigner's?) visit to Moscow.

Chapter 3 argues that postrevolutionary cinema showed a peculiar interest in policing. This chapter dwells on the work of three major filmmakers, Dziga Vertov, Alexander Medvedkin, and Ivan Pyr'ev, who advocated the use of the camera as secret police agent, prosecutor, and criminologist. Their heterodox versions of "kino policing" worked in a variety of ways, from identifying the generic portrait of the Soviet criminal/enemy on screen to capturing particular individuals red-handed through the use of hidden cameras. Furthermore, cinema complexly policed its audiences and their attitudes toward Soviet criminality. Kino police manipulatively cast its viewers in roles as different as sheltered spectator, suspect, witness, and accused in the ongoing political trials and tribulations of the time.

Chapter 4 explores cinematic representations of the Gulag done in collaboration with the secret police. The chapter starts with the analysis of a 1927 documentary about the most infamous camp of the time, Solovki. Next comes *Road to Life*, a sophisticated fictional representation of one of the thorniest issues of the Soviet 1930s, children's labor colonies. The film not only depicts the secret police "reeducation experiment" but engages in experiments of its own: besides being the first full-feature Soviet sound film, *Road to Life* is also to my knowledge the first feature film whose actors were, in the vast majority, child prisoners. The last case study is the multimedia representation of the Belomor Canal labor camp, comprising documentary films, photographs, drawings, and texts coedited by Maxim Gorky and the secret police camp commander Semen Firin. The Belomor project provides rich material for a comparison between the places assigned to word and image in the collaboration between the secret police and the arts. This chapter sustains Chapter 3's focus on the representation of the criminal/enemy and places a particular emphasis on the changing profile of the female criminal. It also continues Chapter 3's exploration of the roles that these films attribute to their audiences.

Chapter 5 explores the relationship between literary theory and the secret police by focusing on the concept of estrangement. I argue that artistic estrangement, long faulted as an apolitical concept, was gradually politicized and radically modified through its entanglements with secret police estrangement. The chapter starts with Viktor Shklovsky's coinage of *ostranenie* (estrange-ment) and revision of the term in his autobiographical works; it then tracks estrangement's conflicted development through Shklovsky's later oeuvre and beyond, in the work of Nicolae Steinhardt and also in secret police interroga-tion and reeducation practices. Both Shklovsky and Steinhardt's reworkings of estrangement in light of their encounters with the secret police take place in autobiographical writings. This is not entirely surprising, for secret police estrangement is mostly directed at the self. What might be more surprising is that these often intimate writings self-consciously evoke standard compo-nents of the secret police file, such as confessions, autobiographies, trial and interrogation depositions, and letters to the government. Through an analysis of these texts, I reveal some of the impact of secret police practices and files on both literary theory and first-person narratives.

The book's core (Chapters 2, 3, and 4) focuses on the intersections between culture and the secret police in the foundational period of the Soviet regime, the 1920s and 1930s. The two framing chapters (1 and 5) open the discussion to the Soviet period at large, and expand it beyond the Soviet Union to consider the latter's larger sphere of influence, through a focus on Romania. The choice of Romania was determined by my linguistic and cultural background as well as by the wealth of materials from the secret police archives that have recently become available. These two chapters follow my intent to describe as wide and deep a range of the intersections between culture and policing as possible, following them through time and across national barriers. I think this cross-cultural perspective illuminates both the Soviet and the Romanian material. We can certainly not understand the Romanian secret police and its records without understanding its explicit model, the Soviet secret police. But the view from the periphery may also reveal quite a bit about the center. On a practical level, it so happens that the archives of some former satellites are significantly more open than Soviet archives, providing invaluable information about sides of Soviet history that are still classified in Russia. But especially in the case of an expansionist institution like the Soviet secret police, the ways it attempted to replicate itself in its various satellites is as important for our understanding as its workings at home. A comprehensive picture of the Soviet secret police and its relationship to contemporary culture requires not only further opening of its archives but also a transnational picture of its enormous area of influence. That will be, of course, a massive, necessarily collective undertaking; the pres-ent book, through its dual focus on the Soviet Union and Romania, attempts to provide one piece of that puzzle.

## CHAPTER ONE

# Arresting Biographies

## The Personal File in
## the Soviet Union and Romania

### Preamble: Fragmentary Archives

*Romanian and Other Eastern European Secret Police Archives*

The story of the partial opening of the secret police archives in Eastern Europe is often as instructive as the declassified files themselves. Anything but relics of the Cold War destined to the dustbin of history, the archives are at the very center of contemporary politics. Indeed, one could write a comparative history of post-1989 Eastern European politics by following their fate. Such an undertaking is well beyond the scope of this study; instead, I will briefly trace the story of my own access to materials used in this chapter, contextualizing that story within the larger discourse on the secret police archives.

The recent fate of these archives in Eastern Europe is a vivid, indeed often lurid, illustration of Jacques Derrida's pronouncement that "there is no political power without control of the archive, if not of memory. Effective democratization can always be measured by this essential criterion: the participation in and the access to the archive, its constitution, and its interpretation."[1] Other theoretical concepts generated in poststructuralist rethinking of the archive, such as the return of the repressed or the death drive, were similarly literalized as Romanian villagers unearthed thousands of pages hastily buried by the secret police. Foucault's thesis that the archive is not just a collection of documents but the whole power structure around them, or Derrida's point about the "house arrest" of res publica by the archons of power, was similarly propelled far from theory books and into tabloid headlines through the story of the secret police heirs' sabotage of the opening of the archives.[2] Starting

with the archives' long anachronic classified status, and continuing with the
delivery of the files into the rain as the successors of the secret police with-
held first the space designed to house them, then the finding aids or reading
know-how needed to decipher them, the story unfolded and still unfolds as
unendingly as the serialized "telenovellas" that competed for transition-weary
audiences.

Throughout Eastern Europe, the more or less reformed successors of the
secret police who inherited the archives proved stubbornly opposed to opening their doors. These were sometimes burst open by public pressure, most
dramatically by angry East Germans who made it inside the STASI archives and
onto television screens worldwide.[3] However, in the rest of Eastern Europe,
early access to the secret police archives often happened behind the scenes,
as well-timed revelations and leakages of the files attempted to compromise
leading political players.[4] The introduction of lustration laws in most Eastern
European countries, with the notable exception of Russia, was designed to
address, or sometimes just feign to address, these problems; but everywhere,
lustration laws brought the archives even closer to the center of contemporary
politics and fueled heated debate.[5] Variously applied in different countries,
lustration laws mandate that the past links of present-day politicians with
the secret police be checked in the latter's archives and made public. The
consequences of these revelations vary, as lustration laws were designed and
implemented differently from country to country, and also within countries in
close relationship to the changing fortunes of the powers that be.

I started my search for secret police files in the late 1990s in Romania. It
took ten years from the 1989 Romanian Revolution for a law to be passed
founding the National Council for the Study of the Securitate Archives (Consiliul Naţional Pentru Studierea Arhivelor Securităţii or CNSAS)[6]; its role was
to allow civil society to check the secret police ties of public figures, from the
president to post-office managers, and also to allow private citizens access to
their own files. CNSAS was to be led by a council of eleven representatives
of the leading political parties. At best, this arrangement signified democratic
pluralism; at its worst, it meant that the council's activity was often nearly para-
lyzed by the wide differences among its leaders, some of whom represented
parties which fought to close CNSAS and all access to the archives. Because
of these internal as well as external pressures, CNSAS often proceeded by fits
and starts and took over the secret police archives slowly and only partially.[7]

In the hope of some edification about gaining research access to the former
archives of the Securitate, I sent e-mails to the webmasters of all eleven political parties asking for the contacts of their CNSAS representatives. I got only
two responses, but they allowed me to contact the representative of the Hun-

garian minority's party, Ladislau Csendes, and then president of the CNSAS, Gheorghe Onişoru. My two contacts, both academics, welcomed my project and invited me to attend the training sessions organized for the employees of CNSAS. This turned out to be an unparalleled opportunity to witness the foundational work of CNSAS. The sessions took place in Ceauşescu's megalo-maniac palace, Casa Poporului, and I remember getting perpetually lost in the labyrinthine hallways, trying to make my way to rooms where senior officers of the former Securitate services were teaching fresh graduates of history depart-ments how to navigate the archives and read files. Everyone looked out of place in the grotesquely oversized private residence, decorated in a boudoir version of socialist realism: the Securitate officers, pacing awkwardly in front of the room, unaccustomed to public lectures; the young historians, visibly excited to have landed their new jobs, although not quite sure what they entailed; and the senior members of CNSAS, many no doubt subjects of secret police files, watching their former watchers expose surveillance methods.

By the summer of 2000 I was working in the archives of the CNSAS. Since the question of research access had not yet been fully settled, I was often the first researcher to gain access to the files of major Romanian writers, such as Nicolae Steinhardt, Marin Preda, and Nichita Stănescu. Besides offering access to personal files from the whole period of communist rule, CNSAS also made available to me internal Securitate regulations regarding the organization of the archives, as well as the conduct of surveillance, arrests, investigation, and informer recruitment. In the meantime, CNSAS publications, such as an extraordinary collection of the Securitate internal regulations used exten-sively in this study; independent publishers; and even SRI (Serviciul Român de Informaţii) publications have made a wealth of secret police documents available for public scrutiny.[8]

### A Case Apart: Russia's Former KGB Archives

Russia never passed a lustration law. Such a law was drafted in 1992, but it failed miserably on the Duma floor.[9] At the same time, the Duma passed laws making it a criminal offense to identify former secret police agents and col-laborators.[10] As a result, access to the archives followed a different route from elsewhere in Eastern Europe. And yet the beginnings had been promising: in 1991, Boris Eltsin established a parliamentary commission to investigate the status of the former secret police archives. The published reports of members of this commission are an invaluable source of information concerning the overall state of the archives. Nikita Petrov reports the commission's finding that in 1991 there were 9.5 million files. He also gives figures for the main types of files (personal or "operational" files, personnel files, files confiscated from

Nazi camps, and administrative files) but warns that these numbers are not reliable since many files have been destroyed, legally or illegally.[11] His view regarding the KGB treatment of the files is summarized in his title: "The KGB Politics Regarding Its Archive Was Criminal." Another important study, cowritten by a commission member, Arsenii Roginskii, with Nikita Okhotin, provides a more detailed description of the typology of the files as well as a thorough account of the activity of the commission and of the power struggles that by 1992 had already hindered the ambitious plans to open the archives to the public.[12]

The archives have instead remained under the jurisdiction of the successor to the KGB, the FSB, which has jealously guarded them from both public and research access. However, alternative sources of information on the archives, when put together, amount to a rather different and highly instructive portrait. The glasnost years saw the first successful efforts to open the archives. Already in 1988, heeding the initiative of Vitalii Shentalinskii, the Writers' Union established a commission aimed at recovering the manuscripts of repressed writers as well as their files. After countless tribulations, supported and hindered at the highest levels of party and KGB leadership, the commission made its way into the archives and emerged with files of leading cultural figures, such as Isaac Babel, Mikhail Bulgakov, Maxim Gorky, Osip Mandel'shtam, and others.[13] Shentalinskii edited these finds in two volumes, which remain to this day an unparalleled source of personal files from the peak of Stalinist repression. Precisely because it was such an extraordinary success, this experience also spelled out the limits of archival access: the commission, backed by the weight of leading cultural figures as well as high-level official sanction, was allowed to see only selected files from the Stalinist period, the safely distant and publicly denounced period of "the cult of personality." Even such selective access was still denied to independent researchers and private individuals.

This changed in 1991 when repressed individuals gained access to their own files according to the law concerning "The Rehabilitation of the Victims of Political Repression."[14] According to the FSB, around two thousand people take advantage of this right every year.[15] Some of them have made files public, either independently or by adding them to collections such as the pioneering Memorial Society archive, thereby filling in gaps of official disclosures by offering information concerning more recent periods of Soviet history.[16] Significant collections of secret police documents, often its correspondence with other institutions which have made their holdings available to researchers, have accumulated into a substantial, if indirect, archive.[17] Furthermore, the partial opening of the archives in certain former Soviet republics, such as Latvia and Estonia, has revealed significant information about the Soviet secret police. Thus, a KGB textbook on the history of the Soviet secret police from 1917 to 1977, which remains top-secret material in Russia, can be accessed online thanks to the opening of Latvian archives.[18] As Peter Holquist wrote in surveying post-Soviet historiography, "the problem is not [primarily] one of archival access to relevant materials, but of our ability to work through them. . . . Tellingly, the most representative genre of post-Soviet historical study is the documentary compilation, bursting with primary source documentation but eschewing interpretation."[19] This chapter takes on the task of analysis and interpretation and offers the first sustained study of the secret police personal file in Soviet times.

We are certainly far from a comprehensive picture of secret police archives in Eastern Europe. In Russia, the near future does not promise much in this respect.[20] Elsewhere in Eastern Europe, the opening of the archives is at best in process, with much yet to be unearthed. But rather than waiting for the heirs of the secret police to invite us to the grand opening of the archives, I think it is time to pick up and analyze the available pieces of declassified or leaked information. When cobbled together, they result in a substantive, if often indirect and fragmentary, archive. With all its drawbacks, this fragmentariness is an instructive antidote to a problematic fantasy of the complete archive.[21] The secret police never kept complete or truthful records, and it has often destroyed the records it did keep. These gaps were often deliberately created to compromise the value of existing archival collections as incriminating evidence to be used in the administration of retroactive justice. It is telling that the successors to the secret police remind us with hardly dissimulated satisfaction that informer records have been partly destroyed.[22] As a result, no one can be absolved of the accusation of having collaborated with the secret police—it might simply be that the informer's file has been destroyed. If we go to these archives to find out the definitive answers about our past, we are bound to come back with the answer that we are all potentially guilty. The relativist position espoused by the heirs of the secret police is self-serving and deeply problematic; but also problematic is the initial question, which even while openly incriminating the secret police, betrays an enduring reliance on its power to give us answers to the hard questions of the past and present. Like the door in Kafka's famous parable, the doors to the secret police archives will not be opened by waiting. And the guard does not have the key. Indeed, there is no one key, just as there is no complete archive; however, the fragments of this incomplete, often indirect, but still sizzlingly active archive give us plenty to explore. So we had better start off.

## A Short Genealogy of the Secret Police File

As the name suggests, the secret police file is a variation on the genre of the criminal record. Walter Benjamin wrote that the challenge of identifying a criminal shielded by the anonymity of the modern masses "is at the origin of the detective story."[23] The elusiveness of the criminal's identity is also at the origin of modern criminology, a discipline that developed in the late nineteenth century around discoveries about matching traces such as fingerprints, bloodstains, and handwriting with the individual who left them. In the 1870s, pioneering criminologist Alphonse Bertillon proposed a method for identifying criminals, which synthesized many of these discoveries.[24] His police records combined mug shots, anthropometric measurements of the body, the verbal portrait (*portrait parlé*), and the record of peculiar characteristics (such as tattoos and accents). By the end of the nineteenth century, the skeleton of the modern police file was already well in place throughout Europe.[25]

Whereas criminal records are usually limited to the investigation of one crime, the Soviet personal file is typically concerned with the extensive biography of the suspect. Already in 1918, Martin Latsis, a leading Chekist, instructed: "Do not look in the materials you have gathered for evidence that a suspect acted or spoke against the Soviet authorities. The first question you should ask him is what class he belongs to, what is his origin, education, profession. These questions should determine his fate. This is the essence of the Red Terror."[26] This speech documents the turning point from the traditional police file, concerned with the particular crime, to the Soviet secret police file, concerned with the whole biography of the accused. Nicolae Steinhardt summarized this condition: "you are not accused for what you have done, but rather for who you are."[27] In line with this fundamental transformation came a shift in the names the secret police called its subjects: the criminal—the perpetrator of a particular crime, often a petty, nonpolitical crime—was eclipsed by the enemy, who was defined by *being* against. Indeed, the figure of the enemy (*vrag* in Russian, *duşman* in Romanian) surpassed the criminal as the most wanted man (or woman) in Soviet times.

The interest in biography also singles out Soviet detective stories (*detektivy*) within the detective story tradition. Just like the Soviet files, Soviet *detektivy* disregarded the particulars of any one crime to focus on the overall character of the suspect. "The Soviet *detektivy* were concerned less with the mechanics of specific crimes and much more with the broader causes of crime itself. Thus, the focus of a book had to be not so much the way in which a particular crime was accomplished, as much as the broader failings and shortcomings in a person that caused him, or her, to wish to bring harm to society."[28] The traditional police file can read like a Western detective story, spurred by a mystery whose solution is ideally crowned with the identification and punishment of the criminal. The Soviet secret police file reads like a peculiar biography.

The penchant for biography that characterizes Soviet personal files is in line with the at-first sight surprising importance of individual biography in communist society, where "a new veneration for the biographical mode" was visible in texts that range from party documents to the canonical socialist realist literature of the time.[29] Thus, in her benchmark book on the socialist realist novel, Katerina Clark argues that "the official models for Socialist Realism have in common a biographical pattern, which structures them."[30] The standard positive biographical pattern was structured around a conversion of an initially imperfect character who in the course of the text attains communist consciousness. Clark notes that "the negative pattern was rather poorly represented in novels," and therefore she decides "to give it little attention."[31] I argue that the negative biographical pattern was not absent but in fact structured the millions of pages of personal files, just as much as the positive biographical pattern structured the socialist realist novel. Featuring the Soviet new man and the Soviet enemy, these biographical patterns appear at first as irreconcilable binary opposites; in fact, as we will soon see, the negative biographical pattern shared a surprising number of key themes and devices with the well-known positive biographical pattern, such as the narrative of conversion and the extreme value assigned to communist consciousness in opposition to a spontaneity that always threatened to turn from ideological naïveté into crime.

A penchant for biography is also discernible at certain moments in the history of Western criminology. The great reform of the modern penitentiary, which originated in eighteenth-century England, "aimed to reshape the life story of each criminal by the application of pleasure and pain within a planned framework. . . . Their aim was the reformation of character through the controlled alteration of material circumstances through time."[32] As a result, criminologists and other penitentiary reformers became extremely interested in recording and rewriting the story of a criminal life. In his history of the penitentiary reform, Michel Foucault notes: "The introduction of the 'biographical' is important in the history of penality. . . . The legal punishment bears upon the act; the punitive technique on a life."[33] Whether they posited their subject as an inborn criminal, a victim of the modern environment, or a free-willing delinquent, the major schools of nineteenth-century criminology had recourse to various narratives—ranging from genealogies to sociologically or psychologically inclined biographies—to express their views of the criminal.[34] However, the biographical interest that sometimes informs Western criminological treatises or penitentiary reform programs is less visible in the more applied genre of the police file, which was mainly used as a practical tool in actual police searches for the perpetrators of particular crimes. Indeed, throughout the nineteenth and twentieth centuries, the Western police file was increasingly developed as a technology of identification: the file was aimed to capture not the detailed story of the criminal, the person's genealogy, life conditions, or psychological development but rather the identifying characteristics of an individual's body. This trend is visible in the development over time of a defining rubric of the modern police file, the distinguishing characteristics. In the nineteenth century, under the influence of phrenology and physiognomy, descriptions of the criminal often tried to link certain body characteristics to character (such as connecting a specific skull shape with "degeneration"). With the adoption of the Bertillon system throughout Europe at the end of the nineteenth century, body markers were no longer recorded in the police file with the expectation that they could reveal anything about character; instead, they were chosen for their ability to distinguish one person from another.[35] The classic apex of this development is the fingerprint, undoubtedly the chief identifying feature throughout the twentieth century.[36] Among newer technologies, the iris scan provides a particularly fit illustration of this trend from symptomatic to synecdochic readings of the body's distinguishing characteristics. The eye, traditionally seen as the window to the soul, is no longer probed for any clue about character. Instead, the eye is chosen as a site, analogous to the fingertip, where random peculiarities of shape and color converge to create unique patterns that distinguish each individual from others in what Allan Sekula memorably described as the modern body archive.[37] As a tool of identification, the modern police file essentially aims to link the fingerprints found at the crime scene with the criminal who left them, and to provide a cogent narrative of a particular crime, not to record or rewrite life stories.

## Surveillance Files: Characterization Through Collation

The mutation from particular crime to overall biography can be traced back to the origin of the Soviet secret police file. While some files were created from voluntary denunciations or from depositions made by suspects during interrogations, thousands of files were created without these personalized forms of suspect identification.[38] A 1935 NKVD circular "urged the Party grassroots organizations to track down any Oppositionist who had ever set foot in their midst so that they could be tried."[39] Similarly, in 1951, foundational internal memos of the Romanian secret police ordered that whole categories of people be automatically endowed with personal files.[40] These categories ranged from members of former political parties to people who had relatives abroad. These memos also gave a comprehensive description of sources for the creation of a secret police file, which included: "informational material [informer reports] or investigation and archive material, material resulting from the opening of correspondence, letters and information received from citizens concerning individuals who are involved in inimical activities."[41] While this succinct list of possible sources flagging an individual as a new file subject takes one short paragraph, the detailed list of categories of people automatically endowed with files takes three full pages.[42] Indeed, before the secret police had knowledge of any particular crime, it typically had the name and some basic incriminating description of the subject. Its first real task was thus not *to identify* the author of a crime but rather *to characterize* suspects.[43]

The 1951 "directives" of the Romanian secret police also detail the protocol for the creation and development of the file, including the description of different types of files. The succession of files outlines the phases of the suspect's characterization. Usually, the first step in the characterization of the suspect and his overall "processing" by the secret police was the opening of a "registration file" (*dosar de evidență operativă*). Registration files could be opened for individuals flagged to be of interest to the secret police by virtue of belonging to blacklisted categories or for other reasons. The purpose of this file was "to keep track of all inimical and suspect elements and to collect necessary data for their identification and characterization, so as not to allow them to work in important institutions," and "to infiltrate their milieu with informers." In case this characterization mentioned "any inimical attitude" (toward the regime), a "verification file" (*dosar de verificare*) was opened.[44] Agents could use "all means available to the security services: trailing, investigations, the verification [sic] of correspondence, surveillance technology, existent informers and the recruitment of new informers" in order to check previous information and further "gather the data that characterizes the individual from all points of view, his political views, his behavior, his relationships, and their character."[45] If the "inimical attitude" was confirmed by the verification file, the latter was closed and the most thorough type of surveillance file, "the informative trailing file" (*dosar de urmărire informativă*, or DUI) was opened. This file aimed at "establishing and documenting, in as much detail as possible, the practical criminal activity of the suspects."[46] The vague, inclusive definition of "criminal activity" in the practice of the secret police, combined with the request for great detail of documentation, meant that in reality agents and informers recorded as much of the activity of the suspects as they could. Their field of interest again overflowed the limits of any particular crime toward a fantasy of full surveillance of the subject.

These types of files and even their peculiar terminology were modeled on the Soviet secret police file and its archiving system.[47] Thus, the Soviet secret police also used the succession of registration file (*delo operativnogo ucheta*), verification file (*delo operativnoi proverki*), and a heightened surveillance file, whose house name, *delo-formuliar*, resists meaning and translation attempts as much as the wooden Romanian phrase *dosar de urmărire informativă*.[48] The DUI and the *delo-formuliar* could, and sometimes did, go on for years and only end when their subjects died. In theory, however, they were supposed to lead to the dropping of the suspect (when no inimical activity was detected) or to arrest. In the latter case, the file was forwarded to a different branch of the secret police, where it became the basis for the investigation. "Investigation files" were standardly archived under different binders, and often under different names: in the Soviet Union, the most common was *sledstvennoe delo*, while in Romania the common name was *dosar de anchetă*.[49]

I distinguish between pre-arrest and post-arrest files, since the arrest served as a crucial turning point in the file, from the perspective of the secret police and from the perspective of the subject. The arrest was usually the climactic moment when the subject was confronted with his or her file and asked to participate in its further development. Furthermore, pre- and post-arrest files were standardly compiled by different branches of the secret police. The first dealt primarily with surveillance. Once the arrest was decided, the file was transferred to the investigating authorities, whose activity was centered on interrogation. Accordingly, hereafter I will call the pre-arrest and post-arrest files surveillance and investigation files, a naming based on the main police activity that defines them. These names are heuristic devices, and one can always find counter-examples: for example, investigation files sometimes contain cellmate informer reports, while surveillance files sometimes contain the record of a warning conversation between a secret police agent and the subject. Nevertheless, while recognizing the imprecision and simplifications unavoidable in dividing thousands of miles of file records into two categories, I believe that the distinction between surveillance and investigation files does on the whole stand, and that it will prove helpful in navigating and understanding these records.

The surveillance file stitched together a variety of materials without much processing or attention to the way they fit. For example, the typical contents of a writer's surveillance file included photographs of manuscripts next to fragments of published works, literary reviews, letters, denunciations, a comprehensive list of all individuals mentioned in the file and their identifying information, and of course, informers' reports.[50] Given the eclectic interests and sources of the secret police, files are characterized by abrupt shifts from one narrative voice to another. Some narrators maintained an impersonal distance, their comments restricted to the professional profile of the subject, his or her writings or public appearances. Other narrators poked through trash, attempting to inspect any traces left by the subject, from illegal contraceptives to aborted manuscripts. Yet others managed to come in direct contact with the subject, recording intimate conversations, gestures, even intonation. The secret police worked hard to recruit the latter, "depth informers" (*agentura de profunzime*) who had "the full possibility to know everything that he (the suspect) does, including his intentions."[51] Besides these precious depth informers, one can and should differentiate between many other types of informers and informer reports, voluntary and coerced, malicious and slyly inane. The secret police had its own way of categorizing its informers. It snubbed voluntary informers as unreliable, and instead developed a mind-boggling network made up of "qualified" and "unqualified informers," "trusted persons" and "supportive persons" (occasional informers), "residents" who collected the information from informers, and "hosts" of meeting houses.[52] Accordingly, the narrative of the surveillance file jumps between miscellaneous angles and points of view, creating a portrait of the subject that is necessarily disjointed and patchy.

Informer reports usually existed in duplicate. The collation of various informers' reports in the subject file appears all the more cacophonous in comparison with the collation of copies of the same reports inside the informers' own files. The police had individual files on its informers, and their reports were usually attached to this file but kept within a separate binder, which in Romania was called a work dossier (*mapă de lucru*).[53] These work dossiers included the totality of the informers' reports: as such, within two covers we encounter one narrative voice depicting one or more characters. It bears noting, however, that the informer file at large looked surprisingly similar to a suspect's surveillance file. Once the secret police set its eyes on a potential informer, it launched a thorough surveillance operation whose purpose was "to collect complete information on these individuals. The data collection will be done patiently, without leaving any question unresolved, following all leads and going all the way to surveillance."[54] And just like in the case of the suspect files, the informer surveillance file was aimed at characterization, which again went beyond any particular actions and instead attempted a totalizing portrait of the subject. "It will be insisted upon that we know in detail the past of the person in question, the actual way of life, the hopes for the immediate and long-term future, weaknesses and qualities, troubles and intimate difficulties."[55] Once this thorough verification was completed, a separate document entitled "characterization (referring to temperament and character)" was added to the file, and the police attempted to recruit the potential informer.[56] The recruit was suddenly in the position to supplement her file but never to change her status as a surveilled object whose biography was being ultimately written by the police. The first step in this transformation was the writing of an autobiography and the informer agreement. Informers were thus granted a rigidly limited role contributing to their own secret police biography at the cost of writing the lives of others. Securitate instructions mention that in case this autobiography and informer agreement were declined, the agent's file was to be closed, but not before a "biography was written," synthesizing all the surveillance and characterization work into one document.[57] Whether they covered suspects, informers, or failed informers, files were designed so that the last word always belonged to biography.

If the one narrative voice of the work dossier foils the cacophony of voices mingling in the surveillance file, a closer examination of the latter also reveals rigid patterns of selection and interpretation that strongly curb heteroglossia. For example, the record of a unique conversation between two major writers is replaced by the bored summary, "In the morning, the subject [Nicolae Steinhardt] has conversed with Stan [code name for writer Alexandru Paleologu] for a very long time on literary and religious themes."[58] Often dormant when it came to long intellectual conversations, the curiosity of both Romanian and Soviet secret services was often sparked by the mention of unfamiliar names, with sometimes unintended comic effect. After a tea party at the house of Lev Tolstoy's daughter, one agent reported that the guests mentioned someone by the name of Socrates. He suggested that this suspicious character be checked since he was not yet identified in police records.[59] The suggestion would have probably amused, but not surprised, contemporary writers like Mikhail Bulgakov, who in *The Master and Margarita* has a character demand in a similar vein that Kant be sent to the Solovki camp.[60] While reading the files, one finds fascinating manuscripts ignored or butchered but for a few lines that the regime singled out as subversive. If at first I was struck by the many voices and points of view that mingle in the police file, the hierarchy among them soon became only too apparent.

The surveillance file was punctuated by "periodical syntheses" and ended with a "general synthesis" written by the chief investigator.[61] This synthesis provided one description of the subject that superseded all previous characterizations. The heterogeneous portrait was here reduced to a cliché from an infamous stock of characters: the spy, the saboteur, the counter-revolutionary, the terrorist, and so on. Thus, the surveillance file was articulated at the intersection of two conflicting practices: that of the informer, denouncer, literary reviewer, and mail censor, who shared an inclination for collecting and recording information; and of the investigator, who collated and synthesized their contributions in a final characterization that reduced their cacophony to one incriminating conclusion. The surveillance file collated and then cut the synthetic portrait of the state enemy. This monster could be many-headed, as multiple accusations piled up on one another: spy, saboteur, kulak, antisocial or anti-Soviet element could coexist. However, all these accusations belonged to the same rhetorical register repeated ad nauseam by the secret police. As such, the many heads were not meant to speak different languages; whatever traces of heteroglossia survived in the hodgepodge collation of the surveillance file were usually dryly stifled in the synthetic portrait. It was the task of the interrogation to "work" the suspect so that he fit this synthetic image, until the one or many heads of the monster all spoke the same secret police language, the ventriloquized language of confession.

## Investigation Files: From Autobiography to Confession

The suspect's synthetic characterization was meant to close the surveillance file and serve as a basis for arrest. The arrest order, often complemented by house and personal search orders, and the list of items confiscated upon the arrest, were the first documents in the investigation file.[62] As mentioned, investigation files were sometimes started under a separate name (*sledstvennoe delo, dosar de anchetă*), and sometimes followed the surveillance materials under the same file name (DUI). The core of the post-arrest investigation file was often constituted by interrogation records. A. Grigoriev accurately explains that "[In] its 'classic' form an interrogation begins by having the prisoner fill out a detailed questionnaire and write his autobiography and a list of his acquaintances."[63] The trajectory of the surveillance files had been like that of a camera panning closer and closer on the suspect. With the house search and the personal search, the records get closer and closer to the physical person of the suspect; with the autobiography, the interior of the subject is breached, and from now on the file will contain first-person accounts of the subject.

Taken upon arrest, the autobiography rarely added any new information to a conscientious surveillance file. Mostly brief and to the point, these autobiographies read like curriculum vitae, except that educational achievements were played down. Next to his fingerprints and his last photograph, Isaac Babel's autobiography starts thus:

> Born, 1894, Odessa. Writer. Not a Party member. Jewish. Last place of work, USSR Children's Film Studio, State Publishing House. Higher education received at Kiev Commercial Institute.
>
> Family: father, a commercial trader, died 1924; mother, Feniia Aronovna Babel, 75, a housewife, lives in Belgium; wife, Antonina Nikolaevna Pirozhkova, 30, engineer with the Metro Construction and Design Institute; children . . .[64]

Most autobiographies adopted a similarly impersonal, bureaucratic tone; a
few, however, used a pathos-ridden, hyperbolic style when reaching certain
episodes, such as one's service in the communist party or in the workplace.
The autobiographies say as much about the suspects' view of the secret police
as they do about the suspects themselves. This view determined the choice
of life events to be included, carefully glossed over, or even excluded from an
autobiography. The differences in tone among the autobiographies reveal a
whole spectrum of perceptions of Soviet power and its repressive apparatus.
The indignant tone of autobiographies that conclude with an address to various forums of Soviet justice attests to a belief that the present abuse was an
isolated accident. At the opposite end of the spectrum lie the resigned, understated autobiographies of those who believed themselves to be just another
victim of a mindlessly repressive regime. The suspect's expectations about the
secret police decisively shaped her way of telling her life story. The remolding
of her life into a police biography was under way.[65]

If the typical interrogation started with an autobiography, it ended on a
confession. While the autobiography reductively presented the portrait of a
socialist citizen, more or less dedicated to the party, with a particular professional and personal history, the confession all too often presented the portrait
of the socialist enemy. The road between is usually described in prison memoirs
as the most painful part of the overall experience of confinement. From the
start, two portraits of the self—the secret police's vague criminal scenario and
the victim's own perception of his life—were pitted against each other. The
balance of power was totally disproportionate, and the individual had value
only inasmuch as he could fill in the details of the secret police case against
him. This relationship between one's self and one's file is recorded in all of its
literal horror in the file of theater director Vsevolod Meierkhold: "[C]onstantly
the interrogator repeated, threateningly, 'If you won't write (invent, in other
words?!), then we shall beat you again, leaving your head and your right hand
untouched but reducing the rest to a hacked, bleeding and shapeless body.' And
I signed everything."[66] The head and the right hand were spared inasmuch as
they were instrumental in the creation of the file. For different reasons, the
head and the right hand are also extremely important in traditional police files,
where they are heavily featured for identification purposes. Indeed, early mug
shots sometimes showed the hand together with the face.[67] Later, the hand
disappeared only to be better showcased in the practice of fingerprinting. The
difference between the identification drive of the traditional police file and the
biographical drive of the Soviet secret police file is saliently exposed in their
distinct uses of these criminal body parts. In Soviet personal files, the head and
the hands are no longer just privileged sites of identification; instead, they are

primarily writing tools co-opted in the penning of a life story whose definitive version the file aimed to record.

This "rewriting" of the suspect in the investigation file was not a passive operation that he underwent. As Meierkhold's words attest, the victim had to carry out this operation himself. In other words, the victim was not just written about or, as in Kafka's *Penal Colony*, written on; rather, he was expected to become the author of his own file. Rather than writing the truth about oneself, the victim attempted to guess and approximate an autobiography that would be satisfactory to the secret police. This required victims to internalize the ideology of the secret police, an accomplishment that did not come easily, even when under the pressure of the investigation victims were ready to write and sign anything. Prisoners often went through tens of drafts before they guessed the criminal scenario that the agent found satisfactory. Indeed, the capacity to concoct such a scenario and identity—whether the victim ended up believing it or not—provided proof that the victim had grasped the logic of the secret police and adopted its rules of composition.

The subject's introjection of police ideology produced a ventriloquized confession. The abstract logic of the secret police took over the body of the victim; it determined not only her perception of the world but also of the self. In other words, ideology became embodied and as such reorganized the victim's feelings and perceptions (*aisthesis*). The secret police's aesthetic reeducation of the socialist man was well under way. The personal file was the artifact where the elusive precepts of this aesthetic were made manifest.

## Stalinist Files: How Many of Those Enemies Were Forged

This blueprint of the file—with its progression from surveillance collation, synthetic characterization, autobiography, through confession and sentence—lasted throughout Soviet times.[68] However, we can trace the development of the personal file through time by following the shift in emphasis on one or another of its constituent parts. The number of interrogation records hit the highest point in the Stalinist period, while surveillance reports overflow from post-Stalinist binders. During the Stalinist purges, surveillance work was often cursory or even entirely skipped.[69] Characterization remained the basis for arrests, but it was often reduced to a bare minimum: people were arrested simply for belonging to a blacklisted group. Being a White, a kulak, or member of a former political party constituted both a sufficient characterization and an accusation.

An extraordinary document made public by the Memorial Foundation gives us a privileged window into the contents and uses of investigation files at the height of Stalinist repression.[70] The document, signed by the head of the secret police, N. Ezhov, in July 1937, orders the liquidation of former kulaks and "other anti-Soviet elements," including members of former political parties and common criminals. The document contains detailed numbers, by region, of people to be arrested, and sets a four-month deadline for the approximately two hundred thousand anticipated arrests. Those targeted were to be arrested on the basis of their adherence to a blacklisted category, and divided into two crass categories—one encompassing "all the more inimical elements" and the second, "the less active, but still inimical members of the above-mentioned categories." The vague difference in these loosely defined categories had crucial consequences: the more active elements were to be "immediately arrested, and, following the review of their cases by the Troika, SHOT [capitals in original]." The "less active elements" were "to be sentenced to eight to ten years of hard labor." Thus, in the Moscow and Leningrad region alone, forty-nine thousand people were to be arrested, out of which nine thousand were destined to be shot and forty thousand to be sent to the camps.

The document establishes the protocol governing the files, giving a typical table of contents and prescribing its trajectory, from its creation by the investigator, to its forwarding to the NKVD troika who passes the sentence, to those responsible for carrying out the sentence, and to the registration-archive department of the NKVD. The protocol starts by ordering that each arrestee is to be endowed with an investigation file (*sledstvennoe delo*) and provides a table of contents for such a file, which is to include: "arrest order, [house and personal] search records, [list of] materials, taken during the search, private documents, the questionnaire of the arrestee [*anketa*], registration forms, interrogation records and a short incriminating conclusion" and to be added later, the sentence and the records concerning the way it was carried out. A special note orders that all criminal links of the arrestee be established and that the family of the arrestee be registered with the secret police. While the cultural figures who are the main subject of my study were usually bound to have more elaborate files than the ones speedily created for hundreds of thousands of people in regional bureaus within the estimated four months of this purge, it is noteworthy that even during such a rush order the NKVD aimed for the creation of a standardized file for each one of its arrestees. And while the laconic table of contents crams the often excruciating road from autobiography to confession into the phrase "interrogation records" and effaces distinctions between the various items in its list, both this list and the protocol at large clearly showcase the emphasis on post-arrest investigation rather than on surveillance work. After all, the first item in the investigation file is supposed to be the arrest order! Even though the protocol advises that "detailed fundamental data" (*podrobnoe ustanovochnye dannye*) are to be collected for individuals in the compromised categories, given the four-month deadline for "processing" hundreds of thousands of cases and the enormous task of sentencing and creating investigation records for all these individuals, surveillance was hardly feasible.

In the absence of costly surveillance work or particular crimes to investigate, secret police agents of the 1930s started first interrogations with the standard question, "Why do you think you were arrested?" The common dismay of those arrested provoked the routine wrath of the interrogator, who asked whether the accused didn't know that the secret police made no mistakes. In order to confirm this axiom, the accused was supposed to discard his life story and instead take guesses at the particulars of a crime that would fit secret police scenarios. Thus, the record of Isaac Babel's first interrogation shows his attempt to answer the famous question haughtily dismissed by the investigator as an "extraordinarily naïve explanation of the fact of his arrest."[71] Babel first guessed that he had been arrested because of his inability to produce "even one sufficiently significant literary work, which could be interpreted as sabotage and lack of desire to write in the [given] Soviet conditions." Babel, once a translator for the secret police, already started the work of reinterpreting and translating his own vision of his shortcomings—his inability to write—into the incriminating language of the police, so that writer's block turns into sabotage in the space of a sentence. Babel's self-incrimination struck even his interrogator as far-fetched (an effect that Babel might have slyly aimed for). Dissatisfied, the interrogator retorted by turning Babel's answer into a rhetorical question, "You mean to say that you were arrested as a writer?" He then returned to the original question, "So what are then the actual causes of your arrest?" until he started getting the kinds of answers he was looking for: "I often traveled abroad and found myself in close relationships with prominent Trotskyists . . ."

Confession became a centerpiece of the Stalinist file. It should then come as no surprise that during the 1930s Mikhail Bakhtin chose the "confession of a person being investigated for trial" as a primary example of an extra-artistic genre deeply relevant to the study of literature. Bakhtin noticed that confession had so far been interpreted only "at the level of laws, ethics and psychology," and called for its interpretation "at the level of the philosophy of language (of discourse)."[72] Bakhtin's prime example was a false confession, Ivan Karamazov's, which he used to raise the question of "the role of the other in formulating discourse, problems surrounding an inquest and so forth."[73] Indeed, the proliferation of false confessions that marked the

1930s offers a troubling example of double-voiced discourse. They testify to a dialogism gone wrong, where the voice of the other does not bring liberating double-voiceness into one's discourse; rather, it takes it over and turns it against its enunciator. Isaac Babel's confession provides a disturbing example that deserves to be quoted at length:

> among my papers can be found the draft I had begun to make of a comedy and of tales about myself that were an attempt at merciless self-denunciation [*samorazoblacheniia*], a desperate and belated attempt to make good the harm that I had done to Soviet Art. A feeling of duty and a sense of public service never guided my literary work. Artists who came into contact with me felt the fatal influence of this emasculated and sterile view of the world.
>
> The harm my activities caused cannot be quantitatively assessed, but it was great. One of the soldiers on the literary front who enjoyed the support and attention of the Soviet reader when he began his work, and who had been guided by Gorky, *the greatest writer of our era, I deserted my post and opened the front of Soviet literature to decadent and defeatist emotions* [emphasis mine].[74]

Babel's confession reproduces *ad literam* some of the clichés of his times, such as "Gorky, the greatest writer of our era." But the confession becomes most disturbing when some of Babel's most profound preoccupations—the relationship between the writer and the soldier as explored in *Red Cavalry* (*Konarmiia*)—blend in with the language of the secret police, so that it is hard to tell who really wrote the last sentence, Babel or the interrogator. This blending was not restricted to the extreme conditions of the interrogation room; rather, Babel admitted to having switched the genre of his creations to self-denunciation even before his arrest. Babel confessed his guilt about contaminating young writers with the destructive influence of his worldview, and atoned for it by taking on the official discourse and letting it impose the new genre of his work—self-denunciation. In essence, Babel's confession revolved around one theme: the mixing of his discourse with that of others. Turning Bakhtin on his head, the sins of dialogism are here atoned for by a conversion to authoritative discourse.

Typically, the Stalinist confession is radically different from the initial file's autobiography, sometimes to the point where it is difficult to believe that they were written by the same person. In sharp opposition to the autobiography, the confession tends to be prolix and muddled with excessive detail, and it often reads like a jumbled mix of fantastic stories. A representative example can again be extracted from Babel's confession, in which he admitted to being a decadent individualist writer, and also a French spy recruited by André Malraux, and also an Austrian spy, and also an associate of the now compromised Ezhov, and also a coconspirator in the latter's wife's "plot" to assassinate Stalin, and finally a terrorist Trotskyist.[75] This splitting of the self into a variety of sometimes mutually exclusive criminals/enemies is a defining characteristic of the confession.

There is a sick logic to this madness, a new definition of crime: "The tsarist government . . . punished people for an already committed crime. Our job is to prevent."[76] Lenin himself supported this idea, proudly explaining to Gorky that some people "are in prison to prevent plots."[77] Thus, the investigation file started with a synthetic characterization—such as bourgeois background—and attempted to match it to all potential criminal profiles: spy, counterrevolution-ary, saboteur, and so on. This was a slippery slope, because according to the extreme voluntarism espoused by Soviet psychology in the 1930s, people could turn into pretty much anything they wanted. In his thorough account of the fashioning of the communist self, Igal Halfin argues that "according to early 1930s Soviet science, plasticity of human nature, its susceptibility to radical reworking, was the key trait that distinguishes proletarian psychology from the bourgeois one."[78] The latter was derided for its exaggerated belief in the influence of the environment on the psyche. In the late 1930s, this voluntarism was taken even further. Soviet people were believed capable of making and remaking themselves, refashioning their old selves into communist New Men. The darker implication of the voluntarist approach was that individuals could just as easily fashion and refashion themselves into various criminal selves.

As Walter Benjamin, and later Michel Foucault, have suggested, modern criminology typically attempted to break up suspicious, threatening crowds and isolate the individual criminal.[79] As such, it was a reductive, linear narrative driven by identification and individuation. At the opposite end, the Stalinist file was sinisterly productive, as it split one individual into a variety of criminal profiles. The diverging orientations of these narratives are based on a radical difference in their understanding of the individual criminal. As John Bender has argued, the development of modern criminology and confinement was founded on a new understanding of the individual as depicted in the realist novel, which charted the development and transformations of changing characters, influenced by their environments.[80] In a parallel fashion, the modern penal system developed gradations of punishment that replaced the domi-nance of the death penalty in the premodern prison system, acting on the belief that each particular crime required a commensurate punishment. Administered in the right doses, these new sentences were conceived not only as punishment but also as a fitting corrective for the malleable character of the criminal.

The Stalinist secret police file did away with gradual narratives to account for the transformation of a socialist citizen into an enemy. The communist psyche, like the Soviet Union in general, was believed to be able to skip whole stages of development; as Halfin argues, "'development . . . was [seen as] a set of qualitative leaps.' Emphasis on revolution in the psyche was not new, of course, but now this transformation was conceptualized as an event, not as a process."[81] By the late 1930s, this attack on the gradual growth of the psyche had reached its apogee, and Stalinist discourse was characterized by an essentialization of moral features.[82] It finally postulated only two human essences: the good and the evil.[83] As a result, the switch from socialist subject to socialist enemy was necessarily dramatic. Those whose false-good masks were stripped by the interrogation to show their evil essence were often called *dvurushniki* (double-dealers), a word that betrays the rigid binary understanding of crime and innocence. As a consequence, Stalinist files showed little interest in observing and recording the individual's every gesture and investigating each particular crime in order to chart a gradual development and instead developed a histrionic rhetoric of unmasking, projecting, and reforging enemies.

## Post-Stalinist Files: The Age of Surveillance

After Stalin's death, Khrushchev's critiques about "past excesses" brought significant changes in the Soviet secret police. The number of arrests was curbed while prisoners started returning home from the camps. In Romania, "the relaxation of the terror" waited until almost a decade later, when most surviving political prisoners were amnestied.[84] At this time, the holdings of the secret police archives also underwent a fundamental change. As repression became less overt, the number of arrests dwindled, and with them the number of interrogation files. At the same time, the relative number of surveillance files soared.[85] As we have seen, in theory surveillance files were meant to provide the basis for opening the interrogation file. However, by this time, surveillance files often dragged on for a lifetime, without leading to arrests. Nicolae Steinhardt's files provide a telling example.[86] They were opened in the late 1950s when Steinhardt was investigated as part of the Noica-Pillat group in the most infamous trial of the intelligentsia to take place in Romania.[87] Steinhardt received a twelve-year prison sentence in 1959 but was amnestied, like many other prisoners, in 1964. The surveillance file continued with cellmate reports while Steinhardt was in prison and throughout Steinhardt's life with small interruptions until March 31, 1989, a day after his death and a few months before the revolution that toppled the communist regime. The file closed laconically on a tapped phone conversation as Steinhardt's maid announced his death to a friend.[88]

Advances in surveillance technology constituted the second major reason for the spectacular increase in the volume of surveillance files. In particular, the 1970s registered an international boom in surveillance technologies and their wide adoption by police agencies.[89] The surveillance of dissident writer

1. OBIECTIVUL „STAN"

2. LEGĂTURA din Sf. NICOLAE LICĂREȚ
   Nr 1 din DATA DE 20.10.1988

Portrait of Nicolae Steinhardt from a surveillance photograph. Steinhardt, marked with a "I," looks into the camera seemingly aware of its presence. *Dosar de urmărire informativă nr. 49342, I 207,* October 20, 1988, Fond Informativ (CNSAS), vol. VIII, p. 197.

Paul Goma by the Romanian secret police between 1972 and 1978 resulted in no fewer than twenty volumes of files, each at least two hundred pages long; that is, over four thousand pages covering six years.[90] The character of Nicolae Steinhardt's files also changes dramatically starting in 1972, when the secret police installed a bugging device in his apartment that allowed them to monitor the suspect's every sound.[91] Lodged in Steinhardt's telephone, the bug captured enough material to fill two separate file volumes.[92] Transcribed without comment, just like all his other conversations, is Steinhardt's wry warning about telephone surveillance delivered to his interlocutor, and likely to his secret police listeners: "Be careful with these phones; you speak here and it's heard elsewhere. That's the definition of the telephone."[93] And yet both Steinhardt and his interlocutors kept on talking, and his listeners kept on transcribing. At this time, the files started to overflow with detailed transcriptions of all daily activities and conversations. These files make cinema verité look fake, the constructed example of an everydayness that cannot but exceed it.

Spanning whole lives in such extraordinary detail, the surveillance file provided endless material for the characterization. At the opposite end of the hasty name-calling of Stalinist files, late surveillance files often attempted to give intimate psychological portraits of the suspect. The use of "depth informers" was emphasized more than ever: "We will continue to emphasize the recruiting of individuals able to penetrate in the intimacy of the surveilled elements, so as to know their plans and illicit intentions."[94] Marin Preda, one of Romania's foremost writers, kept the secret police agents busy with a prolific publication record, three wives, and dozens of schoolmates.[95] In an attempt to find potential informers and blackmail material, the secret police took a field trip to the writer's village to meet his former elementary school friends. The agents returned with a story about Preda's shock at accidentally seeing his father's genitals while the latter urinated. Psychology-savvy agents drew complex analyses of the writer's relationship to his wives, with the account of his last marriage concluding, "weighing the profits and disadvantages of this marriage it is clear that the profits are larger, for Marin Preda and for literature."[96] Preda scholars would likely envy the detailed bibliography of his works and contemporary reviews in his file. The police routinely asked a literary critic to provide a synthesis of these reviews, which often sealed the fate of a book that was their subject. The crafty synthesis of contemporary reviews to Preda's *The Most Beloved of Humans* (*Cel mai iubit dintre pământeni*) would shock the generations of Romanian readers who have considered this novel legendary for its subversiveness: "This volume is a far better propaganda for the present leadership of the country than any other form of ideological agitation, first of all because of the condemnation of an epoch full of abuses [the Stalinist-style precursors of the present government]. Things said in a symbolic manner are better remembered than those said in party meetings or written in newspapers."[97]

Instead of the patchy image of the suspect offered by early files, where a friend's close perspective might have been pasted next to a literary review, late surveillance files provide a steadier picture. The tapping device established the main point of view from which the suspect was observed, and this distance stayed constant day in and day out. With this new form of surveillance came two main types of narrators—the scribes, who simply transcribed the information recorded on the tapping machines, and agents of higher rank, who synthesized it every once in a while. The tape transcriptions were sometimes complemented with the text of a censored letter or an informer's report of a conversation beyond the reach of the tapping devices; literary critics were still asked to come in and comment on a manuscript, while friends and relatives were asked for more personal information. However, the apparent cacophony of informer voices is often drowned out by the impersonal tone set by the new technology.

While Stalinist files rushed in narrative succession along a predictable path—from characterization to autobiography to confession—post-Stalinist files have hardly any narrative progression. It is difficult to distinguish the beginning, middle, and end of a file that was collated from daily records of surveillance. As with some contemporary novels, the reader can justifiably begin reading on any page. Instead of narrative progression, we have a repetitive alternation between surveillance transcripts and periodic syntheses. More often than not, the synthesis does not lead to the opening of an investigation file but to yet another surveillance transcript. Furthermore, many surveillance transcripts accumulated into unwieldy piles of papers in the hundreds before being properly synthesized. These delays mark the opposite end of the spectrum from the far-fetched interpretations, projections, and unmaskings of the Stalinist files, where an innocuous surveillance observation was enough for the creation of a suspect. Stalinist files overworked the little surveillance information they had, tendentiously combining and interpreting it or simply using it as the basis for concocting a far-fetched case. The Stalinist secret police file was a biography that took over the life of the individual, rewriting it into a histrionic, clichéd criminal narrative that as we have seen, radically departed from the realist aesthetic of the modern prison. Post-Stalinist files seem to return to a realist aesthetic based on observation and description. For instance, in the post-Stalinist file the narrative appears to follow dutifully the life of the individual. The denouement often coincides with the (more often natural) death of the suspect. The smallest increments of the file—daily transcripts—were framed by the waking hours of each suspect. Roland Barthes singled out details that do not advance the narrative or easily lend themselves to symbolic interpretation as a key ingredient of what he termed *l'effet de réel* (realist effect).[98] In the post-Stalinist secret police file, the *effet de réel* ran riot as such details proliferated to the point where they choked the hardly visible narrative. The post-Stalinist file often exhibits a singularly drab hyperrealism.

Thanks to the new surveillance technology, the secret police could afford an unremitting, dull containment of the subject that was a far cry from the demonstrative, histrionic rewriting of the Stalinist enemy. This is not to say that the new surveillance was limited to objective recording; it certainly deliberately molded people's behavior, most obviously through intimidation.[99] However, post-Stalinist files represented and remolded the individual in a radically different manner from their Stalinist predecessors. While constantly following suspects up to the most intimate hours of their life, tapping each phone conversation, radio program, or the exact content of the lunch menu, the police rarely solicited the suspect to directly answer its questions. Ventriloquized confessions were no longer extorted from victims during excruciating interrogation sessions. True, the suspect might still enter the scene for an intimidation session at the secret police headquarters. So as to remember that she was constantly followed, the suspect had to confirm a personal detail that the police always (made sure to show they) already knew. These intimidation sessions did not extort the confession or fabrication of crimes unknown to the secret police; rather, they reminded the suspect that all of her actions, criminal or not, were known.

The new surveillance technologies were a good fit for the post-Stalinist turning away from arrest and punishment towards "prevention." Redefining its tasks in 1972, the Securitate issued a whole document on prevention and outlined the main measures to be taken towards the subjects of DUI: manipulation, discreditation, dispersion, and warning or intimidation.[100] The first and last of these measures, manipulation and warning, were part of the same attempt to "positively influence" the suspect through the application of various degrees of pressure. The purpose of the file then was to collect biographical information that, incriminating or not, would be flaunted in front of the suspect so as to intimidate him into changing that biography.

The remaining techniques, the suspect's discreditation and the dispersal of his networks, programmatically aimed to "isolate" the individual to the point of making his activities bear no influence on the world around him.[101] *Isolation* became a key word both in administrative documents and in the files themselves.[102] At this time then the secret police curbed its interest in dramatically reforging the very core of its subjects and instead focused on closely and intimidatingly monitoring him and severing his relationships to the surrounding world. A new division between the personal, the public, and the political took shape, as revealed in Nicolae Steinhardt's seemingly paradoxical defense of his subversive prison memoir. After his manuscript was confiscated in 1972, Steinhardt was called in to the secret police headquarters and questioned about it. He described unapologetically the politically incorrect subject of the journal, namely, his conversion to Christianity during a time of imprisonment that he painted in all its grim details, including unflinching accounts of the widespread use of torture. Steinhardt insisted that this inflammatory journal was a personal matter and as such deserved little attention or reprimand from the secret police. The police appeared to agree. The crime, in their view, was distributing or sharing the contents of the memoir, even if with only one person, the typist. Unapologetic about the incendiary contents of the memoir, Steinhardt showed contrition for hiring a typist instead of doing the typing himself, and never tired of emphasizing the intimate character of his work. Steinhardt's "Statements" (Declarații) constitute a unique document that deserves to be cited at length. On the one hand, they are his most thorough account of the motivations behind the writing of his major work, peppered with his hallmark mix of familiar, bookish, and vintage language; on the other hand, the text also bears some traces of Steinhardt's secret police interlocutors, whose questions shaped his story and whose wooden official language sometimes echoes in Steinhardt's writing. The investigator's two-layered underlining is additionally revealing of what he understood to be relevant or incriminating in Steinhardt's declarations, as in his journal:

> Concerning this manuscript I assert that it represents an intimate journal written by me in my private residence during 1970–71, in which I have tried to depict in a detailed way my religious conversion, i.e., my conversion from Judaism to Christianity. I felt the need to explain to myself this spiritual process, which was so significant for me. . . . Through this Journal I aimed to clarify to myself a spiritual process. The Manuscript was typed by a friend of mine, Yvonne Eseanu, who passed through Romania and who offered to type it. I only own one copy of this Journal, because I did not intend to circulate it in Romania or abroad. The drafts have been partly destroyed, and partly kept together with my other papers, at home.
>
> I did not try to send this manuscript abroad; I neither gave it to anyone else to read nor did I myself read it to anyone.[103] . . .
>
> I aimed to conceal no reality from myself, and instead I recorded on paper the ideas, memories and thoughts which passed through my mind. I never intended to circulate the Journal nor to share it with others. And the idea of sending it abroad seemed to me inconceivable and totally foreign from my beliefs which would have never agreed with anything of the kind.
>
> Leading an isolated life focused on religious practice, I found in this journal a way of exposing to myself in a systematic way an entire interior strife. Since my prison sentence was based exclusively on the fact that I did not agree to serve as a witness for the prosecution, the journal contains sincere expressions of revolt, ending however with the expression of a calm and accepting spiritual state . . . this manuscript . . . does not represent a hostile act toward the regime of my country, but only—I

repeat—an act of spiritual liberation. For someone who has intellectual interests
like me, it was natural to have writing cover this interior spiritual process.[104]

I felt the strong need to elucidate to myself the reasons for my deep religious
conversion. Such an elucidation imposed itself as a deep spiritual necessity. It could
only take the form of writing, which is the only way to clarify. There is however
a danger that such writing could take an artificial, solemn, didactic character, as is
often the case with the religious confessions of former prisoners, which take on a
saccharine air. I did not want to appear to myself in such a light. I therefore tried to
give my confession an authentic and live character, as realist as possible . . . I thought
that joining this spiritual process with the facts of life, its real events, I would be able
to avoid saccharine generalities. That's why I linked the history of my conversion
with childhood memories and especially to the moment when my conversion took
on a real, concrete, form, the time spent by me in prison. . . . The prison was the time
when the conversion took place and as such it plays a very important role.[105] . . .
Regarding the typing of the manuscript I assert that I consider it a mistake on my
side to have had the work typed. It would have been more correct of me to leave
it in handwriting or to type it myself.[106]

Writing trod the thin line between criminal and innocent behavior. As a personal memoir it could be tolerated; however, inasmuch as its existence opened
the possibility of a reader, writing was condemned. In other words, while the
secret police no longer asked the suspect to fully convert to writing in its own
genre, that of the incriminating confession, it still aimed to be the suspect's sole
reader. Even though Steinhardt had long ago been labeled as an "unrepentant
hostile element" and his writings were irremediably subversive, they could be
tolerated so long as they were completely isolated from the exterior world.

This attempt to control and enfeeble the suspect's connections is epitomized by that obligatory item of each file, the detailed list of the suspect's
relationships and all other individuals mentioned in the files. This list, drawn
up by the investigator, was verified and updated by the archivist, who then created registration cards corresponding to each name. As we have seen, already
in 1937 Ezhov insisted that such a list be drawn up, emphasizing the obligatory
inclusion of close family members. Through this list, each file became the
potential originator of other files in an arborescent model that first takes over
the family tree and later threateningly spreads out to "*any* inimical *and* personal
relationships."[107] It is then the relationship that is inimical, whether personal
or otherwise. Or to put it differently, it is the interpersonal that is criminalized
and targeted here.

Confined behind a wall endowed with the best tapping devices, the individual could even express himself. As a child I once eavesdropped on a friend
of my father's who confessed that every night he went home, locked all doors
and windows, hid in the bathroom, and ranted against the regime. As I was
growing up in the 1980s in Romania, this image became my shortcut for that

faceless abstraction, the "socialist man." His rants were most likely carefully recorded. But his precautions probably convinced those who listened that he was harmless. This last remnant of closeted freedom in fact shows the cynical power of the regime, which did not need to spare resources by once and for all stamping out hostile individuals, for it could afford an unending surveillance. Or maybe by the 1980s there were just too many people ranting in their bathrooms. At any rate, the secret police did its best to wall off subversive individuals into helpless isolation.

## A Note on Foucault

The trajectory of my analysis, leading from the histrionic spectacle of Stalinist secrecy and punishment that routinely went as far as bodily torture, to the more subtle practices of post-Stalinist surveillance, might seem to reiterate the famous arch of Foucault's argument in *Discipline and Punish*. In fact, the narrative that I propose here challenges key elements of Foucault's argument. The most obvious of these is the "chronological vector," which as Laura Engelstein reminds us, is never entirely lost in Foucault's thesis: "whatever the overlaps and collusions, Western nations have allegedly proceeded from absolutist monarchies, through Polizeistaat enlightened despotisms, to liberal states that delegate power through social self-regulation and control their citizens through the operational function of individual autonomy."[108] In Eastern Europe, the histrionic spectacle of punishment geared toward the extraction of confession through various extreme practices such as torture took place long after the arrival of a modernity that, in Foucault's chronology, brought more indirect versions of power aimed at the individual's soul rather than body. To reconcile this temporal gap between Eastern European history and Foucault's theoretical model, one might argue that Eastern Europeans arrived late at this narrative of modernization, thus experiencing in the twentieth century phenomena that Western Europeans had ostensibly long left behind. However, it in fact appears that for once, Eastern Europeans made it relatively on time: at least inasmuch as policing was concerned, Russia was largely in line with Western European developments by the end of the nineteenth century. When torture was sanctioned in Soviet criminal investigations in 1937, it was not because the Soviet Union had not yet developed disciplinary methods. In fact, as we shall see in Chapters 4 and 5, Soviet discourse during the 1930s purges explicitly addressed and selectively borrowed from the disciplinary model of both late Tsarist and contemporary Western penal policy, while also using it as a straw man against which it could most favorably present Soviet criminology. Jamming Foucault's linear narrative, Soviet and Eastern European penal history follows more convoluted trajectories, with particular policing techniques and goals—and the related dogmas on human nature—opportunistically and even capriciously introduced, used, discarded, and again revisited. Thus, the preemptive ambitions of Soviet criminology shifted the emphasis away from the practices of identification and individuation that define modern penal practice for Foucault; instead, investigation aimed at matching one individual with all the criminal personae that she could potentially take. In other words, instead of identifying and singling out one suspect from a crowd, preemptive criminology was more interested in splitting an individual into a crowd of potential criminals/enemies. Similarly, the interest in the soul of the prisoner did not supersede the interest in his body; rather, in the 1930s the project of the reforging of the prisoner's soul often relied on bodily torture. Challenging any linear narrative, Eastern European history reminds us that we are never safely lodged in our modernity but rather that "premodern" types of punishment may always reemerge, as they did in the Soviet Union in the 1930s and in the United States in recent years. While using some of Foucault's invaluable insights, my purpose is not to reiterate but rather to renounce the linearity of his narrative. This also means renouncing our privileged place in this narrative, safely ensconced in a modernity from where we can look back into the past toward an age of corporal punishment that appears so remote as to be too facilely exploited for dramatic effect, as it was in the opening paragraph of *Discipline and Punish*.

Read as a biography, the personal file reveals the secret police's ever changing view of its subjects. Taking the biographer's prerogatives to an extreme, the secret police did not stop at passively depicting its subjects but rather attempted to rewrite them. This rewriting was taken to an extreme in the Stalinist file, where the police collated a portrait of the individual to fit its criminal clichés. In the Stalinist practice of confession, the victim was asked to internalize such a cliché and become the author of her file, as well as her new criminal self. Post-Stalinist files renounced this demonstrative Stalinist aesthetic, framed as it was in secrecy and based on unmasking, projections, and ventriloquized confessions. As surveillance files proliferated, post-Stalinist files shifted the emphasis from reforging toward a hyperrealist description of the subject. In its last two decades, the secret police file became a biography that aspired to patiently cover and isolate the life of the subject within its binders.

## CHAPTER TWO

# The Master and Margarita

## The Devil's Secret Police File

As a singularly powerful genre of writing in Soviet times, the secret police file cast a long shadow over contemporary literature. This chapter argues that this shadow extended as far as the most famous novelistic representation of the Soviet 1930s, Mikhail Bulgakov's *The Master and Margarita*. A copious intertextuality riddles Bulgakov's novel, and critics have illuminated, among others, Menippean, Dantesque, Faustian, Gogolian, Orthodox Russian, Gnostic, and Manichaean influences behind characters, themes, and motifs.[1] However, the parts of *The Master and Margarita* written under the shadow of dominant textual practices of its day—such as the secret police file and censorship—have remained so far in the dark. My investigation of *The Master and Margarita*'s complex relationship with the secret police file aims to enrich rather than dispute existing studies of the novel's intertextuality. Similarly, pursuing the novel's relationship to the file is not aimed at disputing the novel's status as a legend of literary subversion. Rather, I aim to show that the influence of the secret police file can be discerned even in the writing of a novel deemed so subversive as to be first published—still partly censored—only in 1966, twenty-six years after the death of its author. In this account, influence is considered in its broad spectrum of meanings, including power, pressure, authority, effect, affect, spell, inspiration, impact, and imprint.[2] Likewise, literature is seen to be shaped *by*, but also *against* and *around*, the influence of the secret police file. Like "any link one establishes" in this babel of a novel, *The Master and Margarita*'s link to the secret police file and censorship "is more of an association than a direct likening or equation"[3]; yet, pursuing this link does illuminate some of the lasting puzzles of the novel.

## The Distinguishing Characteristics of
## the Devil in 1930s Moscow

*The Master and Margarita* recounts the fantastic adventures of Woland—self-identified both as a foreign professor and as the devil—during his stay in 1930s Moscow. What are the sources behind this extraordinary story? The narrator's description of Woland avowedly draws on a variety of sources. Sure, his devil harkens back to the Bible, as any devil ultimately does. But there are more contemporary sources: as the narrator tells us, the first portrait of Woland collates "the reports" presented by "various institutions."[4] For now these various institutions remain unnamed, but any contemporary reader could take a good guess. And this guess is confirmed later in the novel; we are told that it is the secret police that feverishly compiles the reports by pretty much any character or institution even remotely connected to Woland's case. Indeed, the secret police was the one institution that would have certainly not missed drawing a report on the devil's visit to the Soviet Union. In fact, the secret police would have certainly drawn a report on any foreign professor's visit. And in the creation of the report, any bland foreign professor stood a good chance of acquiring evil features nothing short of fantastic. He would be involved in many incredible incidents, which would be dubbed as crimes. These crimes would of course be not just common crimes; they would be beyond belief, the "undermining the social order" kind of crimes. In other words, the professor would be demonized. Demonized in the manner of the day, so that the concoction would be a particular type of Soviet demon—a foreigner, no doubt a spy. Or as his first Moscow interlocutor immediately suspects, Woland might even be a returning émigré, the ultimate embodiment of the Soviet uncanny—the familiar turned strange.[5] If Woland's story makes him stand out from the rich pantheon of literary demons, it fits in very well with thousands of other fantastic stories of demonized foreigners, émigrés, professors, and everymen that filled the secret police files of the time.

Not only does Woland's story fit in with the topics of police cases of the time—a demonized foreigner's visit to Moscow—but even the manner of telling this story recalls contemporaneous police files. Woland's legendary introduction sheds more light on the peculiarities of our narrator's style, and thus deserves a full presentation:

> Afterward, when, frankly speaking, it was already late, *various institutions presented reports* [*predstavili svoi svodki*] describing this man. The *collation* [*slichenie*] of these reports can only cause astonishment. Thus, in the first it was said that this man was short, had gold teeth, and limped on the right leg. In the second, that the man was of enormous height, had platinum crowns, and limped on the left leg. The third

laconically informs that the man had no special *distinguishing characteristics* [*osobykh primet*].

It must be admitted that not one of these reports is worth anything.

First of all: the subject described did not limp on either foot, and was neither short nor enormous, but simply tall. As far as his teeth were concerned, on the left side of the mouth he had platinum crowns, and on the right—gold. He wore an expensive gray suit and foreign shoes of the same color. His gray beret was cocked at a jaunty angle over his ear, and under his arm he carried a stick with a black handle in the form of a poodle's head. By appearance—a little over forty. His mouth was somehow twisted. Clean-shaven. A brunet. His right eye was black, the left, for some reason, green. Black eyebrows, but one higher than the other. In short—a foreigner [my emphasis].[6]

The comical differences between these reports might obscure the fact that it is what ties them together that is most strange. For somehow, out of the myriad details that could be seized on in the description of a human being, the first two reports uncannily pick just three extremely peculiar characteristics: height (short/of enormous height), denture (gold teeth/platinum crowns), and limp (on the right/left foot). The third report, even though the briefest, gives out the most information, indeed the clue to the strangeness of the first two reports. It "laconically informs that the man had no distinguishing characteristics." So that is what the first two peculiar reports were doing; they were trying to report distinguishing characteristics! Indeed, what these three first descriptions of Woland all share, despite their obvious differences, is an attempt to answer the same question, which we can reconstitute rather easily from the peculiar information they give us: Any distinguishing characteristics (such as abnormalities of height, dentures, limps)? Describing a subject through distinguishing characteristics might or might not manage to identify him, but it immediately identifies the institution doing the description as the police. The language of the reports confirms then the first suspicion about the nature of these institutions filing the reports.

Police questionnaires do not just describe as much as they shape their subjects through the questions they pose. For example, while as one criminology manual points out, "people normally see the features of a face in their totality, unless one feature stands out," police questionnaires resist this common way of looking and instead direct respondents to fragment the suspect's body, isolating and focusing on particular body parts (such as ears and noses) and distinguishing characteristics.[7] Respondents, whether eye-witnesses, victims, or police officers, also have their own share in this creation of the suspect by projecting their own vested interests, prejudices, and fears. At some points in history, the skin color of the suspect bled over most other characteristics; at other times, it was class, social origin, or accent. Woland is shaped by a

particular shift in suspect profiling that was taking place in the 1930s in the
Soviet Union, when distrust started shifting "to particular ethnic groups and
foreigners."[8] His portrait also bears the mark of the idiosyncrasies of the day.
If one placed the suspicion-prone promenaders in Patriarch Pond in front
of a standard GPU questionnaire, a collation of their responses about a suspect would likely give no less strange a character than Woland. For here are
some of the rubrics, which of course act as indicators for what one should
look for and remember, used for creating the "verbal portrait" (*slovesnyi portret*) of a Soviet citizen: "distinguishing characteristics: physical abnormalities,
mutilations, injuries; additional features: growths, warts, extra fingers, spots,
welts, scars, abnormal body movements, baldness, asymmetry of the face,
different colored eyes, and others."[9] One can easily imagine the panic-stricken
witness—worried that her vigilance and acumen will be found lacking if she
leaves too many of these blanks blank—fabricating a limp here, a golden
tooth there, and to top it all off, a few asymmetries of the face (different-colored eyes, topped by black eyebrows, one higher than the other). It was then
the job of the investigator to collate these various reports, many of which he
would understandably discard as "worthless," into a verbal portrait (*portrait
parlé*) of some coherence. In his analysis of the rhetoric of the verbal portrait,
Christian Phèline notes that "*le portrait parlé* . . . does not retain but the individual traits which exceed the mean." As a result, just like Woland's portrait,
"the verbal portrait is the verbal equivalent of a caricature."[10]

The investigator's textual practices are surprisingly close to those of our
narrator. To start with, our narrator has access to the reports on Woland and
shares their style and interests. In the third paragraph quoted above, he proudly
replaces the various witnesses' cacophonous reports with his own authoritative
collation. Where possible, the narrator simply combines the previous reports:
thus, he solves the riddle of Woland's teeth, golden in one report and platinum in the other, by affirming that Woland had golden teeth on one side and
platinum on the other. This is a subtle affirmation of his ability to go beyond
a single observer's limited point of view, a modest instance of omnipresence.
Where such easy solutions are impossible, the narrator vehemently and dis-
dainfully affirms his version of the facts, giving no rational explanation for
the superiority of his point of view. It is this mixture of crafty collation and
rhetorical force that imposes his version of the facts before the reader.

With his eye-catching denture, twisted mouth, and different-colored eyes
framed by black eyebrows—one higher than the other—our narrator's Woland
emerges as a caricatural verbal portrait of some of the distinguishing characteristics peculiar to his time, such as the asymmetry of the face, the different-
colored eyes, and any marker of foreignness, from the foreign shoes to the

waxing and waning accent that so baffles Woland's interlocutors. Furthermore, our narrator even notes Woland's not so particular characteristics in the same particular language that at times appears as little less than a transcription of laconic answers to a police questionnaire: "By appearance—a little over forty. . . . Clean-shaven. A brunet." And the legendary conclusion of the description—"in short, a foreigner"—recalls the name-calling that typically ended long, absurd, contradictory subject files by fitting an individual into the scapegoated category of the day; in this case, the foreigner.

## Writer Prototypes: Madmen, Apostles, and Secret Police Investigators

Our narrator himself alludes to the similarities between his own work as a writer putting together the various pieces of Woland's story, and the work of secret police investigators working on Woland's case. This is not for lack of more traditional writer figures that he could compare himself to, which actually abound in his own novel. Indeed, in *The Master and Margarita* the narrator closely follows the fate of several writers and dwells on their varied writing techniques. After promising to quit writing poetry, Ivan Bezdomnyi turns to composing an informer's report addressed to the secret police. In this report Ivan tries to organize his disturbed memories of Woland in a coherent narrative. While Ivan relies mainly on his own testimony, the Master, Ivan's neighbor in the mental hospital, draws largely on historical research in the archives and on the powers of his imagination to compose his historical novel about Jesus. A third writer in the novel, Levi Matvei, practices the genre of the inescapably flawed testimony, following Jeshua and scribbling some version of his words on parchment. Our narrator seems to know something about each of these techniques. He even includes lengthy fragments of these texts in his narrative, but he never limits himself to any one of their approaches. None of the writers in the novel provide any literary model for the collation of stories, narrated at a distance of thousands of years by writers as various as the devil, a regime poet, a retired historian, and an apostle. Such collation remains the hallmark of our narrator. However, at one point in the novel the narrator describes the efforts of a team of twelve investigators who, like him, work on the case of the foreign professor's visit to Moscow by "gathering—as on a knitting needle, all the infernal stitches of this complicated case/file, scattered all over Moscow."[11] The narrator and the twelve investigators all use the same patchwork technique for putting together shreds of Woland's story. Furthermore, the narrator has access not only to the publicized results of their research but also to documents that are confidential parts of their archives, such as "the important material" obtained by the investigator from Ivan's deposition about Woland.[12]

Is our narrator then a secret police investigator? His innuendoes and, even more, his manner of introducing his protagonist in a prose still preserving the identifying features of police questionnaires suggest that this is a possibility. Another possibility would be a writer or, in the manner of the day, a graphomaniac, who alludes to his connections to the secret police in order to give himself and his hardly credible text some authority.[13] In 1930s Moscow these possibilities did not actually exclude each other; instead, they were reunited in a strange hybrid, the secret police agent-writer.[14] Bulgakov had direct contact with one of the earliest representatives of this strange model of the Soviet writer. In 1928, as he was struggling to launch his career as a writer, Bulgakov was asked to edit the stories of Fedor Martynov, a secret police investigator who fancied himself as a writer of short stories, which were based on investigation files. As opposed to Isaac Babel, who made significant changes while editing Martynov's text, Bulgakov limited himself to a few grammatical and stylistic corrections. These editorial marks are the traces of an encounter not just between individuals but also between different models of the Soviet writer. On the one hand, there is the young *intelligent* with a compromising bourgeois past, struggling to make it as a writer in a new, and hostile, literary world. And then there is the poster child of the new order, the secret police investigator, also eager to conquer a literary world, which is so well disposed toward him that it offers the assistance of two brilliant writers to polish the rough edges of his prose. The editing proofs suggest a strange hierarchy: on the one hand, Bulgakov is recognized as a better stylist; but this recognition only places him in an auxiliary position, in a supporting role, to this fledgling model of the Soviet writer—the investigator. The writing of investigation files, even if riddled by bad grammar, turns out to be a more precious prerequisite in the making of a Soviet writer than good style. For a moment, his experience as an investigator gives Martynov a competitive edge over Bulgakov on Moscow's new literary scene.

But only for a moment, since Martynov's stories were, for unknown reasons, never published. However, the figure of the secret police agent-writer was not shelved with those stories. On the contrary, the secret police investigator-writer became a phenomenon of the 1930s through the fascinating figure of Lev Sheinin. Sheinin was recruited to become a state investigator at the time when he was making the first steps toward a career as a writer, studying at the Literature Institute. Expressing his fears that a career in criminal investigation would interfere with his ideal of dedicating his life to literature, Sheinin learned from a more experienced communist that for an aspiring writer a career in criminal investigation was far better than a degree in literary studies.[15] With time, Sheinin came to see his mentor's wisdom, understanding that "there is much in common between a writer and a criminal investigator, the latter coming constantly in contact with diverse characters, conflicts, and dramas" and thus acquiring an unparalleled understanding of human psychology.[16] As the link between his careers in criminal investigation and literature, psychology was a lifelong interest for Sheinin, who was at one time also a collaborator on the renowned Russian psychologist A. R. Luriia's research on the first lie detector.[17] Sheinin quickly rose to an extraordinary career as an investigator and prosecutor. He investigated the most famous political crime of his times, Kirov's murder, assisted Vyshinskii in the prosecution of the 1930s show trials, and was chosen to represent the Soviet Union at the Nuremberg trials. Responsible for landing many in the camps, he also started serving two camp sentences himself but managed miraculously to be freed after relatively short periods of imprisonment. Even though he long refused to talk about his time in the camps, late in life he told a friend an extraordinary story about his first imprisonment.[18] According to Sheinin, his first imprisonment was related to the murder of Solomon Mikhoels, the outstanding director of the Jewish theater and leader of the Jewish community. Asked to investigate Mikhoels's case, Sheinin soon realized that the car accident blamed for his death was nothing more than a cover for Mikhoels's murder by the OGPU. His solution to the case, the story goes, prompted Stalin's wrath and ended in his camp sentence. This would have been quite a story for one of Sheinin's film or theater scripts. However, Sheinin's literary work cautiously drew on his least important work as an investigator: instead of the heads of the Bolshevik Party that he had investigated and prosecuted, Sheinin decided to focus on the petty thieves he came across in his career. His stories, which he started publishing as early as 1928 and which appeared regularly in the most important newspapers of the day, *Pravda* and *Izvestiia*, were collected in a bestseller titled *Notes of an Investigator* (*Zapiski sledovatelia*) in 1938. He is credited as a father of the detective story genre and is the scriptwriter of the first Soviet detective movie, the popular *Engineer Kochin's Mistake* (*Oshibka inzhenera Kochina*). Sheinin continued his dual career as an investigator-writer until 1953, when after his second sentence to the camps he decided to "devote himself fully to literature." A high-visibility popular writer, Sheinin was also well known in the circles of the Soviet literary, theatrical, and cinema elites: Isaac Babel, Grigorii Aleksandrov, Vasilii Grossman, and Roman Karmen, among many others, considered themselves his friends.[19]

Painfully aware of all the intrigues and the who's who of the Moscow literary world, Bulgakov probably knew Sheinin, and quite certainly knew of him.

In any case, through his reworking of Martynov's prose, Bulgakov was one of the first writers to come in such close contact with what was to become a successful prototype of the Soviet writer, the investigator-writer. It has been already noted that around the time of his encounter with Martynov's prose Bulgakov became more interested in criminal subjects.[20] But even more intriguing seems the possible influence of this close encounter with a new model of Soviet writer, the writer-investigator, on a young Bulgakov who was struggling to forge an authorial persona in a literary milieu that he found unwelcoming, indeed often hostile, to an *intelligent* with a White past. Amid the many literary personae that Bulgakov keenly observed on the shifty Moscow literary scene (some on their way in, too many on their way out), Bulgakov witnessed the up-and-coming trajectory of the investigator-writer, from Martynov's shaky beginnings to Sheinin's remarkable political and commercial endorsement. So while *The Master and Margarita* is obviously not a file but a novel, its narrator's allusions to secret police sources for his prose actually mirror a real-life phenomenon of the times, the investigator-writer and his use of investigation files as a basis for literature, a basis that was meant to give the resulting literature a claim on real-life status as well as unique authority and cachet.

While the narrator spends considerable effort weaving and obscuring his links to the secret police, these links can never be fully disclosed, because as the etymology suggests, *cachet* relies on secrecy. In the root of the word *cachet* we find the French verb *cacher*, to hide, or the noun *cache*, which can refer to the secret itself or to the container of the secret, the place where the secret is kept. Fittingly, *cachet* can also be "the covering of paste, gelatine, or other digestible material" enclosing unpalatable contents of a medicine—or by extension, a story.[21] In connection to writing, as in the phrase "letter of cachet" (*lettre de cachet*), *cachet* showcases the relationship between secrecy and power, often of a repressive kind since it originally referred to "a letter under the private seal of the French king, containing an order, often of exile or imprisonment." But there are probably few times when cachet was so linked to secrecy, or when secrecy had such cachet, as in 1930s' Moscow. If *cachet* is also originally "a stamp or a distinguishing mark," at this time there was no stamp that was conferring more of a certain type of cachet than the "strictly secret" stamp that was the distinguishing mark of the secret police.[22] Secrecy was the name of the game in those years; so while our narrator strongly signals a relationship to the secret police, it is only suitable that this relationship can never be fully stated or unequivocally proven. And yet it is precisely this lingering mystery, this carefully crafted aura of secrecy, that most convincingly links our narrator's writing practices to those of the secret police.

The narrator's link to the secret police may in fact turn out to be the long-missing link needed to solve the novel's greatest remaining puzzle: the mystery of its narrative voices. For indeed, the novel as a whole has the appearance of a puzzle bringing together disparate fragments of stories.[23] Some of these stories are narrated by the devil; some are dreamt by a disturbed poet; some are mysteriously excerpted from an unpublished and later burned novel; and some are written down by Matthew the Levite. This puzzle of the narrative voices has accordingly attracted much of the critical attention dedicated to the novel.[24] Generally focused on identifying the "real, hidden narrator," the discussion of narrative voices has produced a number of suspects but "no earth-shaking conclusions."[25] The novel's mysterious narrator puts together all the various stories in a coherent, if stylistically discordant, text. He gives patchy information about his access to such improbable sources. Furthermore, the narrator never brushes over the ill-fitting edges of his puzzle; rather, he teasingly draws our attention to them. Far from solving the mystery of the narrative voices, the narrator seems intent on kindling it. And as if to revenge his lack of cooperation, critics seem to have conspired to do away with him. Instead, they have proposed one of the novel's characters, usually either Ivan Bezdomnyi or the Master, as "the true narrator."[26] However, these provocative solutions to the narrative puzzle risk disregarding the stylistic characteristics of the text at large and reducing its defining heterogeneity to one unifying voice. The hypothesis of the would-be investigator-narrator collating various texts related to Woland's case into a coherent, if stylistically jagged, story is consistent with the novel's carefully crafted patchwork of narrative voices; at the same time it returns the focus to the novel's main, if long–glossed-over narrator.

## Censorship and the Authority of the Word

Bulgakov's encounters with the secret police continued past his editing of Martynov's stories through the time he wrote *The Master and Margarita*, which he worked on from 1928 to his death in 1940, a dozen years that saw the end of the New Economic Policy (NEP) of liberalization and then the height of the terror. The ominous steps of secret police agents that the novel's characters hear while inhabiting the fictional representation of the writer's own apartment at 50 Sadovaia Street were actually heard in 1934 when Osip Mandel'shtam was arrested from Bulgakov's building.[27] Bulgakov's own harassment by the secret police and the powers that be is well documented; it's not surprising that, as J. A. Curtis has argued, *The Master and Margarita* "brims over with allusions to the police state." Just the succinct enumeration of these allusions by Curtis takes a couple of pages. Examples include the paranoid "suspicion of for-eigners"; a suggestion that Immanuel Kant be sent to the Solovki labor camp; "the 'inexplicable' disappearances . . . , many arrests"; and Bosoi's "show trial" dream.[28] And a lot is left to add: the close "working" relationship between the psychiatric hospital and the OGPU, more or less voluntary statements, denunciations, interrogations, and torture. While many of these allusions come down to us, contemporaries were bound to make even more connections. As Curtis convincingly shows, "the dominating presence of the OGPU is indi-cated largely through euphemisms" that we might miss but that most readers at the time would have certainly picked up.[29] For example, "the OGPU head-quarters are continually characterized with the elliptical phrases such as 'there' or 'another place.'"[30] The story of the last two unnamed guests at Woland's ball, "which involves one of them obliging the other to spray the walls of his successor's office with poison," might not ring a bell for us, but according to Lamperini and Piper, "the anecdote would have been immediately recogniz-able to a contemporary audience," since this charge was made in 1938 against Genrikh Iagoda, the outgoing head of the secret police, who was accused of having his subordinate poison the office of his successor, Ezhov.[31] Curtis insightfully, if ever too fleetingly, mentions that "the atmosphere of the police state pervades even the neutral omniscience of the Moscow chapters, some of which appear to be couched mockingly in the language of a police report."[32] I will argue that the secret police does not just supply the novel with anecdotes, themes, or inspiration for a superficial mockery of "the language of a police report." Instead, the shadow of the secret police significantly shapes the writ-ing of the novel, from the selectively strange punctuation, through some of the most innovative narrative devices, and up to the fundamental question of the position and authority of the word.

With his plays viciously attacked in the press, mangled by censors, and often withdrawn from the stage, Bulgakov saw censorship affect his ability both to make a living and to write, to such an extent that he requested permission to leave the country, where his existence as a writer was "unthinkable." While Bulgakov's suffering under censorship was particularly severe, it was by no means isolated. During the time Bulgakov worked on *The Master and Margarita*, the heightening of censorship dealt blow after blow to the authority of literary, religious, and scientific discourses. At the same time, some words were gaining more and more power: as we have seen in the previous chapter, in the secret police files words not only described but actually dramatically shaped their subjects' lives, or put a full stop to them. This split in the authority of the word is the very fulcrum on which *The Master and Margarita* pivots. On the one hand, the novel dramatizes the crumbling of the authority of the word—as the basic unit of both literary and religious discourse—in a world ruled by censorship and atheistic ideology. Searching for a way out of this crisis of authority, the novel appropriates the power of words from the one place where it actually existed (if anything, in excess): the secret police file.

The novel opens on an act of censorship. The first dialogue, featuring the editor Berlioz and the young poet Ivan Bezdomnyi, revolves around a "critique" of a poem about Jesus Christ. The editor had asked Ivan "to write a long anti-religious poem for the coming issue of his journal" and is now "not at all pleased with it."[33]

The "poet's basic error" is that

> his Jesus turned out ... well, altogether alive—the Jesus who had existed once upon a time, although invested, it is true, with a full range of negative characteristics. Berlioz, on the other hand, wanted to prove to the poet that the main point was not whether Jesus had been good or bad, but that he had never existed as an individual, and that all the stories about him were simple *inventions, the most common myth* [my emphasis].[34]

The object of Berlioz's censorship is the idea underlying—even if involuntarily—the text, not its words, whose proliferation he supports. Berlioz departs from the typical profile of the narrow-minded censor, whose activity consists mainly in cutting undesired passages. He is, above all, "eloquent," and this quality is not accidental but defining for his activity as an editor-censor. Looking for consolation after Berlioz's death, Ivan tells himself, "There will be another editor, and maybe he'll be even more eloquent than the last one."[35] Indeed, Berlioz is willing to preserve Ivan's words on one condition: that they have lost their meaning and history and are ready to become myths. If Berlioz will be dead by the end of this scene, his model of censorship will last for well over fifty years. In 1989, less than a couple of months before the fall of Ceauşescu's dictatorship in Romania, another censored writer, Stelian Tănase, described the workings and effects of an era of eloquent censorship:

> Censorship is not just the reign of the lie, but in particular that of fiction and unreality in civil society and in the state. Everything is a lie. But another level is also created, a parareality. Censorship does not limit itself to interdicting, to cutting some passages, etc. It asks for the creation of myths, themes, etc., which it projects (like a film on a screen) onto reality. We have been living in this fiction for fifty years, in a mystified reality, in which truth and lie are indecipherable [*indescifrabile*].[36]

Bulgakov's novel begins thus at the critical point where Ivan's poem about Jesus is censored and the mythologizing eloquence of Berlioz is in full swing. Ivan is silenced: "The poet, to whom everything the editor said was new, listened ... attentively, staring at Mikhail Aleksandrovich ... and merely hiccupped from time to time."[37] It is at this point that Woland appears and attempts to offer the seventh proof for the existence of God, through both word and deed. The narrator follows him faithfully, attempting not only to tell the extraordinary story but also to convince the reader of its truth. However, both the narrator and Woland seem acutely aware of the difficulty of their task. Indeed, the novel opens, and the devil materializes, on the dramatization of this difficulty in suspending disbelief. In his initial appearance, Woland tries to counterbalance Berlioz's attack on Ivan's poem and claim the existence of Jesus by telling a story about Jesus' encounter with Pontius Pilate. But however brilliant Woland's storytelling might be, his audience is hardly convinced. Berlioz expresses his serious doubts as to the authenticity of the story, which leaves it with the status of apocrypha. Rather than gaining any authority as the narrator of such an extraordinary story, Woland only convinces the two literati that he is an insane foreigner, better dealt with by the police or put away in a mental institution. Far from rescuing the endangered idea underlying Ivan's poem, Woland sees his own story discredited.

As Ivan and Berlioz show no sign of taking his arguments about God or the devil seriously, Woland identifies their polemical strategy: "No matter what you name here, it doesn't exist."[38] His attempt to suspend disbelief thus begins with an attack on words emptied of meaning, which will in time lead to a veritable reform in the Muscovites' ways of using language. Initially, phrases such as the recurring refrain of the novel, "the devil knows," or Margarita's "I am ready to go to the devil himself" have the status Berlioz aspires to give words: clichés emptied of meaning.[39] However, as a result of Woland's visit, such words are radically transformed. After she regains her lover on account of her visit to the devil, Margarita responds to the Master's reckless use of words—"Only the devil knows what this is all about, the devil, the devil, the devil!"—by saying, "You just involuntarily spoke the truth. . . . The devil does know what this is all about, and believe me, the devil will arrange everything."[40] This belief is shared by the reader, who has just read in the previous chapter how the "Fate of Master and Margarita [was] decided" by Woland. Throughout the novel, Woland literalizes metaphors and clichés, offering himself as a referent for previously empty phrases.

The devil has a weak spot for the literal; yet faced with the difficult challenge of convincing contemporary Muscovites of the truth behind his words, he doesn't shy away from rhetoric. Once his story about Jesus and Pilate is met with disbelief and derision, the devil learns his lesson, and changes tactics. He will henceforth attempt to suggest God's existence through conjuring God's traditional negative, the devil. This triangulation marks the devil's strategic embrace of a peculiar rhetorical device—litotes. A figure of speech in which an affirmative is expressed by the negation of its opposite (as in saying "not uncensored," to mean "censored"), litotes is complexly tied to the times. The turn to litotes follows Woland's experience with the specifically contemporary vulnerability of his story, as well as of Ivan's text, before Berlioz's censorship and before the declared atheism of the Muscovites. Michael Holquist draws attention to the practice of litotic reading triggered by censorship: "necessarily focusing attention on what it denies, censorship defines itself as a version of litotes, a radical form of meiosis with political teeth."[41] Censorship leaves its traces not only on the (crumbling) authority of the word but also on the litotic character of Woland's response to this challenge.

The novel is thus founded on an absence, namely, Ivan's censored text, the poem about Jesus that we will never read. Opening the novel by alluding to the absence of a censored text is by no means accidental: throughout the novel are many censored or mutilated texts ostensibly lying behind what we read. The Master's novel, parts of which are inserted into the text we read, is the most salient example; his attempt to publish the novel prompts his "catastrophe," the beginning of his road to the madhouse. On taking the novel to an editor, the Master is looked at "as if [his] cheek were blown-up with a tooth infection" and is asked, "Who had given me the idea of writing a novel on such a strange subject?"[42] What hides under this vague formulation is soon made clear in the storm of articles condemning the fragment of the novel finally published as an "apology for Jesus Christ."[43] The question that everyone is asking is how this "religious freak" managed to "sneak (that damned word again) it [the novel] into print."[44] The Master's novel is in fact the subject of a famous censorship scandal, so famous that Ivan remembers it years later. Indeed, his novel is the second text about Jesus Christ (and Pilate) whose absence is recorded in Bulgakov's text. The two remaining chapters of the Master's novel, together with the detailed story of the peripeteias leading to the absence of the rest of the novel, again dramatize the image of a vulnerable, violated text. Unable to suspend the disbelief of its readers, the text, together with its author, becomes their victim.

Censorship insinuates itself between the word of God and the stories of the Gospels, as Jeshua's conversation with Pilate makes clear:

> There is one [Levi Matvei] who follows, follows me around everywhere, always writing on goatskin parchment. And once I happened to see the parchment and was aghast. Absolutely nothing that was written there did I ever say. I begged him: "For God's sake burn your parchment!" But he snatched it out of my hands and ran away.[45]

Levi Matvei might have been trying to be faithful, but as the narrator suggests, what he writes is what he hears and understands—not what Jeshua preaches.

Left out of Levi's manuscript, Jeshua's words are forever lost, and the Gospels' authority is fundamentally challenged. Insinuating itself in this description of the Gospels in the making, censorship—inescapable if involuntary—challenges the idea of a universal, unique sacred language and replaces the original, now compromised, by apocrypha.[46] In so doing, censorship illuminates the absence of a legitimizing authority of the text, both that of God and that of the establishment, and leaves the text open to its own influence, to a reading that reserves for itself the right to change the text.

Vaguely traceable to a variety of often unidentifiable narrators, these series of censored texts, whose partial absence is repeatedly mentioned and whose questionable fragments are patched together to form *The Master and Margarita*, give the novel the appearance of a palimpsest. As such, the crisis prompted by censorship's effects on the other texts—the Master's, Ivan's, and Jeshua's—moves to the core of the novel, undermining the idea of a unified, reliable, and credible work, as well as that of traditional authorship. By drawing attention to its numerous partial, inaccessible, censored, or distorted narratives, the novel seems to reenact this questioning of the status of the text.

## Stalinist "Fantastic Reality" and Its Textual Practices

Having set out to tell a story whose lesson, according to its authoritative protagonist, is that "He [Jesus] simply existed, and that is all," the narrator finds himself confined to a language that as all the writers in the novel discover, is compromised, vulnerable, and lacks authority.[47] The story of Levi Matvei shows that this is hardly a new crisis. The solution is not new either but hinted at already by Ivan Karamazov's devil: "Does proving that there's a devil prove that there's a God?" . . . "It's reactionary to believe in God nowadays, . . . but I'm the devil, so I may be believed in. Who doesn't believe in the devil?"[48] Indeed, this legendary devil also relies heavily on litotes, which he calls his "special method." The devil implements this method in order to convince skeptical moderns of his existence. He claims that he does not really exist, and while talking about this he forces his audience to draw the opposite conclusion.[49] In his attempt to paint the most convincing and "realistic" picture of the underworld, the devil pauses on one of its institutions, the secret police: "We even have gossip, as much as here [on earth], maybe a bit more, and finally we also have denunciations (*donosy*) and we also have one department, where they receive certain 'information' ('*svedeniia*')."[50] Ivan's interlocutor intimates the existence of God by dwelling on the type of supernatural that he thinks is most credible—the devil and the secret police. Maybe the reason the devil comes to Moscow in the 1930s is that this is a unique place to put into practice his ideas about litotes and the secret police.

As the "capital of rationalism," Moscow does not leave many doors open to the supernatural, condemning the bourgeois reading and writing of decadent fantastic literature to replacement by socialist realism. However, it still offers a fantastic of its own: "fantastic reality itself was prompted by the epoch of Stalin, flying saucers as an element of history. . . . Life itself had become fantastic and in order to convey that, I had resort to the fantastic," declared Andrei Siniavskii. He then went on to call *The Master and Margarita* "the one work that capture[d]" the nature of this fantastic growing out of the nighttime world orchestrated by Stalin.[51] In Edwards's analysis of the irrational in Bulgakov's work, starting with *Diaboliad* (an early short story about the devil) and ending with *The Master and Margarita*, he affirms in the same vein that "fantastic events grow naturally out of the absurdities of everyday life in the post-revolutionary confusion."[52] Edwards suggests that the denunciations, disappearances, and executions are the liaisons between the real and the fantastic in *The Master and Margarita*.

This Stalinist fantastic gives a new twist to the genre famously described by Tzvetan Todorov. It "produces feelings of insecurity about the natural order of things," by transgressing the space of reading and shaping everyday reality. Furthermore, it creates "profound fear and terror" by intimating "the existence of unsuspected worlds and powers" not only to a subjective reader but also to a whole community.[53] This police state supernatural is appropriated by Woland, who plays on this last, extremely dangerous deviation from rationalism to "sneak in" his idea of the supernatural, that is, to convince the Muscovites of the existence of God. Adapting Woland's approach to his own literary project, the narrator appears to playfully appropriate the type of writing and reading that such a fantastic entails in order to legitimize his suspect text. An examination of *The Master and Margarita* next to Bulgakov's own file, passed from the Cheka to the KGB, shows an uncanny similarity in the organization of the narratives.

## Mikhail Bulgakov's Personal File

A reconstruction of Bulgakov's file from the documents released by the former KGB reveals the usual contents of a writer's file: multiple copies of his diary and novella *The Heart of a Dog (Sobach'e serdtse)*, surveillance and informers' reports, records of the two questioning sessions that Bulgakov had to undergo, and OGPU notes and decisions.[54] More uncommon file fare are the two letters by Bulgakov openly directed to the OGPU, one requesting the return of his confiscated manuscripts, and one asking them "not to obstruct the submission of his letter of 28th March 1930 to the Soviet Government."[55] The letter in question was a courageous cri de coeur that Bulgakov wrote to the government, complaining of being politically persecuted and asking either to be allowed to work or to emigrate. The letter indeed made it to the Soviet government, as well as to the OGPU, whose head, Iagoda, read and carefully marked its contents before instructing that Bulgakov be given "the opportunity to work where he wants." These letters prove the writer's acute and accurate awareness of the OGPU's interest in him. Bulgakov's confiscated manuscripts were returned to him in 1929, when the writer allegedly proceeded to burn his incriminating diary and vowed to never keep one again. His dramatic renunciation of diary writing seems only fitting at a time when first-person narratives were becoming the most dangerous type of literature, one easily converted into conclusive evidence against their author.[56] In this light, the change convincingly traced by Edythe Haber in the profile of Bulgakov's narrator from a vulnerable, largely autobiographical intellectual to a more elusive and satirical narrator can be seen as a defense strategy.[57] I will argue that the carefully crafted puzzle of the narrative voices in Bulgakov's last novel is the culmination of this process. The enigmatic narrator of *The Master and Margarita* is a mask designed to double as a shield protecting the vulnerable author by mimicking his threatening adversary, a secret police agent.

A noteworthy document in Bulgakov's file is an informer's report "written by someone close to literary and theatrical circles."[58] Vitalii Shentalinskii notes that "it seems clear that the author was not personally close to Bulgakov because he used the service of others."[59] The informer recounts the rumors that were circulating among writers about Bulgakov's letter to the government and his phone conversation with Stalin. His treatment of the subject is quite imaginative. Although he had obviously not been present but heard the story as a series of rumors, this informer chooses dialogues, not related speech, when recounting the story of Bulgakov's phone conversation with Stalin. His report draws on a series of complex, often diverging stories that he edits together into a coherent narrative ended by a univocal conclusion, most flattering for "the first reader": "It should be said, that the popularity of Stalin has developed a simply extraordinary form. He is spoken of with warmth and affection, and the legendary story of Bulgakov's letter is being retold in various forms."[60] This informer's interests decidedly lean toward literary gossip rather than literature or even fact, since the police knew the actual content of the phone call. Overall, this report provides a representative example of the appropriation of stock fictional techniques into the writing of the files.

The opening scene of Bulgakov's novel reverses the sense of this appropriation, echoing the tone and conventions of such informer's reports and the investigator syntheses based on them. The scene is Patriarchs' Pond, a Moscow park where the narrator, as well as any of his contemporary readers, could go for a walk and happen upon the characters. Indeed, the first description of the characters gives the impression that they are two unknown citizens walking into our narrator's field of vision. His description is strictly limited to physical appearance and consists of an enumeration of the same attributes: age, height, figure, hair, dress. "At the hour of sunset, on a hot spring day, two citizens appeared in the Patriarchs' Ponds Park. One, about forty, in a gray summer suit, was short, plump, dark-haired and partly bald."[61] The second paragraph further identifies the two citizens, in a peculiar way: name, pseudonym, and function. "The first was none other than Mikhail Aleksandrovich Berlioz, editor of an important literary journal and chairman. . . . His young companion was the poet Ivan Nikolaevich Ponyrev, who wrote under the pen name Homeless."[62] While sticking to the factual, this time the narrator introduces information that could not be gleaned just through on-the-spot observation of his characters. Furthermore, listening in on their conversation, the narrator misses certain points but fills in the gaps with subsequent information: "'Well then,' he [Berlioz] continued the conversation interrupted by the drinking of the apricot soda. This conversation, as was learned subsequently, was about Jesus Christ."[63] Our narrator's account of his characters is then not completely spontaneous; rather, it is admittedly a report drawing on information from different sources. What the narrator couldn't hear, someone else could, or maybe one of the interlocutors later disclosed. Our narrator's power lies in his ability to access these different accounts and thus provide us with quite interesting, and often secret, information.

On the subject of informers, it bears noting that most narratives in *The Master and Margarita* are written from the point of view of an insignificant character. These characters often change, and their presence in the narrative rarely has any meaningful relationship to the events narrated from their point of view. Their justification for being our means of transportation around Moscow and around the story is their contingent presence at the scene of an important event. These episodic characters fragment the flow of the story. Moreover, the narrator admits that they are far from ideal in their access to the events. Levi Matvei, who is our reference point in the crucial story of Jesus' crucifixion, literally found himself in the worst position from which to view the events: "Yes, he had chosen the worst rather than the best position for watching the execution. Nevertheless . . . this was evidently enough for the man, who clearly wished to remain unnoticed and unmolested by anyone."[64] The bookkeeper

Vasilii Stepanovich is a modest picaro traveling through three Moscow offices. In one, the devil's tricks have kidnapped the director and left his suit to receive visitors; in the second, the whole office cannot stop singing compulsively. Vasilii Stepanovich ends up in a third office, interrogated by the police. Indeed, most of our episodic narrators, such as Nikanor Ivanovich, the chairman of the house committee, or Ivan Bezdomnyi, end up writing reports for the police, whether in their headquarters or in the psychiatric hospital, which the investigators visit at leisure.[65] Our narrator produces an ingenious compilation of their stories, a compilation that shows traces of multiple observers and levels of discernment.

The reliance on various limited, even flawed accounts is partly responsible for the curiously patchy character of the narrative. For our narrator, despite his overall power and ability to follow any relevant plot, builds on partial accounts that he puts together. Unlike the traditional models of omnipresence or omniscience, God or the realist author, our narrator's power is not visible in each detail. As we will see, he can lose important fragments of conversation when the characters whisper or shut a door. His power resides in the collation of the disparate stories of the various insignificant narrators featured in the novel, a collation that he consequently dwells on. With their summaries and reports that combine novice or experienced literary expression with police jargon, these insignificant narrators fit well the shady profile of the informer as preserved in Bulgakov's own file.

## Repetitions with Suspect Differences: The Writer as Copyist

Another key stylistic peculiarity visible at the novel's seams, that is, at the transition between chapters, is the repetition of the last phrase of the previous chapter at the start of the following chapter. All five chapters of the Jerusalem story begin on a slightly modified repetition of the last phrase of the previous chapter. Thus, the last sentence of chapter 15 reads, "But soon they were silent, and he began to dream that the sun was already setting over the Bald Mountain, and the mountain was surrounded by a double cordon . . ."[66] The beginning of the next chapter cuts the first part of the sentence and changes its punctuation: "The sun was already setting over Bald Mountain, and the mountain was surrounded by a double cordon."[67] Similarly, chapter 24 ends thus: "The darkness which had come from the Mediterranean shrouded the city hated by the Procurator . . . Yes, the darkness . . ."[68] The next chapter exhibits an even subtler difference, the disappearance of the phrase "Yes, the darkness . . ." There is no explicit reason for these repetitions, but there are certain pointers for their interpretation. Before the first chapter ends, Woland's accent wanes and disappears as he starts telling the story. Although the words themselves remain identical in most of these fragments, the punctuation changes in all of them, replacing suspension points with periods. Different markers of orality, as the repetition "Yes, the darkness," as well as the words marking the presence of the storyteller, are also erased from the repeated version of the phrases. The seemingly redundant repetitions mark thus a certain change toward a more "neutral," formal, written style. In each case, the narrator carefully stages the pretext for the beginning of the story: the first episode, Pilate's conversation with Jeshua, is supposedly told by Woland during his encounter with Ivan and Berlioz. The second part of the story, the crucifixion, is dreamt by Ivan; the other two chapters are read by Margarita from the Master's restored manuscript. Each of these pretexts is introduced somewhat seamlessly in the narrative, although the question of how fragments of such different provenance end up composing a coherent story is left open. The repetitions emphasize that question. They do away with the narrative masks of Woland, Ivan, or Margarita and thus raise again the question of who is telling, or rather writing, or maybe just transcribing the text that we read. It is fitting that in the censored version of the novel "Yes, the darkness" was cut. Thus, the difference between the two passages, as well as the question mark that such a puzzling disappearance of the phrase in the following chapter could raise, were carefully airbrushed from the first Soviet version.[69]

Another curious narrative device used by Bulgakov, in his novella *Heart of a Dog*, could potentially shed some light on the strange repetitions or transcriptions in *The Master and Margarita*. In *Heart of a Dog*, the young doctor Bormental' keeps a diary of an experiment initiated by his mentor, Professor Preobradzenskii. Aiming at the improvement of the human species, this experiment goes awry and transforms a perfectly decent dog into an opportunistic communist. Given the extraordinary outcome of the situation, the professor is visited by a group of mysterious and threatening officials, probably the police. Anticipating such visits, the young doctor Bormental' burns his diary—the way Bulgakov will in a few years' time. The question, of course, is how this diary, whose owner did everything to keep from others, appears in front of us, the readers. Similarly, the narrative attempts to reproduce the conversations of the characters at times when they are afraid to be heard by informers eavesdropping behind the door. When they speak in a low voice or in a foreign language, the narration is interrupted or only catches short, isolated words.

Filip Filipovich was suddenly on the alert. He raised his finger.
"Wait . . . I heard footsteps . . ."
Both listened intently, but there was silence in the corridor.

"It seemed to me," said Filip Filipovich, and then started heatedly speaking in German. In his words several times rang the Russian word "crime."[70]

In *The Master and Margarita*, as Curtis notes, "the Master describes his experiences with the OGPU in a whisper as inaudible, it seems, to the narrator as it is to the reader.[71] Our narrator is quite limited in his knowledge to what he can eavesdrop on or copy. No explanation is given when Bormental's journal is reproduced for us. However, the reproduction makes it obvious that this is not the actual diary we are reading but rather someone's copy of it: cuts are made where too-abstract medical material appears, and strangely, the punctuation marks are not actually used but rather represented by words: "Laboratory dog approximately two years old. Male. Breed—mongrel. Name—Sharik. Weight—8 kg (*exclamation mark*)."[72] The one paragraph in which the narrator introduces the journal points to a matter-of-fact, meticulous copyist: "FROM DOCTOR BORMENTAL'S JOURNAL. Thin writing pad. Written in Bormental's hand. On the first two pages he is accurate and clean, on the following pages he writes in nervous bold hand, and leaves many blots."[73] This preface-summary mysteriously frames the journal, inciting the reader to ask who could have gained access to the compromising journal and further offered it to us.

The slight yet carefully underscored differences between the original and the version of the diary that we read suggest transcription. A similar type of summary prefaced copies of letters, manuscripts, and other documents found in secret police files. Given the secret police habit of making copies of the original, it was most relevant for the copyist to mention the characteristics of the original that would have been lost in the copy, such as handwriting versus typewriting. Bulgakov seems to allude to one of the most common practices of the secret police regarding confiscated manuscripts, that of copying most or all of the document and keeping the copy after sometimes returning the original. This was indeed common practice to the point where a significant part of putting together a secret police file must have consisted of copy work. The often incomplete, tendentious copies superseded the original, which was either destroyed or returned to its owner. The copy became the final variant of the text, for the original manuscript, even if returned to its author, became so suspect once confiscated that it was practically unpublishable. One such example, discussed in detail in Chapter 5, is Nicolae Steinhardt's *Happiness Journal* (*Jurnalul Fericirii*), which was first secretly photographed by the secret police in Steinhardt's home and then confiscated and copied by the secret police before being returned to its author.[74] Among the literary texts that, like *Happiness Journal*, finally came down to us thanks to the copies made by the secret police, Bulgakov's *Diary* is arguably the most famous. Confiscated in 1926, the diary was copied by the secret police and then returned to Bulgakov, who as mentioned before, proceeded to burn it as a tainted, compromising document.[75] The *Diary* was first published in 1990, shortly after it surfaced from the KGB archives.[76]

In this light, the small variations in *The Master and Margarita* might similarly draw attention to the narrator's work in copying, compiling, and collating the fragments of stories. The neat sequencing of seemingly random fragments of stories—Ivan's dream picking up at the very point where the devil's story left off; and Margarita happening on the very chapter in the Master's manuscript that continues Ivan's story—might turn out to be less miraculous than it would first appear. Indeed, it could be the result of diligent copy and collation work on the part of a narrator. Despite their widely different provenance, these three fragments of the Jerusalem narrative have something in common: all of them would have been likely to end up in a secret police archive. We are explicitly told that Woland's appearance in Moscow has been profusely documented in police reports by witnesses and informers. We watch Ivan at pains to write a coherent and comprehensive report of his meeting and conversation with Woland, including the latter's story about Jeshua. Thus involved in the case and confined in a mental hospital, Ivan's dreams might well have made the subject of a conversation with Professor Stanislavskii, whose psychiatric ward appears throughout the novel as a complement to the police headquarters. Our narrator has access not only to the police reports but also to the research of a "team of expert psychiatrists," most likely involving the most respected Moscow psychiatrist, the same Professor Stanislavskii. As the Master himself recounts, his scandalous novel traveled through numerous editorial as well as censorship offices. According to a contemporary practice well known to Bulgakov, such a text would have been most likely copied and stored for permanent retention before the manuscript was returned to its compromised author.

As both Bulgakov and his Master saw with their own eyes, manuscripts do burn. But beyond the writer's control, copies are made; slightly distorted, they eventually reach the reader. The repetitions and singular transitions of *The Master and Margarita* show the narrator at work copying various texts and, more importantly, copying the very practice of copying. This practice characterizes a genre that threatened to confiscate and incorporate Bulgakov's own manuscripts—the secret police file. To respond to this threat, the author fashioned his text as a copy, and mimicked the appearance of the file. *The Master and Margarita*'s main characters are introduced in the language of police sketches, through personal history and distinguishing characteristics. Our narrator's eye seems all-seeing, but examined up close his vision appears more like the careful collation of imperfect observations made by eavesdroppers, passers-by, and bookkeepers, all very likely to be informers. Endowed with his peculiar brand of omniscience, the shady narrator stitches together reports. Boasting over his patchwork, he challenges competitors working on the same piece: these competitors turn out to be not local babushkas but rather secret police agents, busy at work on Woland's case. While mimicking their work on the secret police file, the narrator attempts to appropriate the power of this emerging genre and to restore the authority of the literary text by appealing to the very practices that have started to endanger it. The mimicry of the police file in *The Master and Margarita* never fully exposes its model. The narrator crafts subtle references to this model at the same time that he carefully covers his traces. In the case of the police file, such obfuscation of its mechanisms grounds its power, a power from which the text borrows. Nevertheless, the novel's mimicry of the secret police file points to some of its key features and sheds light on its deep impact upon the literary imagination of the time.

Painstakingly woven and obscured, this link between our narrator and the secret police points to a relationship between writing and policing that goes far beyond the old model of censorship, where art is the helpless victim of all-powerful policing; instead, it opens toward a more complex model where art engages with policing through mimicry, appropriation, and *détournement* of its powers. In this world of investigator-writers and writer-investigators, art and policing put on each other's masks, step into each other's shoes, but do not necessarily walk the same walk. A narrator who alludes to his links to the secret police to gain authority says something about the precarious authority of literature; but the crafty use of the very same narrator also embodies the gutsy and ingenious ploys that literature can devise to get back at the police. After all, Bulgakov's shady narrator is just a device, indeed a tool, in the hands of his author.

## CHAPTER THREE

# Early Soviet Cinema's
# Shots at Policing

Reminiscing about the Soviet cinema of the early 1920s, Moisei Aleinikov, head of the Rus film studio, recounted the story of legendary director Lev Kuleshov's "montage people," who, "wearing leather jackets and carrying revolvers, used to 'arrest' old film negatives in the studio, in order to re-edit this 'rubbish ... filmed by the bourgeoisie' into new revolutionary film—there being no raw film in the country."[1] The next two chapters will follow the clue left dormant in the uncanny image of the filmmaker impersonating a secret police agent (for who else would carry out "arrests" outfitted with leather jacket and revolver rather than a regular police uniform?) and explore a type of cinema that I believe defined the foundational decades of Soviet filmmaking: kino police. I will argue that filmmakers took on more than the look of the secret police: they were instrumental in its major projects, such as identifying the new profile of the socialist criminal/enemy and molding the public response to it. That cinema was a weapon in the hands of the Soviet state was a leading cliché of the time; some filmmakers took it to heart, others to the letter. Dziga Vertov, whose experiments with capturing and editing the image of the criminal/state-enemy we will follow shortly, strikingly described his camera as "a gun apparatus direct[ing] its muzzle over the city."[2] Alexander Medvedkin actually built and wielded a camera-gun; later, his "cineinvestigations" tracked "evildoers" across the country and landed some of them in jail. Ivan Pyr'ev's popular portrayal of the Soviet enemy in *The Party Card (Partiinyi bilet)* induced audience members to conduct searches on each other lest they mingle with enemies of the people potentially teeming in the darkness of the cinemas.[3] Following this chapter, which explores the pioneering, if sometimes heterodox, versions of kino police, we will move to a chapter that dwells on the secret police's own involvement with cinema, focusing on newsreels and documentaries, as well as an OGPU fiction blockbuster, *The Road to Life*.

## Filmmaking and Fingerprinting: Dziga Vertov's Film Theory and Practice

In the plastic language that characterized his manifestos, Dziga Vertov compared "the work of the movie camera" with "the work of GPU agents, who do not know what awaits them but who always have a definite task: from the thick tangle of life they must single out and investigate such and such a question, such and such a matter."[4] Vertov's striking comparison of the camera with the secret police agent is part of a larger rhetorical web that links the cinema with policing in his manifestos and theoretical writings. He attacked traditional fiction films as bourgeois crime, passed "a death sentence" on them, and touted his newsreels as a fight against this ideologically suspect cinema.[5] He credited his cameramen as reconnaissance agents (*razvedchiki*) and repeatedly described the working of his kino-eye as "the careful reconnaissance mission of the camera."[6] Proudly boasting to have found the path of new revolutionary cinema, Vertov claimed it led past the roofs of film studios "into genuine reality full of its own drama and detective plots."[7] The path that Vertov claimed to have found in 1923 had been suggested just a few months before by leading Bolshevik ideologist Nikolai Bukharin. Confessing to a weakness for detective flicks and reminding his audience that "Marx himself had a passion for crime novels," Bukharin asked for the creation of a Red Pinkerton, a Red detective genre.[8] To turn the Pinkerton into a local Red, Soviet writers and filmmakers were advised to leave fiction behind and instead to use "real material," such as "the activity of the Cheka, the Red Army and the Red Guards as material for revolutionary novels" and a new "corresponding cinema."[9] Vertov's rhetoric, and in particular his turn towards a reality defined by its wealth of detective plots, both echoes and outdoes Bukharin's call for the cinema to illustrate the actual work of the Cheka, since for Vertov the filmmaker should not only portray but actually emulate the secret police agent's work and approach to reality.

The 1920s are known for over-the-top rhetoric, and Vertov's manifestos offer some of the more flaming examples of rhetorical excess. So to what extent does Vertov's film practice justify the comparison of the camera with the secret police agent? An examination of the film that Vertov made around the time of these pronouncements, *Kino-Eye* (*Kino-Glaz*, 1924), reveals some scenes offering captivating glimpses of the local underworld that could compete with his dynamic editing in "grabbing the attention of the viewer" and "cooling his thirst for 'detective stories.'"[10] Following the title "Shady Business" we get tantalizing shots of hands furtively exchanging money. Having captured the speculators red-handed, the camera tilts up to reveal their faces.

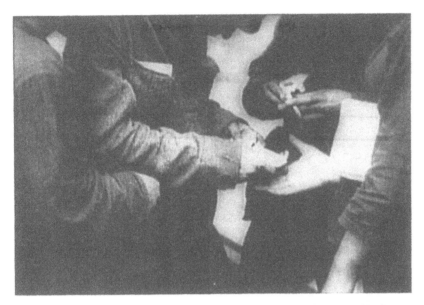

The hands of speculators followed by their faces. *Kino-Eye,* 1924, frame enlargements.

Women of the underworld. *Kino-Eye*, 1924, frame enlargements.

Seemingly unaware of the camera shooting them from a strange high angle, a man intent on hiding his face exchanges money with a woman. Having again closely captured their shady dealings, the camera demonstratively backs out, thus drawing attention to its own hidden position, perched somewhere on a high wall or rooftop. The couple is still visible in long shot, now arrestingly framed through barbed wire. Another beautiful young woman leans against a wall, smoking. Stuck into the underworld chapter of the movie, her image can scarcely escape becoming the iconic representation of a 1920s prostitute. While these shots are ostensibly examples of hidden camera footage, the iconic images and histrionic gestures of the underworld chapter of the film suggest that Vertov might have compensated for the difficulty of catching lowlifes unawares by some staging and manipulative editing, thus creating enemies onscreen rather than capturing them live. Ironically, such questionable creation of fictional evildoers, which passes itself off as the apprehension of actual criminals, would only bring Vertov closer to the actual practices of the Soviet secret police.

The hands of speculators exchanging money appear again in *Stride, Soviet!* (*Shagai, Sovet!* 1926), as does the peculiar mode of character presentation that starts with the hand and then moves to the face. In fact this device becomes a striking visual signature in *Stride, Soviet!*: hands filing papers, sorting through seized illegal goods, counting and exchanging money, handling food, sterilizing themselves, palpating a pregnant belly, cleaning, flushing toilets, taking a body's measurements for a new suit, or writing, typing, drawing, and burning books appear first; the faces that go with them usually appear in the follow-up shot, although sometimes they are skipped altogether. What explains this obsession with hands? One might say hands were in the air of the times. In her diary entry of November 24, 1927, constructivist Varvara Stepanova wrote that Alexander Rodchenko, her husband and Vertov's close collaborator, talked about "a film telling the story of an object; for example, a ten rouble note. Try to show it without people. Just hands. . . . A whole film out of close-ups, very close ones."[11] Vertov himself wrote an étude titled "Hands," consisting of a numbered list of 127 "shots" of hands—"on a piano," "a policeman's hand," "a manicure," "a hand plunges a dagger," "a hand pulls on gloves," and so on.[12] Strangely, only the "policeman's hand" appears twice, as numbers 8 and 101. At times, *Stride, Soviet!* appears the closest Vertov got to putting this bold idea into practice. But still this does not explain the strange emphasis on hands and, more specifically, the device so coherently used in *Stride, Soviet!* of showing the hands before the face when introducing the filmed subject. In his commentary on a section of *Man with the Movie Camera*, Yuri Tsivian cogently notes an opposition between hands and faces—the hands stand for work or production while the face stands for services or leisure.[13] Given Vertov's Marxist worldview, these associations certainly privilege the hand over the face.[14] But what should we make of the mysterious hand holding a revolver that flashes so briefly on the screen of *Man with the Movie Camera* that one wonders if it is really there? What does this armed hand stand for—the work of the police, or the crime of the lawbreaker? Maybe this ambiguous image is a leftover from *Hands*, or from *Stride, Soviet!*, where both hands and faces are more multivalent, standing for work, leisure, and even crime.

Vertov's early use of this "hands first" device for the representation of criminals in *Kino-Eye* might contain a clue, one that is confirmed by the most striking shots of hands in *Stride, Soviet!* in a sequence that meticulously follows the process of fingerprinting. As strange as it might appear in the context of film history, Vertov's consistent privileging of the hand over the face to represent his criminal subjects is completely in line with fingerprinting—the system of criminal subject representation then recently adopted by those whose official business it was to capture and record these criminal subjects—the police. Fingerprinting is the one system of subject representation in which the hand trumps the face, or any other part of the body. While we marvel at the peculiarity of Vertov's privileging of the hand over the face in representing his criminal subjects, the ubiquity of fingerprinting in modern policing makes it easy to take for granted its equally strange reconfiguration of the policed body, a reconfiguration that moved the emphasis to—of all body parts—the modest fingertip. Fingerprinting revolutionized the modern ways of looking at and representing the long-elusive criminal identity. Refusing to be pinned down by those who had attempted to peer deeply into the soul for inborn character traits, or by those who had transferred the body's measurements to paper charts and then engaged in arcane calculations, criminal identity proved most susceptible to being captured by those willing to look attentively at the minute web of lines and curves that had lain the whole time at their own fingertips. Fingerprinting reconfigured the human body not only by shifting the emphasis of particular body parts but also by moving toward different ways of looking at, recording, classifying, and recalling (visual) information. In other words, the fingertip not only displaced the head from its former position at the center of criminal identity; its new centrality also required the brain and the eyes to undergo significant retraining and refocusing. To use Jacques Rancière's term, the worldwide adoption of fingerprinting was enabled by and further enabled a true shift in *the distribution of the sensible*.

It was in the 1920s, at the time when Vertov was filming his *Kino-Eye* and *Stride, Soviet!*, that fingerprinting was decisively adopted by police agencies worldwide, beating out late nineteenth-century photographs of the face or anthropometric measurements of the body.[15] Fingerprinting was in fact sensational news at the time, as police around the world advertised its uses in the resolution of previously unsolvable criminal cases.[16] In the Soviet Union, fingerprinting made both serious and sensational news in the 1910s and 1920s as a new technology able to both "scientifically" prove guilt and save the innocent from unjust sentences.[17] The stories of dactyloscopy exculpating two sons from the charge of killing their mother, or restoring a misclaimed child to his rightful mother fed straight into the melodramatic imagination.[18] Popular attention was also drawn to the spectacle of the hitherto invisible traces of guilt, the "latent fingerprints" left on broken mirrors, shiny lamps, or greasy newspapers at the scene of the crime. Since "most latent prints are colorless," they were "'developed,' or made visible, by brushing them with various gray or black powders"; then they were "preserved as evidence by photography."[19] Fingerprinting did not just prove guilt but also made it spectacularly visible by "developing" and preserving its traces in ways that inextricably linked this new police technology to the other indexical modes of representation of the times: photography and film.

Vertov, who was famous for drawing parallels between his own filmmaking and other types of work presented in his films, from assembly work to coal mining, certainly did not miss the closer parallels between filmmaking and fingerprinting. While detailing the process of fingerprinting, Vertov closely focuses on two pairs of hands, the black leather-gloved hands of the police agent and the hands of the suspect—at first unremarkable then starkly ink-marked. After a close-up of the suspect's face and a medium shot of the policeman and suspect together, we return to the close-up of the hands. The sequence ends as the camera closely scrutinizes the resulting police report, which just like the film preserves the dramatic imprint of both the suspect's handprints and the police agent's handwriting. This scene presents the work of the filmmaker and policemen as analogous: fingerprinting, like filmmaking, is an indexical mode of representation, a recording on paper or film of the actual traces left by an object.[20] Since in this case the object is the index itself, fingerprinting might well have claim to the status of *the* indexical means of representation par excellence. In this scene of fingerprinting, Vertov certainly prefigures the link later drawn by André Bazin between the photographic image and the fingerprint. According to Bazin, "the photograph as such and the object itself share a common being, after the fashion of the fingerprint."[21] Bazin's comment has been repeatedly revisited in a recent film theory "heavily marked . . . by the image of the photographic index."[22] Thus, Laura Mulvey writes, "An index . . . is a sign produced by the 'thing' it represents . . . something must leave, or have left, a mark or trace of its physical presence. Whether it

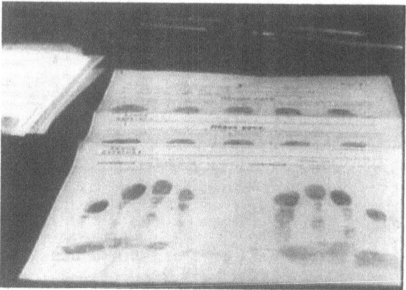

Fingerprinting. *Forward Soviet!*, 1926, frame enlargements.

persists, as in the then-ness of the fingerprint, or not, as in the now-ness of the sundial, the 'thing' inscribes its sign at a specific moment of time."[23] Lev Manovich reformulates Bazin's famous statement in his very definition of cinema, although this time the stand-in for the index is not the fingerprint but the footprint: "Cinema is the art of the index. It is an attempt to make art out of a footprint."[24] Vertov's film theory and practice show that the fingerprint is not just an innocent illustration for the indexical nature of cinema, one that could be just as well replaced by the footprint or the shadow. In Vertov's work, the fingerprint points not only to cinema's indexical nature but also to cinema's relationship to policing, a link that is overlooked in Bazin as well as in more recent work on the cinematic index. In portraying fingerprinting, Vertov follows Bukharin's call by illustrating the work of the police. But in the very same shot sequence Vertov is also true to his own idea that the filmmaker does not only illustrate but also emulates the work of policing. In capturing the indexical traces of the criminal body, filmmaking does not only portray fingerprinting; it itself becomes a form of fingerprinting. Vertov's striking privileging of the hand over the face in the representation of his subjects in *Stride, Soviet!* might well be a cinematic ripple effect of fingerprinting, the main twentieth-century method of criminal identification, which made news in the 1910s and 1920s. This would not be the first time that a mode of identification and representation first developed for criminals stretches its initial limits to apply to others such as foreigners, minorities, political opponents, and then the population at large. The history of fingerprinting in fact provides a textbook illustration of this trend.[25] What is more interesting here is the possible reach of this representation strategy outside of its original policing domain into cinema, at the moment when a criminal identification technique morphs into an innovative film device.

## Hidden and Artfully Exhibited Cameras

Vertov's comparison of the film camera with the secret police agent is justified not only by particular scenes from his movies; it echoes in one of the central ambitions of his cinema, the desire to replace the fallible vision of the human eye with the disclosures of his perfect camera eye. He described this *kino-eye* as "an x-ray eye . . . able to show people without masks, without makeup . . . to read their thoughts, laid bare by the camera. Kino-eye as the possibility of making the invisible visible, the unclear clear, the hidden manifest, the disguised overt."[26] To turn these metaphors into reality, Vertov and his brother-cameraman Mikhail Kaufman devoted part of their prodigious creative efforts to developing hidden camera techniques. They used telephoto lenses and false cameras cranking loudly to distract the attention of the filmed subjects while the actual smaller cameras were filming them unawares.[27] A contemporary critic credited them with "climbing into the attic and making a hole in the ceiling for the camera lens."[28] They went so far as to disguise themselves as phone operators, and built tents to hide the cameras.[29] It is fitting that in recalling the origins of his career, Vertov's "man with a movie camera," Mikhail Kaufman, singled out for description one of the first photographs he took as a child: snapped unawares, the photograph showed another "pupil passing an answer to someone."[30] Uncannily foreshadowing the complications of Vertov's and Kaufman's later rapport with the powers-that-be, the hidden camera picture through which Kaufman captured a small illicit act boomeranged, bringing him not the gratitude but the wrath of the authorities: he was expelled from school.[31]

And yet, Vertov repeatedly and self-consciously aligned his hidden camera with state power, of the repressive kind to boot. His "general instructions" for "invisible camera" techniques in his *Kinok's Field Manual* started: "1). Filming unawares—an old military rule: gauging, speed, attack."[32] The comparison was taken over by one of his contemporary reviewers, who noted that "overall, the kinocs, *as in war*, make wide use of the practice of masking the lens."[33] Vertov's illustrated notes for the iconic sequence of the camera overlooking the city in *Man with a Movie Camera* reveal another striking comparison. This time the camera was likened to a gun, a comparison that Vertov elaborated throughout the description of the shot sequence, which started: "gun apparatus directs its muzzle towards the city. 1. [Camera] lens with a device, filmed as a gun, lengthways—moves tentatively over the city."[34] The climax of this original description compared the "camera racing over the city" with the infamous symbol of despotic state power, the frighteningly animated statue of Peter the Great haunting the city and its little men in Pushkin's poem *The Bronze Horseman*.[35]

The camera then does not just incidentally turn into a gun in the hands of the state when it runs into criminals and captures them red-handed. The kind of look that one might believe to be reserved for criminals is extended over the whole city, and acting as a gun becomes the camera's proudly advertised modus operandi. In fact, the shots intercut with the camera hovering over the city like a gun detail the registration of marriage and divorce, the state regulation of private life. In the divorce scene, the woman clumsily signs the paper as she tries to cover her face with her purse. The image of people covering their face is in fact a leitmotif spanning Vertov's movies. But as Vertov reminded his audience, thanks to his ingenious hidden camera techniques, "in the end not one viewer can be sure he has not been captured on film in this part of

"Gun apparatus directs its muzzle towards the city." *Man with a Movie Camera*, 1928, frame enlargement.

*Kino-Eye* or another."[36] This point was given a positive spin by Vertov's most famous contemporary reviewer, Walter Benjamin, who wrote:

> With the invention of the modern press, an increasing number of writers became readers... Thus, the distinction between author and reader is about to lose its basic character. All this can be equally applied to film. .... In cinematic practice, particularly in Russia, this change-over has partially become established reality. .... Some of the players whom we meet in Russian films are not actors in our sense but people who portray *themselves*. .... In Western Europe the capitalistic exploitation of the film denies consideration to modern man's legitimate claim to being reproduced [represented].[37]

Benjamin's prime example was Vertov, the foremost representative of "unplayed film" in the Soviet Union. "The newsreel offers everyone the opportunity to rise from passer-by to movie-extra. In this way any man might find himself part of a work of art, as witness Vertoff's *Three Songs of Lenin*."[38] Vertov certainly did dramatically undermine the separation between audience and filmed subject, most famously in the beginning of *Man with a Movie Camera*, in which he filmed the audience taking their seats in the movie house. While some of Vertov's films embody Benjamin's utopia, others are a far cry from it. Vertov's subjects did not all have equal rights over the means of representation, even though some of them famously looked back at the camera, thus displaying an awareness of its presence and, implicitly, some degree of agency over their own portrayal.

The hidden camera, a literalized version of a cinema that catches life off guard, is the very negation of the gaze into the camera. The prostitutes and speculators ostensibly filmed by Vertov with the hidden camera could not return his gaze. Vertov's camera was deliberately not the medium through which these people represented themselves but the medium that caught them off guard and exposed them. While his criminal subjects may have (mis)appropriated the "means of production," they certainly did not appropriate the means of mechanical reproduction. It is most emphatically the "film troika"—director, cinematographer, and editor—who portray people without their consent or even against their will. Annette Michelson wrote about the politically subversive and "destabilizing effect" of Vertov's assertion of "the truth value of cinema in its converting of the invisible into the visible, in its rendering of the hidden manifest, in its revelation of disguise, and in its conversion of falsehood into truth."[39] His "decoding of communist reality," she cogently argues, explains much of the establishment's hostility towards him, a hostility that later in his career turned into outright harassment. But while priding itself on bringing criminals to light, creating them when they appeared in short supply, or approaching the whole city as a criminal subject under the gun, Vertov's hidden or artfully exhibited cameras brought out a more problematic side of his cinematic conversion of the invisible into the visible, one that self-consciously emulated, rather than subverted, the work of the police.

## The Original Show Trial Film and Its Audience

Vertov was one of the first filmmakers to record political prisoners. He used large parts of the first eight editions of his newsreel *Kino-Pravda* to cover the 1922 trial of the Socialist Revolutionaries (SR). The trial was a major Soviet and international media spectacle, "the reigning model of the Soviet show trial throughout the 1920s."[40] At first the authorities found little use for cinema in the courtroom. Vertov had to fight hard for permission to film and was initially refused.[41] Indeed, the first *Kino-Pravda* showed only street scenes of demonstrators requesting drastic measures against the SR. But once he finally received permission to film inside the court, Vertov produced a memorable coverage of the trial. As opposed to the drawn-out footage of 1930s show trials, where the camera droned as mechanically as the other participants in the trial, Vertov's 1922 coverage engages through its sharp structure and dynamic editing. It presents in swift succession the defining moments of the trial: the arrival of the defendants and members of the court, witness testimonies, and defense and prosecution speeches. The terse intertitles effectively punctuate this narrative and identify the key players. Vertov had already experimented with the trial newsreel in the very beginning of his career. His *The Trial of Mironov* (*Protsess Mironova*, 1919) showed deft appropriation of the courtroom drama into a well-structured filmic narrative.[42] The early film already exhibited the striking focus on the audience that would define Vertov's coverage of the SR trial, while also presenting a sight that would be carefully edited from the later trial: the image of the defiant defender.[43]

Watching Vertov's newsreels taught the audience how a trial proceeded, and that it was fascinating to be at one. The latter impression was reinforced by the strong focus on the reactions of the courtroom audience. In *The Trial of Mironov*, a group of men climb on top of one another to get a better view, in a spectacular shot that was probably staged for the camera. In the *Kino-Pravda*s, a spectator jumps out of his seat from excitement at the prosecutor's speech while another watches intently through opera glasses. Even the court secretaries forget about professional distance and excitedly delve into a thick file, likely the work of the secret police (see the first photograph in the Introduction). A woman stretches herself forward to get a better look. The extreme close-up of her back, which allows us to count the minuscule buttons that keep her blouse together, unambiguously and temptingly places us in the seat right behind her. The camera both lures and enables its audience to see the trial from the position of the courtroom audience. Further assisted by the design of the courtroom, which was "modeled on a theatrical stage," the film's identification of the on- and offscreen audience was less innocuous than it might seem.[44]

Julie Cassiday has documented the state's extreme preoccupation with the population's reaction to the SR trial. The courtroom audience was handpicked from loyal trade union and party members. "Common Soviet citizens interested in attending the trial found it impossible if their names did not appear on a predetermined list of audience members."[45] Furthermore, OGPU agents were deployed among the trial's spectators with the task of modeling the right reactions while at the same time monitoring the audience.[46] The authorities also made great efforts to extend outside of the courtroom this manipulation of the trial's reception. Together with carefully orchestrated mass demonstrations and partisan newspaper coverage, Vertov's film played a major role in this molding of the public's opinion about the trial. The last scene of Vertov's trial coverage explicitly addresses his concern with bringing the trial to the general public, as well as his willingness to work together with the newspapers. The

Trial audiences. *The Trial of Mironov*, 1919, *Kino-Pravda 8*, 1922, frame enlargements.

scene dramatizes precisely the relationship between the courtroom and the outside audience: a group of smiling stenographers takes down the speech of the prosecutor, which is immediately printed in *Pravda*. The camera leaves the courtroom and positions itself in front of a newsstand in expectation of *Pravda*'s arrival. As the newspaper arrives, our film crew is there to pick up the first copies. A man, who turns out to be no one else but Dziga Vertov, leans out of a tram to buy his copy of *Pravda* from a running newspaper boy. He opens the newspaper and, turning to a beautiful woman seated next to him, excitedly shares the news while pointing at the paper. The trial news turns out to be the perfect pick-up line: the woman smiles, flattered and self-conscious, tilting her head toward Vertov and his paper. The camera discreetly leaves them as they launch into an animated conversation.

This conclusion of the trial newsreel is most unusual: Vertov, the adamant champion of unplayed film, stages a dramatization where he himself plays the lead role. The director of the trial newsreel poses as just another passer-by getting his news of the trial from the newspaper. Vertov's act literally models the reception of the trial by the man in the street and seduces others into sharing his reactions. Watching his excitement and the woman's giddy laughter, it is almost impossible to remember that their reactions are provoked by a prosecutor's speech asking for no less than the death sentence for all the accused in a political show trial. Even the (actual) *Pravda* reviewer considered that the other elaborate dramatization which ends the coverage of the trial, "the footage of two young 'gentlemen' betting on whether the men will be shot or not is not at all serious, and quite inappropriate."[47] This was ungrateful, since "the two young gentlemen" modeled the excitement of the man in the street for the trial *and* for the reading of the *Pravda* itself. Indeed, the sequence should be adopted by any campaign promoting reading, since never has reading in general, let alone reading the soporific *Pravda*, appeared as such adrenaline-boosting fun as in this sequence: the two men grab the newspaper from each other as close-ups of the typed verdict—the SR were condemned to be shot, but their sentence was conditionally commuted—give their suspense-building bet a dramatic turning of the tables. As we have seen, this is the third episode of two people excitedly reading together in this newsreel, and there is more than just an air of flirtation here around reading, even if a (secret police?) file and the *Pravda* have replaced Francesca and Paolo's Arthurian romances as the Soviet Gallehault. For those in the know, the excitement must have been boosted by the recognition of two dashing members of Vertov's crew, Mikhail Kaufman and Ivan Beliakov. But for most men in the street, these crew members probably remained a better-dressed, charismatic, and in a word, cinematic, version of themselves.

Cassiday cogently argues that Vertov worked with the Soviet authorities to

script the response of the audience to the SR trial by censoring the defiant
self-presentation of the accused in the SR trial. "It proved a simple task of
editing to delete the SR's denunciations [of the Bolsheviks] from newsreels
distributed across the Soviet Union."[48] I believe that Vertov went far beyond
manipulating the image of the accused to mold the audience's response to the
trial: he artfully manipulated the image of the audience.[49] His trial coverage
stands out for the large number of audience reaction shots, most of them
repeated at least twice in different *Kino-Pravda*s. The repetitions raise questions
about editing. What is this man trying to hear by cupping his ear: the attorney's
speech, as shown in *Kino-Pravda No. 4*; the contrite defendant's testimony, as
shown in *Kino-Pravda No. 8*; or the defiant defendant's speech, edited out of all
the *Kino-Pravda*s? Maybe this eager listener even belonged in a different trial,
or in a theater hall; it is hard to know. The close-ups of members of the audience make the shots more arresting, and also allow the editor to insert them
as reaction shots whenever they are needed rather than where they originally
belonged. Furthermore, the film rallies its most sophisticated and original
cinematic moves—such as the dramatic modeling of the trial's reception by
Vertov himself and his crew—to entice its audience to identify with the courtroom audience and view the trial as an entertaining spectacle.

The significance of this artful casting of the audience comes into sharper
relief when compared to the roles attributed to the audience in other films.
Carol J. Clover has shown that the norm in Hollywood trial films is to assign
the audience the role of jurors.[50] The audience watches the debate of the two
sides from a distance and deliberates the verdict. As we will see, Soviet kino
police casts its audience in a much wider variety of roles. Indeed, the ever-
changing interpellation of the audience defines kino police as much, or more,
than the interpellation of the criminal subject. With his knack for cinematic
pioneering, Vertov breached different directions to be taken by kino police: his
camera caught criminals/enemies off guard, indexed them, edited their public
images, and maybe even made them up when in short supply, while also casting
the audience in a carefully scripted role.

## Alexander Medvedkin: Cinema as Public Prosecutor

Alexander Medvedkin launched his artistic career in the military. A soldier
in the Red Army, he rose through the ranks because of his success directing
the army theater. In 1930, Medvedkin joined the military studio Gosvoyen-
kino, where he started making military training films.[51] Soon after he became a
key player in one of the most fascinating cinematic experiments of the 1920s:

the film train. After the Revolution, film trains and ships traveled the vast expanse of the Soviet Union bringing propaganda shorts from the center and recording the everyday life of the provinces.[52] The idea of the agit-train was born in the Military Department of the All-Russian Central Executive Committee (V. Ts. I. K.). The experiment was first confined to agitational activity among the military[53]; however, within months the government understood its propaganda potential for the population at large. Lenin allocated special funds for the film trains. In 1919, his wife, Nadezhda Krupskaia, headed the film section of the agitational ship *Krasnaia zvezda*.[54] At this time of extreme poverty, when most film theaters in the capital were closed, the mobile cinema brought its propaganda to millions of people.[55]

Medvedkin recalled that in the very beginning, his train films differed little from the standard fare of informational newsreel. But soon "the character of his 'Kinojournals' changed. Critical topics started to increase."[56] Medvedkin's film crew "traveled on wheels to wherever there was something wrong."[57] They went after "bad workers, absentees, drunks, and other 'concrete carriers of evil' [*konkretnykh nositelei zla*]."[58] Capturing the first drunkard on camera took days of stalking him, but finally the cameraman managed "to catch the drunk off-guard" (*vrasplokh*).[59] As a result of the film, the worker was chased out of his work. Encouraged by their first successes, Medvedkin's cameramen started embarking on a "real cineinvestigation" (*nastoiashchee kinoissledovanie*) of bigger cases, whose public showings led to harsher punishments: people not only lost their jobs but were also "put into prison."[60] "The film train," boasted Medvedkin, "imposed itself as an arbiter, as a judge, as an inspector. . . . Our films more and more often appeared as passionate prosecutors [*strastnye obviniteli*]."[61] This time, the use of legal and judicial terms was no longer just metaphorical: those condemned to prison could certainly testify to that. Medvedkin's cinema literally performed a variety of functions: it conducted investigations, articulated accusations, and demanded punishment. Even this confusion between various roles—particularly amongst the investigator, judge, and prosecutor—speaks of the kinship of this cinema to the (il)legal practices of the times.

Of all the roles his versatile cinema could perform, Medvedkin came to prefer that of prosecutor: "it was rather like the prosecutor's speech in the courtroom: it showed what was wrong on screen."[62] If Medvedkin's admirers missed the prosecuting gesture of his films, his subjects were certainly most aware of it. Medvedkin repeatedly testified to the "fear" that his camera instilled in its subjects. People made desperate attempts to avoid its intrusive gaze. One worker changed his whole daily routine so that he would only go out when darkness shielded him from the camera. Others simply ran away,

The prosecutor's camera. *Journal no. 4*, frame enlargements.

leaving Medvedkin's cameramen with plenty of back shots.[63] When caught, the workers and their families routinely came to beg the film crew to cut them out of the movie.[64] They certainly did not share Benjamin's admiration for the tendency of unplayed Soviet film to transform a passer-by into a film subject. Indeed, Medvedkin gave a new meaning to this transformation. Unlike Benjamin, Medvedkin was not interested in cinema's potential as a means of not only mechanical but also political representation. Rather, he was interested in what he repeatedly hailed as "cinema's denunciatory power" (*oblichitel'naia sila ekrana*).[65] He understood full well that "any man is interested in seeing one's friends, factory, street on the screen."[66] But this was old news, already exploited in 1895 in the very first film shown to a commercial audience, the Lumière Brothers' famous short of workers leaving their factory (*La sortie des usines Lumière*). Inspired by this historic model, "factory gate" films quickly proliferated and then remained popular through the 1910s by playing on the desire of local audiences to see themselves depicted on the screen.[67] Medvedkin's film trains revisited this "factory gate" tradition but introduced a self-conscious twist: "Except that we showed the viewer not only his factory and his friends, but also the shortcomings of his work, his factory when experiencing a breakdown, his friends among the idlers and the absentees."[68] Medvedkin's cameramen were intent on catching the workers with their pants down, as is made graphically clear in *"How Do You Live, Comrade Miner?"* ("Kak zhivesh', tovarishch gorniak?"), a film in which the camera follows a worker to an outhouse that, conveniently, has no door to block the view.

The erosion of the boundary between audience and filmed subject was not confined to the moment of shooting, when the passer-by walked into the camera's field of vision or as she was caught running away from it. It was Medvedkin's careful direction of the viewing experience during the film's projection that most forcefully defined his relationship to the audience. From his first experiments in the military theater, Medvedkin started to devise ingenious techniques for breaking the fourth wall between the actors and the audience. In a show that presented evidence of soldiers maltreating their horses, Medvedkin planted trained actors in the audience. When a culprit's name was mentioned, the plants shouted, "'He's sitting here in the audience.' . . . 'Where? Stand up.'"[69] Taken by surprise, the culprit stood up, admitted to his crimes, and thus became a critical part of the show. During the film train projections, Medvedkin devised another revealing technique. Whenever the camera unmasked a problem, "this was always accompanied by a title addressing the audience: 'What are you doing, dear comrades, what are *you* doing?'" (original emphasis).[70] The audience members whom the camera did not catch red-handed were not allowed to sit back and enjoy their luck and the spectacle of someone else's misfortune. In some cases, Medvedkin would stop the projection right after the incriminating intertitle, turn on the lights, and ask the audience to provide solutions to the problems on-screen. The audience was denied the anonymity traditionally offered by film theaters and was instead literally placed in the spotlight. They were asked to take an active part in the show, either as prosecutors unmasking somebody else or as contrite culprits. In keeping with the times, these roles were easily interchangeable as the spotlight could always turn to unsuspecting members of the audience. Medvedkin thus carefully cast his audience in the role of prosecutor or culprit, at the same time casting out the very possibility of the audience's distance from the show in favor of passionate, if often forced, engagement. If Vertov enticed his film audience to identify with the courtroom audience in viewing the trial as an entertaining spectacle, Medvedkin's cinema staged trials where the film audience was often placed in the role of the accused. The excitement, often trepidation, came from the possibility of being caught in the spotlight of the public prosecutor camera.

In the last phase of the film trains, the camera's prosecuting gaze radically enlarged its frame from "negative elements" to the whole population, including the very heroes of the new world, the workers. Medvedkin recalls this phase as the ultimate achievement of his film trains: "If you had been told to produce certain instruments and you had not done so we would film you. After this *people* were seized with terror. *People* worked in front of our camera as if it were a machine-gun."[71] Medvedkin was certainly one of the earliest advocates of cinema as a preemptive weapon of mass terror. But he was not the first to advocate the use of cinema for the control of workers. Instead, had Medvedkin read his Lenin, he would have found an unsettling antecedent. In Lenin's article "Taylor's System—The Enslavement of the Worker to the Machine" (Sistema Teilora—Poraboshchenie cheloveka mashinoi) he described how in Taylorism

> Cinema is systematically employed for studying the work of the best operatives and increasing its intensity, i.e., speeding up workers . . . a newly engaged worker is taken to the factory cinema where he is shown a "model" performance of his job: the worker is made to "catch up" with that performance. A week later he is taken to the cinema again and shown pictures of his own performance, which is then compared with the "model."
> All these vast improvements are introduced in the *detriment of* the workers, for they lead to their still greater oppression and exploitation.[72]

Lenin was no longer alive at the time when Medvedkin unwittingly reenacted Taylor's cinematic experiments. By 1931 the establishment's view on the role of cinema had significantly changed. The resolutions of the historic Party Conference on the Cinema of March 1928 stated, "In the period of socialist construction cinema should be the most powerful weapon for the deepening of class-consciousness of the workers, and for the political re-education of all the non-proletarian strata of the population, and above all the peasantry."[73] As this resolution shows, by 1928 the population was clearly divided between proletarians and nonproletarians, and cinema was expected to treat these two categories differently. Had Medvedkin turned his prosecuting camera towards the uncooperative peasantry, the establishment would have likely supported him. Cinematic denunciations of kulaks, including footage of kulak trials in which the camera identified with the prosecution, were common in newsreels from the 1930s. This is how Graham Roberts describes the shooting of such a kulak trial: "The filming of the trial is carefully managed. The camera does not move from its position behind the questioner's table. The only variation of shot is the use of close-ups of the accused."[74] Medvedkin, however, came under strong criticism for pointing his denunciatory camera toward workers. Even Medvedkin's strongest supporter, Anatolii Lunacharskii, chided, "You knock your own side and others. But you should not knock your own people. You have to knock the others without touching your own people."[75] But despite the threat of having his films banned because of "the carelessness of [his] aim," Medvedkin continued his experiments until he himself came to realize that the film train had gone too far.[76] In 1932, "the severity of our denunciatory cinematograph" started to "worry" him, and as a result he "firmly decided to also make comedies in the train."[77]

This last laugh and the eventual demise of the film trains did not however change Medvedkin's view of the essence of his film trains. Looking back in old age on his career, he categorically stated, "So much has been written about the train since then but it has all missed the point. It was a kind of public prosecutor's cinema."[78] For Medvedkin, just one other definition of cinema competed with, and ultimately complemented, this prosecutor's cinema: cinema as a weapon. In the same late assessment of his career, Medvedkin self-consciously completed his credo: "what I wanted, and what I still want from cinema is that it should be a weapon of attack, an offensive weapon in the battle against evil."[79] Medvedkin even laid claim to the origin of the cliché, arguing that in the early 1930s, just before embarking on the film train, he "made a special pronouncement that cinema is a weapon. . . . So you see that I advocated using cinema as nobody else used it."[80] Fewer clichés were more abused in the 1920s and 1930s than cinema as a weapon, so Medvedkin's claim to its origin seems almost absurd. But his originality, as he was well aware, consisted of his use of cinema, not as a weapon in a "'general' sense . . . , but in a concrete sense."[81] While he did not originate the cliché of cinema as a weapon, he was the first to take the cliché literally and make an *ars poetica* out of it.

Recollecting his beginnings in the movies, Medvedkin told a revealing war story. As a young soldier, he used to ask his comrades to ambush an enemy so that he could film the capture live. During the ambush, Medvedkin's role was double: he had to cover his comrade by pointing a gun at the enemy while at the same time filming the ambush. So he concocted a practical solution: he mounted his camera on the gun and pointed them both at the enemy. In his film trains, Medvedkin had no need for a real gun anymore, since the camera fulfilled both functions by itself. But Medvedkin never abandoned the image of cinema as a weapon; in the last account of his career, the phrase appears over twenty times in eleven pages. Dwelling on this image did not elicit any new, no less, critical, reflections. Medvedkin lovingly preserved his camera-gun through the tumultuous decades of his life; the strange contraption is proudly exhibited in Chris Marker's documentary *The Last Bolshevik* (*Le tombeau d'Alexandre*, 1992).

Medvedkin's camera-gun is not an isolated curiosity but rather a symptomatic episode in the complicated relationship of the camera to the gun. A camera-gun was already shooting as cinema was being born, at the very moment when still images were inserted in a series of consecutive shots designed to capture movement. In a letter regarding Eadweard Muybridge's photography, another cinema pioneer, Étienne-Jules Marey, confessed that he had been "dreaming of a kind of *fusil photographique*, to seize the bird in a pose or, even better, in a series of poses marking the successive phases of the movement of its wings."[82] In February 1882 the dream had already turned into reality, and Marey wrote to his mother that he had "a photographic gun that has nothing murderous about it."[83] Marey's early attempt to diffuse the metaphorical associations between cameras and guns has since been often counteracted, maybe most famously in Susan Sontag's critique of photography:

> The camera/gun does not kill, so the ominous metaphor seems to be all bluff. . . . Still there is something predatory in the act of taking a picture. To photograph people is to violate them, by seeing them as they never see themselves . . . it turns people into objects that can by symbolically possessed. Just as the camera is a sublimation of the gun, to photograph someone is a sublimated murder.[84]

The actual history of the relationship between guns and cameras, memorably sketched by Paul Virilio, shows that their pairing is more than symbolic and that the ensuing murders are not always quite as sublimated as Sontag thought.[85] Already in World War I, film cameras became instrumental in warfare, decisively shaping the new ways war was to be waged in the twentieth century. The

Medvedkin's camera-gun. *The Last Bolshevik,* 1992, frame enlargement.

synchronized camera–machine guns on the biplanes of that time were driving forces in the "growing derealization of military engagement" that defined a century where face-to-face combat was to be replaced by massive long-distance killing of people transformed on enemy screens into faceless targets.[86] If the metaphor of the camera-gun has wings, the historical development and uses of the actual contraption, first designed by Marey to capture the elusive flight of birds, has caught up with the most improbable flights of fancy and rhetoric.[87] Medvedkin's coupling of the camera and the gun is one of the primal scenes in the complicated marriage between war and cinema, a primal scene that the left-bank avant-garde largely repressed when claiming Medvedkin as a predecessor.

## The Indistinguishable Crowd: Criminal Challenges to Vision and Visual Technologies

In the 1930s, Soviet cinema became more than ever preoccupied with showing the face of the Soviet antihero on screen: about one out of six of the over three hundred films released in the Soviet Union between 1933 and 1940 prominently featured class enemies, wreckers, saboteurs, and spies.[88] However, both the image of the criminal and cinema's attitude toward its task changed significantly. Anyone who had read Maxim Gorky's 1934 description of Moscow in the new model socialist realist book, *Belomor Canal*, knew that going out into the city with a camera in the hope of catching criminals off guard, or even setting up a hidden camera on a busy city corner was likely to produce nothing but footage of a sea of unreadable faces. Looking back to the beginning of the 1930s, Gorky described a society undergoing major transformations, where

> the content of people had changed radically, but their appearance had still not managed to change, and for that reason the crowd in 1931 was so indistinguishable [*malo razlichima*]. . . . In Moscow the street crowd changed in 1931. . . . It is almost impossible to make out this crowd. One simply has no idea—is this a worker's face, an administrator's face, the large forehead of the scholar, the energetic chin of the engineer, about which they write abroad?[89]

This radical disjuncture between "appearance" and "content" becomes unsettling as the narrator focuses on particular faces and starts wondering about what they might hide. Gorky, whose main concern in the book is the reeducation of Soviet criminals, starts his narrative in two classic haunts of the modern criminal—the railroad and the capital city. Gorky presents Moscow and the railroad as the double-sided topoi of a dynamic society in both literal and figurative transit; on the one hand, they are two great achievements of the new Soviet State, and on the other, they act as potential hiding places and escape routes for its enemies. Intent on meeting "the heroes of his narrative"—the criminals—Gorky scans the anonymous crowds in railway stations, on the trains, and in the city's restaurants, cinemas, and metro stations. But how can one tell these evildoers apart in this "indistinguishable" crowd? The problem is old, as any reader of nineteenth-century literature knows, but for Gorky it becomes more acute as old solutions appear discredited. The first such outdated solutions he alludes to are physiognomy and phrenology, nineteenth-century criminological responses to the problem of identification that were based on the assumption of a clear relationship between visual appearance and criminal character. Gorky mockingly cites from the latest German work on anthropometrics, adding, "a foreign anthropometrist would be at a complete loss [in the Moscow crowd], incapable of understanding a thing."[90] What is more alarming is that even "experienced Soviet people," who have their own ways of carefully "sifting through the thick of this crowd of people by special, contemporary signs" that lead them to verdicts such as, "our man, they say, watching carefully. Or—not ours," can be mistaken.[91] For even their distinctions, inasmuch as they are based on visible, "exterior signs" and visual examination, no matter how attentive, are only "relative."[92] The unreliability of visual appearance becomes a leitmotif of a book where everything from anonymity to smallpox scars, glasses, beards, wrinkles, or even the condensed water in a laundry room that covers the face of a woman worker becomes a potential mask. Gorky had long been fascinated with the idea of penetrating behind the elusive appearance of people and reading their minds. In 1896, he fantasized apropos of the invention of the x-ray:

> Imagine that someone wants to know you better. He takes a picture of your skull, and if this skull contained some thoughts, the negative will reveal them as black blots, or snakelike spirals, of some other unattractive form.
> If he wishes, he can try to photograph your conscience, and the negative will also show all the excrescences and blots.[93]

By 1934, Gorky's version of that "someone" who could read people's dirty minds was no longer the x-ray photographer but rather the secret police agent. In *Belomor Canal*, the various petty criminals or threatening enemies who hide behind the passers-by Gorky puzzles over, with little help from foreign criminological science or experienced Bolshevik street smarts, are all identified by the OGPU. It is not close observation of their physical appearance but surveillance at work and at home, searches, and informer reports provided by Gorky's secret police coauthors that help the narrator identify evildoers in the overwhelming crowds. Take the passing "engineer dressed in a Russian peasant shirt, his speech peppered with slogans, his face open and earnest."[94] His appearance puts him in the "our man" Bolshevik category, but eavesdropping behind the doors of his apartment results in compromising information, and a secret police investigation of his work leads to his arrest as a saboteur.[95]

What role can vision and its various prostheses, in particular cinema, play in identifying criminals/enemies or capturing them on the screen when visual appearance and content no longer match? A film started in the same year as *Belomor Canal* and released to great popular success in 1936, *The Party Card*, posed this question in stark visual terms and decisively answered it through its memorable portrayal of "the enemy" on screen.[96] The film's director, Ivan Pyr'ev, explained that the film's ultimate task was to identify "the distinguishing characteristics" (*opoznavatel'nye znaki*) and "offensive tactic" (*nastupatel'naia taktika*) of the class enemy on-screen, and further teach the spectator "vigilance" (*bditel'nost'*) and the ability to identify enemies in his everyday life.[97] Pyr'ev's use of police jargon to describe the task of his film recalls Vertov's comparison of the filmmaker with the secret police agent. But unlike Vertov, who modeled his activity on that of the investigative agent, sifting through the crowds in the hope of catching this or that particular criminal off guard, Pyr'ev appears to emulate the activities of a different police role model, the criminologist. According to Christian Phéline, the foundational ambition of criminology was to identify the image of the criminal, singling out his visible characteristics at a time when the anonymity of the modern crowds and the rise in criminality made any stranger a potential criminal.[98] Criminology thus attempted to use anthropometry—the measurements of the human body— or the pseudo-scientific theories of degeneration and in-born criminality to identify and expose visible traits of criminality (a certain shape of the forehead, a certain ratio of facial features). Phéline argues that whether "'the criminal type' is conceived as a mainly biological or as a 'socio-professional' reality, the criminologist is always engaged in researching the *manifest* characteristics of culpability. Whether it is the physical stigma of atavism or the identifying characteristics of the recruits of 'the army of crime,' it's always the appearance that makes the delinquent" (original emphasis).[99] A crucial part of the criminological project then was to teach certain techniques of looking at, measuring, and deciphering the human body that could help detect a criminality threatening to elude the untrained naked eye. Even when the search for a "criminal type" became a compromising skeleton in the closet of the history of criminology, the discipline maintained its defining preoccupation with making crime and the criminal visible. *Visible Proofs: Forensic Views of the Body*, a recent exhibit on the history of forensics at the National Library of Medicine, aimed, according to the library's director, Donald A. B. Lindberg, "to reach all the way back to medieval times to show how medical professionals around the world have, over the centuries, developed methods for seeing inside the body and making visible what the untrained, unequipped eye cannot."[100] The review of the exhibit similarly emphasizes the ways in which criminologists and their newer avatars, forensic experts, "strove to make their findings as easy to see as possible": "thus came the specialized camera-microscopes designed to photograph tiny fibers of hair and samples of blood; a test for arsenic that yielded a simple, visible result (a silvery substrate on a glass tube); fingerprint analysis; and even crime scene photography: all of these served both as crucial investigative tools and as props for dramatizing a case to a jury."[101] The curator, Michael Sappol, articulates the exhibit's lesson: "There was a lot of theater involved. The scientist was making himself visible, as well as the evidence."[102]

By the 1930s, at the time Pyr'ev was making his film, criminology was coming under serious criticism in the Soviet Union after a decade of lively development in the 1920s. The history of the State Institute for the Study of Crime and Criminality pointedly illustrates the fate of the discipline.[103] Founded in 1925 under the auspices of the NKVD, the institute came under attack starting in 1929 for concentrating on the individual criminal rather than on the social phenomenon of crime and criminality. As with criminology in general, the institute was also accused of espousing by now unorthodox psychological approaches to crime alongside the politically correct socioeconomic approach.[104] By 1934, the state institute was reorganized to reflect a sharp narrowing of the acceptable scope of criminology, which had been reduced to the study of crime prevention, on the one hand, and punishment and rehabilitation, on the other.[105] In between these two closely delineated fields stood the gaping excluded middle of criminal identification, apprehension, and investigation, all major traditional areas of criminology. At the time when, according to Gorky's officially sanctioned description, criminals were becoming more and more elusive in the mobile crowd, while criminology was losing its authority to provide a solution to this crisis, Pyr'ev's film de facto took over the classic criminological project of rendering the enemy visible. What justifies the filmmaker's grand criminological claim to identifying the distinguishing characteristics of the enemy and creating a generic portrait that, disseminated through film, would teach Soviet citizens to see through "the sophisticated disguises" of real-life enemies?

## The Forged *Party Card*: Detaching Photographs, Names, and Identities

The premiere of *The Party Card* in May 1936 could not have been more topical, as the whole country was in the middle of the "party card exchange" campaign (*obmen*). Since 1933, the party had been aware of the poor state of its records, but it was only in 1935 that a formal campaign was launched to remedy this.[106] Between 1931 and 1933, 1.4 million people became party members; party cards were given out hastily and without much careful recording.[107] Furthermore, given the "vast numbers [of people] . . . moving around in the early 1930s as a result of industrialization, party organizations were unable to keep track of 'real' party members."[108] Since a party card entitled its owner to important privileges, such as access to special rations of food and clothing, access to government and party buildings, and even immunity from arrest by civil authorities, many did what they could to obtain the valuable document, whether authentic or forged: "nearly half the party cards checked in Leningrad in 1935 were either invalid or false."[109] Sheila Fitzpatrick finds that

> archival evidence now makes clear that . . . the black market trade in party cards and other identification documents was huge. . . . In the 1920s and 1930s there was a flourishing black market trade in blank sheets of paper with institutional letterhead, institutional stamps, and false identity documents of all kinds—party and Komsomol membership cards, trade union cards, work records, passports, residence permits, *spravki* from local Soviets attesting to an individual's identity and social position, and so on.[110]

This "relative ease of forgery" was especially troublesome given the great significance of bureaucratic records at the time: "Soviet society in the 1930s placed a high value on literacy and the written record, for personal identity was constructed bureaucratically, through such documents as internal passports, autobiographical testimonies, and work papers."[111]

The press and internal party documents warned that passive elements, "opponents, enemies, and even foreign agents" took advantage of the privileges bestowed by the possession of a party card.[112] Attempting to rid itself of such nefarious elements, the party initiated a campaign of verification of its members (*proverka*) in 1935; the dissatisfaction with its results led in the beginning of 1936 to the launching of another campaign, which aimed to exchange all old party cards for more reliable documents. Chief among the security features of a new party card was an obligatory photograph. "Each party card was to have affixed on it the photograph of one member—otherwise it was void."[113]

*The Party Card* epitomizes this escalation in the already heightened preoccupation with identity, identification, and misidentification that defined the first decades of Soviet power.[114] In particular, *The Party Card* makes the disjunction between visual appearance and character, as well as the related disjunction between visual, textual, and political representation, into its central crisis. Above all, the film addresses the challenges that contemporary criminality posed to vision. The protagonist of this political melodrama, the dedicated young communist Anna Kulikova, fails to see that her own husband is an enemy of the people, a murderer and spy who hides under a false name (Pavel Kuganov) and who uses her reputation as just another one of his disguises. Through her inability to see his real face, Anna also loses face: her husband steals her party card and gives it to a foreign female spy, who uses it to penetrate into high-security buildings. Without even knowing it, Anna harms the party, becoming herself an enemy. In the dramatic climax of the movie, the party confronts Anna with her forged party card: opening her card, she discovers in shock the photograph of a different face, the face of a spy, next to her name. Seeing the dramatic alteration of her identity card, Anna's face is in turn disfigured by horror: she not only discovers that her party identity card no longer adequately represents her; she also discovers that she is no longer the person she thought she was—a reputable party member. Instead, she has unwittingly become a negligent liability to the party, which no longer recognizes her as its own, and formally excludes her. Unable to control her own visual and political representation, Anna is herself changed by them: her "content," her identity, is forever altered by the alteration made in her party card. The film thus takes the disjunction between appearance and content described by Gorky to a whole new level. It is not only enemies like Kuganov, who misrepresent themselves through false names and fabricated autobiographies; even honest individuals like Anna are unable to control the relationship between their "content" and their visual, verbal, and political representations—names, photographs, identity cards. Furthermore, false representations are not only used to cover up dangerous "contents"; they can indeed actually impact and transform good "contents" beyond recognition. Identity is contaminated by the instability and vulnerability to perversion that afflict representation.

If Anna is a victim of the radical instability of both representation and identity depicted by the film, Pavel Kuganov is its main catalyst. Presented as a sophisticated master of disguises, Kuganov poses the film's greatest identification challenge. The film carefully sets up this challenge, spending as much effort laying out the difficulty of its task as responding to it. The opening sequence introduces Pavel Kuganov as a riddle. In one of the most striking cinematic images of 1930s Moscow, the city celebrates May first, International Workers' Day, at night. The triumphant geography of Soviet power pierces the pitch-black night: boats festively decorated with electrically lit slogans float by the Moscow embankments, and the Kremlin lights glitter in the not-so-distant background. The film deftly exploits the eye-catching contrast between light and darkness. But no sooner is the eye caught in the spectacle of the Stalinist night than the limitations of vision become painfully clear. The viewer can see little of the celebration in this darkness, except when searchlights ominously tease with flashes of briefly illuminated scenes. As the camera draws closer to a boat and approaches the faces of the celebrants, lights flicker, briefly revealing a sideways glance or smile; but the darkness and the frenzied dancing make it impossible to distinguish any particular face, "any hero of our story." All of a sudden, a voice calls from the unlit embankments, and Pavel Kuganov runs toward the boat as all eyes, including the camera's, now nestled in the middle of the crowd, turn in the direction of the cry, just in time to capture a close-up of his face lit by a flash of light. Nearly falling into the dark waters as he tries to step into the moving boat, Pavel is helped on by a young man, Iasha, who articulates the question already visible in the crowd's curious looks: "What kind of a man are you?" Pavel tries to laugh the question away but inadvertently gives a portentous answer, when turning the attention to his wet clothes, he mutters, "Nothing, the devil . . ." The camera puts the same question in visual terms as it searchingly moves closer to his face. The unanswered question returns in the next scene when Pavel is again cast as an intruder, interrupting Anna and Iasha's flirtation. Annoyed with his presence, the couple turns toward him and again asks who he is. Pavel once more fails to give his name, instead mentioning that he is a newcomer from Siberia and "a true man of the people." As he (mis)identifies himself, a searchlight demonically glitters in his eyes, and Anna looks at him with open suspicion, which he immediately notices and counteracts with the words, "What, you don't believe me?"

Suspicion is the spontaneous first reaction to Kuganov, a suspicion shared by the young couple and the camera. So it does not come as too much of a surprise when the camera follows Pavel around as he travels the dark city and makes a late appearance in the house of old acquaintances. The first characters who actually know Kuganov's identity, his hosts do not resolve its mystery but exacerbate previous suspicions: the man, backed by a portrait of Stalin, who gazes sternly from the wall, throws Kuganov out of the house, while his wife acts as if seeing an apparition. But while our suspicions have been increasing, Iasha and Anna's have been all but forgotten in their mutual infatuation. Wandering through romantically lit streets, Iasha declares his love to Anna, whose response leaves him skipping for joy—right into Kuganov's path. Blinded by his love, Iasha takes the homeless Kuganov into his house and "opens himself to the friendship with a man, whom he knew and verified too little, thus committing a mistake that will lead to his private drama"—losing Anna.[115] For Anna, in her turn, also becomes blinded by love. Her fall for Pavel is explicitly depicted as a loss of vision. Hearing Pavel play a love song on his guitar, Anna literally closes her eyes to Iasha and their party work, and falls into a strange catatonic state that Iasha cannot break or understand. It is not just the young protagonists of the film that are fooled by Pavel: the three experienced Bolsheviks portrayed in the film, Anna's father, an old worker who examines Pavel's technical prowess, and the party secretary, all meet Pavel with the usual open suspicion but are in time fooled into accepting him into their family and workplace. The party secretary's difficulties in seeing through Anna and Pavel weigh on him so much that as the film progresses he develops a nervous tic around his eyeglasses, which he obsessively takes off and puts back on with little benefit to his political clairvoyance.

Just as the film characters lose their suspicion and clairvoyance, the audience is offered more and more visual clues and evidence that incriminate Pavel. Thrilled by his acceptance into Iasha's work brigade, Pavel takes out a pocket mirror and approvingly checks his appearance, then turns to the audience with an ingratiating, contrived smile. This act of audience seduction is interrupted by Maria, Pavel's old village fiancée, now turned cleaning woman in the factory, who eerily calls out to him from a dark corner of the workshop. Visibly startled, Pavel approaches her conspiratorially, and threateningly warns her "not to jabber." From now on, the audience knows that Pavel's carefully monitored pleasant appearance hides something compromising. We are a step ahead of all characters in the film, including Anna, who soon finds out from Maria that "Pavel is not the person he pretends to be." Confronting Pavel, Anna learns that he has hidden his kulak social origin, a serious offense that once made public would unquestionably constitute grounds for party exclusion.[116] In order to stop Anna from sharing his compromising social background with Iasha, Pavel causes a fire in the factory, which he then also puts out. While the film audience sees Pavel committing his crime, none of the characters are aware of it. One of the film's most powerful scenes contrasts our privileged knowledge of Pavel's crime with the partial and misleading view of a whole crowd of workers who, seeing Pavel emerge from the fire wounded, declare him a hero. The montage of workers' voices singing Pavel's praises and Iasha's declaration that "he always trusted Pavel" silence Anna's doubts. The next shots display official documents that testify to Pavel's act of heroism, his inclusion in the party, and his marriage to Anna. The film dramatically shows that not only an infatuated young woman but whole workers' communities and party organizations are incapable of seeing the true face of Kuganov; at the same time, the film offers its audience a privileged point of view that unambiguously identifies Kuganov as a "double-dealer" and a "saboteur."

The film pits its own masterful exposure of the enemy against its characters' difficulties at seeing through both Pavel and themselves. The last in this series of privileged disclosures shows Pavel to be a spy plotting with the chief of a foreign intelligence agency to steal Anna's party card. As a result, the audience has been given proof that Pavel is a spy long before Anna and Iasha come to make their own discoveries about his misidentification. Furthermore, not only are the characters' roads toward discovering Pavel's true nature tortuous and full of blind spots and alleys, but even their detection of his true identity is only fortuitous and partial. While both Iasha and Anna finally expose Pavel Kuganov as the kulak murderer Dziubin, to the end they fail to expose the most dangerous of his criminal personae—the spy. Anna stumbles into her partial discovery of Kuganov's true identity when putting order into the thick bundle of "papers, portraits, and photographs" that Kuganov demonstratively uses to support his working-hero identity. Suspicious of the familiar ring in the name of a letter's signatory, Dziubin, Anna digs deep into her memory until she makes the association with the name of a murderer described in Iasha's letters. It is by reading suspiciously and by serendipitously putting together two pieces of information that were completely harmless within their original context that Anna finally reaches her incriminating conclusion: her husband is the murderer Dziubin. Iasha also accidentally discovers Pavel's identity by researching the murder of a young communist by a class enemy in the Komsomol archives. The files that contain the resolution of the crime—presumably secret police files since the crime is presented as a political crime—contain a photograph of the runaway murderer named Dziubin, whom Iasha recognizes as Kuganov. It is the serendipitous cooperation between the work of the police and that of a studious vigilante that finally brings the murderer to justice. Just as in the case of Anna's mutilated party card, the imposter is exposed when the alleged relationship between name and photograph is questioned. *The Party Card* goes one step beyond the new *obmen* policy, already warning that the authority bestowed onto written documents by the attachment of a photograph may itself be fraudulent. Instead, the film suggests that both verbal *and* visual representations of identity should be treated with suspicion.

## Vigilance: The Look of High Stalinism

The protagonists' revelations give the audience a double lesson in interpretation: the more far-fetched, the better. In a world where nothing is what it seems, faces, texts, and images should be distrusted on principle. Since these signifiers are so complexly and often deceptively linked to meaning, finding the truth requires suspicion in order to break those misleading links and the far-fetched rerouting of signifiers so that they lead to previously obscured meanings. Anna and Iasha's exposures of Kuganov therefore reinforce the film's overall suspicion towards empirical observation and the unreliability of appearances, and promote a way of looking that peers through deceptive appearances by employing complicated processes of decipherment and speculation. *The Party Card* is first and foremost the promotion flick for this way of looking, most fashionable in the Stalinist thirties: *bditel'nost'*. Translated as "watchfulness" or "vigilance," *bditel'nost'* is not so much a kind of vision as suspicion towards vision and the visible, doubled by the urge to peer through the surface of reality in nervous expectation of the worst.

Sheila Fitzpatrick asserts that "in the first two decades after 1917, 'vigilance' in identifying and exposing . . . enemies of the revolutionary was one of the cardinal virtues of the communist."[117] The changing entries on *bditel'nost'* in the various editions of *The Great Soviet Encyclopedia* tersely encapsulate a revealing cultural and political history of the term. *Bditel'nost'* does not appear at all in the first (1927) edition of the encyclopedia; however, the next edition, published in 1947, features the term at great length.[118] Here *bditel'nost'* is defined in opposition to "political blindness" (*politicheskaia slepota*). The reader is informed that to meet the need for vigilance and the exposure of the enemies of the Revolution, the state created the Cheka. The secret police is thus presented as the institutionalization of vigilance: the *bditel'nost'* entry contains a short history of the secret police and its successive reorganizations and renamings. In creating the genealogy of the term, the 1947 encyclopedia tries to make up for its predecessor's omission, reaching back to revolutionary times and arguing that the quality of socialist vigilance was developed during the revolutionary struggle. However, the encyclopedia entry emphasizes that the present day requires a new kind of increased vigilance. Compared to revolutionary and civil war times, when the enemy engaged in open political and military fights with Soviet power, today's enemies, the encyclopedia informs, are harder to identify, since they "have stopped acting as political movements and instead transformed themselves into the agents of Fascist counterintelligence, spies, saboteurs, murderers and diversionists, traitors of the motherland."[119] As a result, the identification of these enemies is much more difficult, requiring unprecedented vigilance. It soon becomes clear that *bditel'nost'* is truly a Stalinist quality and that the excursion to the time of the Revolution is little more than a pious genealogical fiction. Indeed, while the entry mentions Lenin alongside Stalin, all the quotations explicitly exhorting communists to vigilance come from the latter's speeches, in particular from a 1937 speech that the encyclopedia links to Kirov's murder. The 1970s reprint of the encyclopedia still features *bditel'nost'*, but its links with Stalin are carefully erased, while the reader is warned against the inclusion of "unfounded distrust and suspicion" under the rubric of vigilance.[120] Having cut Stalin's explicit discourses on vigilance, the encyclopedia proposes Marx, Engels, and Lenin as the originators of the call to vigilance, although it cannot muster any direct references to *bditel'nost'* in any of their works. With its timely criminal—disguised kulak, murderer, spy, saboteur, and enemy of the motherland, all in one—and with its scene of party exclusion overseen by the portrait of the assassinated Kirov, *The Party Card* epitomizes the distinctive version of vigilance promoted during the Stalinist purges.[121]

The promotion of *bditel'nost'* is a key strategy in what Hannah Arendt identified as a shared Soviet and Nazi propaganda strategy to manipulate "one of the chief characteristics of the modern masses. They do not believe in anything visible, in the reality of their own experience; they do not trust their eyes and ears but only their imaginations, which may be caught by anything that is at once universal and consistent in itself."[122] *The Party Card* masterfully taps into this suspicion, but it does not take it for granted. Instead, the film goes all out to inculcate this suspicion and bring it to record levels. This extra care seems more than warranted by the sheer ambition of the movie, which targets nothing less than the subject's trust in her eyes to see the true face of the closest human being, in Anna's case, her husband. It is one thing when propaganda convinces its audience that some more or less abstract political figures or ethnic groups are, even against any visible evidence to the contrary, enemies. It is a different thing when propaganda manages to convince individuals that all their accumulated knowledge of their closest relations is worthless: when husbands, sons, and movie-going companions turn overnight into murderers, spies, and other no less fantastical creatures. We have plentiful evidence that Soviet propaganda attempted and partly managed to pull off this incredible feat. The measure of *The Party Card*'s success at such propaganda is given by contemporary audience members, like A. T. Mironova, who commented that while watching the movie it "became very clear to her that we—women—communists—must be especially careful. We must not lose class vigilance even against the ones we love, unless we become tools in the hands of a fierce enemy."[123] The paranoia certainly crossed gender lines, with film director Fridrikh Ermler confessing to his colleague Leonid Trauberg, "I saw this film and now, more than anything, I'm afraid for my party card, what if someone stole it? You won't believe it, but at night I check under my wife's pillow, to see maybe it's there."[124] If *The Party Card* turned out to be such a successful propaganda film, it was because Pyr'ev understood so well that in order to impose his film's paranoid vision of the "dangerous, well-masked criminal," he first needed to thoroughly undermine both the characters' and his audience's trust in their own ability to see things for themselves.

## Legitimizing Cinematic Vision: Socialist Realism, Depth Style, and *The Party Card*

Having so carefully set up this crisis, the film helpfully offers a solution, or rather offers itself as a solution. If one has difficulty spotting the enemy lurking between the dramatic shadows cast in the Stalinist night, why not go to the movies, and in particular, why not see *The Party Card*? The viewer can then share in the movie's privileged vision and see the masterful exposure of the enemy shown "whole and from all points of view." His film's main task, Pyr'ev also announces, is to present the viewers with "a clear image of the aggressive enemy."[125] Furthermore, Pyr'ev makes "the crystal-clarity of the film's idea" to "the multimillion viewers" into the newest aesthetic imperative of the day, pitching *The Party Card*'s promotion article like a rallying call, titled "Remember the Viewer," which he addresses to the whole Soviet cinema industry.[126] It might seem that Pyr'ev is offering *The Party Card* as a consolation-prize crystal ball for what he has convinced us is the opacity of the world. But he has far larger claims for his film. The climax of Pyr'ev's whole article is the call to "breaking any partitions, even if they are very thin, even if they are glass partitions" that separate the viewer from the film.[127] The film's ideological fiction breaks out of its crystal ball, and its protagonist, "the enemy, becomes completely real" (*sovershenno real'nym*).[128] Pyr'ev invokes here the ultimate propaganda fantasy, the moment when its fiction takes over reality. The film's review in *Kino-gazeta* not only approvingly echoed this fantasy but also declared it fulfilled: "this realistic film . . . is a part of our reality, life itself."[129] Of course, despite such critical sanction, inasmuch as Kuganov could never actually step out of the screen and mingle with his spectators, the vision of the film metamorphosing into life itself remains no more than a telling fantasy. However, to the extent that *The Party Card* managed to convince its viewers of the existence of hidden enemies, and insofar as it recast the familiar face of family, friends, and coworkers into a potential mask for the enemy, the fantasy came dangerously close to reality. Pyr'ev certainly realized that the success of his project was predicated not just on raising suspicion in visible reality but also on instilling belief in the propagandistic vision it puts forth. "If the viewer does not believe in this enemy, does not believe in his strength and aggressive tactics," then the film will cause "the opposite effect."[130]

To secure the authority of his film's vision of the enemy, Pyr'ev foils it against his characters' deceptive vision and also, more ambitiously, against a wide range of visual styles and techniques, which he viciously attacks: "And the decision stood before us, that here [in *The Party Card*] will not be tolerated petty trifles, superfluous details, short, fast montage, high-flown phrases and phrases, whispered to the camera . . . Not details, not static . . . not impressionistic shot constructions, this is not important." Pyr'ev justifies his accusations, exhaustive enough to encompass most 1920s cinematic experiments, as a preoccupation with a viewer unable to understand a film's ideological message unless carefully guided by the director. Of course, Pyr'ev's call for a cinema able to guide the viewer through a reality that is visually challenging for the fallible human eye has more in common with the tradition he attacks than he would want to admit. The film camera's mission to expand the limits of the imperfect human eye, in ways similar to the telescope or microscope, is the cornerstone of Dziga Vertov's kino-eye theory. The difference is that while Vertov's kino-eye goes out into a visually challenging reality and attempts to capture its heterogeneity, speed, and strangeness and offer them as both visual pleasure and a jolt to political action, Pyr'ev's cinema censors that messy reality and instead offers the bewildered and fallible human eye a simplified vision of the world where the details and the grays have disappeared to leave place for a black-and-white, didactic, character-centered melodrama. "We wanted to make this film with simple, stern means that would be completely clear to the viewer. . . . What is important is the person, what is important—is the actor—who through his work, led by the director, has to reveal his character."[131]

Pyr'ev deftly presents his film as a representative of a larger turning point from the varied styles of the 1920s towards a new orthodoxy. And indeed, the main components of his film's visual language correspond to recognized landmarks of cinematic socialist realism. According to David Bordwell, socialist realism departed from 1920s cinema in several major directions. It replaced strong directorial presence, expressed in techniques like direct audience address, with a more impersonal point of view.[132] Pyr'ev strikingly expresses this new trend when he describes his work in *The Party Card*: "The directorial work in this film needs to allow the viewer to see the actor in his entirety and from all sides, not noticing the director."[133] *The Party Card* similarly illustrates other main changes in cinematic practice that defined the emergence of socialist realism as described by Bordwell. The film moved the locale of political struggle from the street to the interior, here a female communist's bedroom and psyche. It shifted the focus from crowds to larger-than-life individuals, and from "montage editing that had been well suited to suggest mass movement sweeping across cities and continents" towards "a new depth style which could present more intimate scenes and focus on individual characters while also inflating them and their enterprises."[134] Related to this last point, Bordwell notes that Soviet socialist realist films of the late 1930s "remarkably anticipated" a visual style defined by "exaggerated use of depth" that has been traditionally associated with the work of Hollywood directors such as Orson Welles's *Citizen Kane* (1941).[135] Without attempting to give a "fine-grained causal account of why depth-staging of this sort emerged so saliently in the USSR in the late 1930s," Bordwell does offer some elucidation: the existence of technical preconditions, such as wide-angle lenses, sensitive film stock, and powerful lighting; the strong influence of Sergei Eisenstein's teaching; and the capacity of this new visual style "to amplify and aggrandize" the filmed subject, which fit the monumentalizing drive of socialist realism.[136]

I think that this major innovation, quite rare in the history of a largely conservative visual style like socialist realism, is also deeply rooted in the Stalinist obsession with developing a vision that can see past the foreground, past the misleading surface of reality, and into its deepest recesses. If we look close enough at the muses that inspired the emergence of depth style, we might well spot the shadow of Stalinist vigilance. Depth style emerged from the intersection of two cinematic techniques, deep space and deep focus, which closely fit the Stalinist conception of a thickly layered reality and its accompanying fantasy of a gaze able to see through those layers. Deep space is a variety of mise-en-scène where the special arrangement of set design, character, and dramatic action emphasizes the rich layers of space behind the foreground. Deep focus is a filming technique that makes use of special lenses to allow the objects and events in the backgrounds of deep space to appear as clearly as those in the foreground. *The Party Card* is a foundational film in a politicized history of depth style. The film masterfully realizes the potential of depth style to depict the high Stalinist view of the world. In *The Party Card*, the contemporary obsession with exposing the enemy is consistently expressed through a dramatic tension between a revealing background and a misleading foreground. When Anna, already suspicious of her husband, watches him hang up the poster announcing his candidacy for party membership, his stark shadow dramatically projected on the background wall warns the viewer of the dark side hidden behind his ingratiating foreground smile. In another crucial scene of the movie, Maria, Pavel's former fiancée, emerges from the dark background to shed doubt on Pavel, who in the foreground self-consciously works on his false smile, projecting it forward into a mirror and past it, toward the audience.

Pyr'ev's presentation of *The Party Card* in "Remember the Viewer" carefully secures his film to the pillars of socialist realist aesthetics. However, in legitimizing his film, Pyr'ev goes beyond aligning it with official aesthetics, which as he had ample opportunity to learn during the making of *The Party Card*, was subject to interpretation and constant revision. Despite the clarity of his depiction of the enemy, the film was at first shelved as politically and aesthetically unsound.[137] In his promotion of the film, Pyr'ev does not gloss over this unpleasant episode. On the contrary, he gives it full prominence and turns it into the ultimate legitimization of his film. He modestly explains that at first he had been carried away with his heroine; instead of stopping at her climactic unmasking of her husband as a murderer, he stepped over the limit and "overdeveloped her psychological experiences, making them melodramatic." As a result, in the first version of the film "Anna killed her husband with her own hands, thus making yet another mistake towards the party and the government." Pyr'ev loudly announces that the party and the leadership of the cinema association advised that this ending be cut and replaced with another. It then follows that the last version of the film is no longer the result of the fallible vision of the director: censorship has cut the excesses, and the party and cinema leadership have provided a corrective. In a masterful stroke, Pyr'ev ends by noting that while witnessing the audience reactions, he understood how "sharp-sighted [*prozorlivyi*], and aesthetically-politically correct" the party's reworking of the movie had been. In a paragraph, Pyr'ev recasts himself from the dangerous role of censored director to that of admiring witness of a film that reflects the party's sharp vision and ability to see eye to eye with the audience. The director's self-erasure makes the movie into the work of the party, thus giving it the highest legitimization.

## Stalin as Scriptwriter and His Chekist Protagonist

How exactly did *The Party Card* acquire its authoritative vision? Pyr'ev's description only gestures to the higher power's corrective work but remains coyly vague about the details of the creative process. It turns out that while Pyr'ev might have been self-serving in assigning authorship of his film to the highest powers in the state, he hardly exaggerated. The record of a conversation between Stalin and the head of the cinema industry, Boris Shumiatskii, documents that it was Stalin himself who literally authored the first and last words of *The Party Card*'s script. After a private Kremlin viewing of the film shown without its previously censored ending, Stalin changed the title from *Anna* to *The Party Card* and dictated its ending:

> When Anna, already in her apartment, exposes Pavel to be Dziubin and the killer of the Komsomol leader, aiming her revolver at him, and he starts crawling [at her feet], enter Iasha and the Party secretary.
> Anna tells them:
> "Look, this is Dziubin, the killer of the Komsomol leader."
> The Secretary responds:
> "He not only killed the Komsomol leader, he is also a spy and a traitor of our government . . ."
> During this time standing in the background two red army soldiers and a NKVD commissar arrest Pavel (and in the darkness, holding him by the arms, take him away).[138]

Stalin's script changes curb the excessive heroine, removing her from the title, halting her pistol in midair, and denying her the ultimate insight into her husband. Stalin's intervention also explicitly curbs the power of the director and significantly, if more subtly, alters the film's claim to omniscience and privileged vision. We have seen that, as opposed to the characters whose vision remains partial, the camera offers its spectators unfailingly reliable, privileged vision. The scene where the camera follows Pavel into his secret meeting with a foreign spy is the ultimate example of this privileged vision. The camera's extraordinary knowledge cannot be explained in diegetic terms, and instead seems to function as the defining mark of a particular aesthetic of omniscient narration. The last lines of Stalin's ending work as an understated coup de grace for this aesthetic. Stalin's addition of the NKVD commissar to the film introduces the character who has the ultimate insight into Pavel Kuganov. His presence realistically justifies the film's previously mysterious insights into Kuganov. This does not necessarily diminish the film's power; sharing secrets with the secret police might even boost the film's authority. But it denies the independence of the film's knowledge from that of the state, tying aesthetics and policing by showing a cinematic device—omniscience—to be just a temporary cover for police surveillance.

This does not mean that *The Party Card* should be seen as the representative of autonomous aesthetics being forcefully tied to the political police through Stalin's heavy-handed intervention. We have already seen that the loudly trumpeted task of the film, that of displaying the identifying characteristics of the enemy, closely echoed the preoccupations and even jargon of the secret police, positing the film as a form of policing before Stalin's intervention. Furthermore, the film did not just try to emulate the work of the secret police but also embedded the powerful institution inside its plot, casting it as a shadowy force that drives Pavel's diegetic exposure from behind the scenes. Behind the party secretary, who shows Anna her mutilated party card, suggestively looms the shadow of the secret police, for who else could have caught a foreign spy and confiscated her forged documents? Iasha's discovery of Kuganov's true identity as Dziubin is also grounded in the investigation, most likely carried out by the secret police, of the murder of the Komsomol leader by a class enemy. But while the film discreetly invokes the secret police as a behind-the-scenes helper in its own quest to expose the enemy, Stalin brings the secret police agent out onto the screen. In so doing, he decisively recasts the relationship between the film and the police and their roles in helping the spectator see through the misleading appearances of the world.

## Melodrama and the Police

To understand the stakes of this shift, it is important to remember that this relationship is much older than *The Party Card*; indeed, it is deeply rooted in the melodramatic imagination, which according to Peter Brooks, is defined precisely by the drive to see "beyond the surface of reality [in]to the truer, hidden reality."[139] Both melodrama and the modern police were born in the wake of the French Revolution as attempts to provide clear answers at a time when traditional values were violently uprooted and signs and their meanings disjointed by massive historical change. Brooks starts his classic study, *The Melodramatic Imagination*, with a quotation from Balzac's *Peau de chagrin*, which presents the narrator's attempt "to interrogate" "the surface of reality" in relationship with the interrogation of that same reality by the police. Searching for the hidden meaning of the hat checkroom at the entrance of a gambling house, the narrator wonders, "Is it some scriptural and providential parable? Isn't it rather a way of concluding a diabolical contract by extracting from you a certain security? . . . Is it the police, lurking in the sewers of the society, trying to find your hatter's name, or your own, if you've inscribed it on the headband?"[140] The narrator's oscillation between Providence and the police as the power able to see through the surface of reality is symptomatic of the shift from classical melodrama to its modern reincarnations. Classical melodrama, which Brooks dates from the wake of the French Revolution to the 1830s, relied on Providence to expose "the moral order . . . occluded behind the deceptive play of signs."[141] Tom Gunning has shown that as Providence loses its credibility in a rapidly modernizing world, melodrama's drive toward "seeking truth beneath the surface, pushing the gaze even deeper into the surface of things" ties in with contemporary legal and medical discourses.[142] Jointly responsible for dealing with deviance, legal and medical discourses of the time share with melodrama the obsessive preoccupation with exposing the villain by acquiring a penetrating gaze able to cut through the surface of reality. Gunning argues that "as melodrama enters the 20th century, the discourses of republican law and modern medicine become particularly problematic elements [in melodrama], since they partake of the same ambition as the form itself: exposing and speaking the truth," an ambition that proves more and more unrealizable as time progresses. Thus, when in the theater of the Grand Guignol, melodrama spectacularly confesses its failure to reveal the meaning and truth behind a radically desacralized and illegible reality, it also makes sure to show that its rivals—the police, the judiciary, and medicine—fail just as miserably. As an illustration, Gunning cites the ending of a Grand Guignol play, *L'Acquitée*, where an examining magistrate and a doctor/hypnotist watch helplessly as the villain walks away free, proving the limits of Providence, poetic justice, and legal justice alike.

This brief historical excursion shows the police and melodrama's deeply entangled relationship. Grounding their relationship is a shared mission—exposing the villain—and a more general effort to respond to seismic historical change with an attempt to expose the deeper, darker truth behind a reality that is conceived as a misleading, shifty surface cover. It is certainly not accidental that not only were both melodrama and modern police born in the wake of the French Revolution but that they both underwent a rebirth after the Russian Revolution. Their relationship is extremely dynamic, as witnessed by the changing invocations of the police in melodramas, invocations that range from calls for assistance or legitimization, to taunting challenge, and

The secret police enters the film following Stalin's script and stage directions. *The Party Card,* 1936, frame enlargement.

even subversion. Stalin's rewriting of the ending of *The Party Card* provides one possible denouement to this long and complicated relationship between melodrama and the police. The last melodramatic unmasking is that of poetic justice, which is shown to be just a cover for police justice—a shifty, potentially treacherous cover, one that alludes to the police powers behind it for legitimization but is then ready to overstep its bounds and take full credit for the villain's exposure and punishment. As Anna reaches for her husband's pistol, she triggers the expectation of personal as well as poetic justice, which classically proclaims that the villain's own weapons will turn against him as justice is served. This is, of course, why Stalin intervenes to rein in the excesses of personal and poetic justice before they usurp the prerogatives of the police, who are instead given exclusive rights not only to the villain's ultimate exposure as a spy but also to his punishment.

In a chapter that tracked filmmakers with a penchant for wielding rhetorical as well as literal weapons, the last celluloid gun is fittingly displayed by the secret police. Rather than doing the policing itself, cinema is reduced to showing the police doing the job. But that is itself a delicate task, one that requires careful supervision. Any film featuring the secret police had to be viewed at its headquarters and was only released once the secret police, ever careful of its public image, put its stamp of approval. So when ushering the NKVD com-

The melodramatic climax: the villain is brought to light; the chekist remains "in the background." *The Party Card*, 1936, frame enlargement.

missar into kino police, Stalin not only limited cinema's meddling into polic-ing but also implicitly sanctioned the police's meddling into the cinema. With regard to *The Party Card*, Stalin took the task into his own hands, even adding stage directions to his usually laconic script dictations. The NKVD commis-sar is to be framed "in the background," "in the darkness," silent while the party secretary, his mouthpiece, announces the results of the investigation.[143] In the film's grand finale, according to melodramatic conventions the moment of pure visibility when misleading appearances are pierced to finally expose the hidden truth, the NKVD commissar is to remain in the dark background. The police is carefully framed here not simply as the agency that brings the occluded mystery into the light but as the mystery itself. The "moral occult," long lodged in that privileged space of traditional melodrama—the back-ground behind the misleading play of appearances—has been expropriated by the police occult, by the police as the occult.

## Vision, Visual Technologies, and Policing

Before we part with *The Party Card*, I would like to return to the question of the particular relationship between vision, visual technologies—especially photography and film—and policing. Most of the influential theoretical work on this question has focused on photography, with some mentions of early film. Writing on this subject, both Alan Sekula and Tom Gunning have seen photography as playing two distinct, often opposing roles in relationship to modernity. On the one hand, photography is, as Alan Sekula memorably put it, "modernity run riot."[144] Photography illustrated and accelerated the problems of identity that we have seen haunting the modern metropolis from the nineteenth century on, by divorcing images from their referents, be it in the postcards that circulated images of exotic places and peoples, in the mortuary portrait, or most alarmingly, in the false identity card. As Jonathan Crary argued, photography "reshaped an entire modern territory" on which "signs and images, each effectively severed from a referent, circulate and proliferate."[145] Opposing this side of mechanical reproduction and multiplication of photographic images, which "undermined traditional understanding of identity, within the practice of criminology and detective fiction the photograph could also be used as a guarantor of identity and as a means of establishing guilt and innocence."[146] In the practice of police photography, the image was used "to facilitate the arrest of its referent," "tying the separable image back to its bodily source."[147] Photography could not on its own fulfill this task of establishing identity by reconnecting the image and its referent. Indeed, by itself, photography could only produce thousands of images that crowded early nineteenth-century police headquarters but proved largely useless in establishing the identity of that most wanted criminal on the early criminology's list: the repeat offender. For how was the photograph of a freshly arrested repeat offender hiding under a false name going to help identify him with one of the thousands of images of former criminals previously taken by the police? The latest scientific and technological advances were called on to make legible these befuddling photographs by translating them into words and then into numbers, which could be neatly filed in a way that would link each photograph to one criminal. Indeed, as Alan Sekula brilliantly showed, early proponents of police photography, such as Alphonse Bertillon, "sought to break the professional criminal's mastery of disguises, false identities, multiple biographies, and alibis" "by yoking anthropometrics, the optical precision of the camera, a refined physiognomic vocabulary, and statistics."[148]

As we have seen, the problem of identity and identification is at the very core of Pyr'ev's film, as Stalin's title, *The Party Card*, announces from the very beginning and as the various instances of misaligned person, photograph, and word repeatedly prove. But while Sekula and Gunning hold that the police uses visual technologies like photography in order to quell the play of signifiers and to forcefully attach image and referent—the mug shot and the criminal—Pyr'ev's version of kino policing spends most of its rhetorical force doing precisely the opposite. *The Party Card* is first deeply invested in demonstrating, to the point of caricatural overstatement, the disjuncture between image, word, and identity. The film relentlessly inculcates in its audience vigilance as a heightened form of suspicion towards vision, visual appearance, and visual technologies. The film proves to its audience that this suspicion is especially warranted when directed against photography: even in its officially sanctioned uses in identity cards or police records—the epitome of the medium's indexical function—photography not only fails to break the criminal's mastery of disguises but is instead easily appropriated by the criminal and put to work at misrepresenting identity.

However, while regular vision and photography can be deceiving, the film itself confidently offers the definite solution to the mystery, conclusively seeing through Pavel's many-layered disguises. Like the police photography described by Sekula or Gunning, *The Party Card*, as an instance of kino policing, does end by demonstratively reattaching the disjointed bond between image and referent and making the enemy visible. More specifically, *The Party Card* self-consciously aligns itself with particular contemporary state and police attempts to control the relationship between identity cards and their referents. The 1936 introduction of obligatory photographs in party cards is probably the main such practice with which the film unambiguously engages. (Internal passport photographs also became obligatory in 1938).[149] The role of the secret police in this effort to realign names, images, and their referents is made graphically clear in a 1936 regulation, which held that new blank party cards as well as the old discarded party cards could only travel from Moscow to local party organizations through the special NKVD courier service.[150] The secret police was thus put in charge of the circulation of the visual and textual representations of a population whose mobility and chameleonism appeared threatening to the state.

Nevertheless, Pyr'ev's greatest ambition reaches far beyond this triumphant ending, aiming to extend suspicion beyond the screen by inducing the audience to question the relationship between image and referent not only in the film but also in life. As a result of seeing the film, suspicion of one's closest relations opens the possibility that the face of a colleague, movie-going companion, or spouse is just a mask hiding a Pavel Kuganov. While the film resolves the puzzle of Pavel Kuganov's identity, it never attempts to resolve the suspicion towards the other, which it tries so hard to inculcate in its audience, nor does it give its audience the tools to do so on its own. Indeed, even though the film shares the criminological project of exposing the criminal by peering through her deceiving masks, it does not share the basic criminological premise that as scientific techniques, observing, measuring, describing, and seeing through the criminal could in theory be learned by anyone. Unlike popular *bditel'nost'*, penetrating vision (*prozorlivost'*) belongs to the selected few, an authority vaguely identified as the party leadership and de facto embodied by Stalin. So while this carefully cultivated suspicion opens the audience to the possibility that anyone, including oneself, might be hiding an enemy inside, it is only the special vision of the state that can see through the last mask, decisively giving the answer. As such, this 1936 film prepares the reception of the purges' shocking exposures of state enemies hiding under the mask of pretty much anyone by simultaneously inculcating suspicion towards one's own vision and suspension of disbelief towards the penetrating vision of the state. The most ambitious undertaking of this kino policing is then not the classic quest for solving the crisis that modern criminality poses relative to empirical vision—the disjuncture between image and referent—but rather the manipulative escalation of that crisis to unprecedented levels.

## The Many Ways Film Directors Took Shots at Policing

Kino police went far beyond identifying the portrait of the Soviet criminal on-screen; it engaged in an ongoing redefinition of the place of cinema, filmed subject, and spectator in the foundational decades of the Soviet State. Dziga Vertov can be credited with breaching the two main directions to be taken by kino police: exposing criminals and molding the audience in the direction desired by the secret police. Vertov's involvement with kino police was a fleeting youth affair, quickly abandoned in his search for myriad other innovations, including a complex and dynamic articulation of the audience's roles. But kino police continued on, as Alexander Medvedkin developed the denunciatory powers of cinema, turning his camera into a prosecutor and, when needed, a weapon. With Ivan Pyr'ev's *Party Card*, we see cinema emulating another side of policing, the criminological project of identifying the distinguishing marks of the Soviet enemy to the public. In part, these various types of kino policing keep pace with the major contemporary trends in policing, such as the shift in emphasis from an early model of the investigative agent, who goes out into the world to capture criminals off guard, to the much more theatrical policing style of the 1930s, primarily concerned with exposing and parading the enemy in elaborate public displays, in particular show trials but also film showings. At other times, kino policing seems out of step with its times: Alexander Medvedkin's attempt to create a critical denunciatory cinema that would document problems wherever they are found, at the time when official

artistic dogma was moving toward socialist realism and its ideals of showing reality as it should be rather than as it was, is a case in point. And yet at
other times, kino policing seems to take over sides of traditional policing that
have become somehow discredited, as in the case of Pyr'ev's criminological
project, undertaken at the time when criminology as a scientific discipline had
been largely silenced. While it seems important to uncover the long-neglected
policing fantasies at the core of these cinematic experiments, it is also crucial
to distinguish between the various examples of kino policing reviewed here.
In some instances, and in particular in *The Party Card*, cinema appears strongly
tainted by its attempts to emulate and glorify the secret police at its worst. At
the other end of the spectrum stands the filmmaker who gives policing a shot
for his own purposes, which can run parallel or even go against those of the
police. After all, misappropriating a police uniform is a serious crime, which
was quite common in the Soviet 1920s, when not only filmmakers but also various professional criminals made a habit of impersonating the secret police.[151]
So it is no surprise that the state, and the secret police in particular, had a wide
range of reactions to these attempts at kino policing, from ignoring them, to
outright banning them, to censoring their excesses, editing, and supporting
them. As we will see in the next chapter, it was not long until the secret police
took kino policing into its own hands.

## CHAPTER FOUR

# Secret Police Shots at Filmmaking

## *The Gulag and Cinema*

In the years following the October Revolution, the secret police appeared to have oscillated in viewing cinema as something between a suspect and a potentially useful propagandist. A 1923 *Pravda* article tersely summarizes this ambivalence:

> The cinema has become a very important factor in the development of crime and the judicial organs are establishing a direct and indirect connection between one adolescent's crime or another and the picture he has seen at the cinema. The cinema, which in our hands can and must become a most powerful weapon for the spread of knowledge, education and propaganda, has been turned into a weapon for the corruption of adolescents.[1]

Critically addressing the commissar of cultural affairs, A. Lunacharskii, the *Pravda* article argued that contemporary cinema was far from living up to its revolutionary potential, and went so far as to argue that "the parlous state of the Soviet cinema [was] largely responsible for the delinquent element of Soviet society."[2] Discussing "the influence of cinema on the sexual arousal of adolescents," another contemporary study writes, "We know, for example, of 10 to 15 visits to the same picture because of a feeling of sexual arousal stimulated by the appearance of the hero and heroine."[3] Besides arousing, cinema also "satisfies, engulfs like drunkenness, and as a result we see innumerable thefts carried out by adolescents and juveniles to get the money for the cinema ticket."[4] The 1919 Cheka document placing artists at the top of the surveillance list noted that "variety and cinema artists" should be "under special observation," since they worked with contemporary themes and could thus easily engage in "[counter-revolutionary] agitation."[5] Before the Revolution, cinemas had also engaged in the illegal showing of pornographic films after the regular program ended; the vigilant new authorities immediately cracked down on these nocturnal sessions.[6] At a more fundamental level, the difficult nationalization of the cinema industry posed a persistent challenge to the secret police.[7]

At the same time, cinema was critical in turning Soviet leaders, including the often-featured head of the secret police, Felix Dzerzhinsky, into "living realities" for a vast population.[8] By 1925, the secret police seemed well aware of the importance of cinema for the new Soviet State. On July 24, an OGPU decree established the Society of Friends of Soviet Cinema (Obshchestvo druzei sovetskogo kino—ODSK), and Felix Dzerzhinsky himself became its head. The organization was to have "the widest possible membership" and "was supposed to reform cinema through mass involvement."[9] ODSK worked on the premise that reforming Soviet cinema did not mean only censoring improper films and encouraging ideologically sound ones; ODSK was singularly focused on molding the audience to assure proper reception: "We cannot have a situation in which the cinema organization merely shows the film and the audience, our Soviet audience, merely watches. Intimate contact with the mass audience is necessary."[10] To this end, members of the ODSK introduced the films, explained the titles, led ensuing discussions, and reported back to the center "on the reception of films among rural audiences."[11] Indeed, ODSK pioneered "scientific" viewer studies and audience surveys.[12] Set on "transforming the cinema into a real weapon for the cultural influencing of the masses," ODSK promoted didactic films, adamantly supporting the enlightenment over the entertainment side of the debate about cinema's role in Soviet society.[13]

## The Camp as Soviet Exotica: *Solovki*

The 1928 release of A. Cherkasov's *Solovki*, a feature-length documentary film about the most infamous secret police camp of the time, the eponymous Solovki, marks a new stage in the agency's position toward cinema and its audience.[14] The very existence of the film testifies to the close collaboration between the secret police and the filmmakers. The access of the camera into a high-security camp bursting at the seams with thousands of prisoners had to be allowed, if not fully choreographed, by the agency running the camp. The OGPU did not only open its vast domain to the camera; a large number of OGPU agents participated in the shooting of the film. The agents played model versions of themselves, and according to contemporary accounts of the shooting, they also played the roles of well-fed, compliant prisoners.[15] In exchange, the film was explicitly framed as a grateful eulogy to the secret police. In the beginning of the film, terse intertitles announce that socialism is quickly advancing but that there are still wreckers who would like to stall the tempo of its development. The audience is reminded that the defense of the Soviet Union is in "the reliable hands of the Army and Fleet" and that "next to them, stands guard the watchful eye [*nedremliushchee oko*] of the Party." The film ceremoniously introduces this eye of the party as the GPU, and goes so far as to document its founding act by cutting to the cover page of the constitution and then dwelling in close-up on chapter 9 concerning "the unification of the fight against the counterrevolution, spying, and sabotage" under the GPU. It is the vision of this vigilant eye keeping watch over the criminal side of Soviet society that the film follows in training its camera eye on the ordinarily inaccessible camp.

*Solovki* presents its audience with a vision of a Soviet camp that is diverting in both senses of the world: as a manipulative distraction from the actual reality of the camp and as entertainment. *Solovki* was part of a larger campaign to disprove recent revelations about the camp published in England by Solovki fugitive Sergei Malsagov.[16] The horrors of this camp have since been described in detail in a rich memoir literature.[17] Suffice it to say that at the time the film was made and released, life on Solovki was at its very worst: typhoid fever raged, killing up to half of the camp population, and prisoner abuse by the camp guards and administration reached an all-time high.[18] Indeed, the situation was so dire that the OGPU itself was moved to send out a commission, which investigated the abuse and punished some of the culprits.[19] In Cherkasov's film, however, Solovki appears as little less than an exotic summer vacation resort, offering comfortable living accommodations, delicious food, and a full range of cultural attractions such as theater, variety shows, museums, newspapers, and libraries. But *Solovki* does more than just cover up and sanitize the unpleasant realities of the camp; it exoticizes the camp, presenting it as a strange and entertaining spectacle. The main exhibit piece in this portrait of the camp is its population. In the words of camp commander Berman, at Solovki "the counter-revolution was collected as in a good museum. . . . In our camp there are living counts, living landowners, princesses, maids of honor of his Majesty's court. There are also spies."[20] Safely quarantined in the camp, and further so in the film, this exhaustive collection of model "others" of the Soviet State was paraded in *Solovki* for the edification and diversion of its audience.

The idea that crime and criminals would make for good museum exhibits was not an OGPU invention. Indeed, crime museums had appeared and quickly spread throughout Europe as the discipline of criminology took flight at the end of the nineteenth century. In Russia, a museum of criminology was founded in 1900 in Petersburg and soon became one of the most sought-after sightseeing attractions in Petersburg; it became a fad to take foreigners visiting the Russian capital to the museum, and its first-class rogues' gallery—an extensive collection of criminals' photographs—soon became world famous.[21] During the October Revolution some of the museum holdings had disappeared, and the museum was officially closed for seven years. However, the 1920s were an era of unparalleled development in Soviet criminology; the museum reopened in 1925 after having recovered the best of its exhibits and acquired some new ones. Among the most lurid new acquisitions was the decapitated head of Petersburg's infamous criminal, Len'ka Panteleev.[22] Panteleev had been shot in 1923 by the Cheka, and after a few months of having his head displayed in a shop window on Nevskii Prospekt, the authorities moved it to the Criminology Museum. Museums and museumgoers elsewhere in Europe were no less fascinated with criminal bodies, but most had to content themselves with photographic representations or with less "capital" body parts, such as hands or fragments of tattooed skin. Berman's image of the camp museum played on this public curiosity for criminal bodies but one-upped traditional criminology museums with its loudly trumpeted ability to display "living" criminals.

Besides feeding off a larger culture of displaying criminality, the idea of a camp museum was also firmly founded in the particulars of Soviet criminology dogma of the 1920s, which held that criminality was caused by social and economic inequality, a phenomenon that was bound to disappear in an equal socialist society. Thus, Maxim Gorky explained in his 1929 reportage about Solovki, "In the Soviet Union, it is established that a 'criminal' is formed by the class-based society, and that 'criminality' is a social illness growing in the rotten soil of the system of private property. Criminality will be easily eliminated if one eliminates the condition that created this illness, which is the old, rotten economic basis of the class-based society."[23] Indeed, it was widely asserted in the 1920s that criminals were a species expected soon to become extinct in the Soviet Union. According to this dogma, the Solovki camp did not hold just any criminals but the last generation of criminals in the Soviet Union. It was their imminent fate as historical curiosities (or "vestiges of the past" as Gorky called them) that best qualified them as museum pieces. This idea is echoed almost literally in Sergei Eisenstein's film *Bezhin Meadow* (*Bezhin lug*), in which a Bolshevik castigated the retrograde kulaks who had set fire to communal property and would end up killing Pavel Morozov, by exclaiming, "Oh, oh, brother . . . these are the last ones! They should be shown in a museum!"[24] The museum is here a transparent euphemism for the camp, since in reality all those suspected of such crimes were typically sent to the camps. But this is also a very particular euphemism, one that suggests that criminals should not only be put away but also publicly displayed.

But how does one publicly display a camp? Having the public visit the camps would have been a rather impractical, and also potentially dangerous, idea. People might see things they need not see, and miss out on some carefully prepared exhibits. Film turned out to be a great solution to this problem. As Eisenstein showed in a famous description of visiting the Acropolis, film is a striking substitute for sightseeing, as it allows its audience to mimic the experience of a tourist's moving gaze while dispensing with the need to travel.[25] By authorizing a film about the camps, the secret police thus killed two birds in one shooting spree: it completely controlled the sightseeing experience while binding the public to its cinema seats. Other arts were also enlisted to the task: photographers, painters, and writers were employed by the secret police to present the camp's image. Party and secret police bosses received lavish photography albums and playing cards painted with images of the camp; a set of postcards with painted views of Solovki was published in the camp in 1926.[26] The Kirov Museum in Saint Petersburg still holds a collection of 148 photographs of the Solovki camp presented by the secret police to Kirov in 1930. Painting also literally covered up the actual view of the camp for the inmates: a monumental image of a new Soviet city sprawled on the walls of the monastery now turned prisoner living quarters.[27] Cherkasov's film was the most ambitious of all these attempts to cover the camps in the 1920s, both by mustering the most extensive resources and by addressing the largest public.

If early cinema functioned, as film scholars have convincingly argued, as a "means of transportation" promising to take its audiences to faraway, otherwise inaccessible places, few cinematic trips could rival a 1928 trip to Solovki.[28] An archipelago rising from the waters of the White Sea in the Soviet far north, Solovki boasts a fourteenth-century monastery that has long been recognized as one of the most stunning architectural ensembles in the world. Indeed, Solovki was about as dramatic a location as any film could have. In the Soviet imaginary, the archipelago occupied a no less dramatic place. Even after the fall of communism, Solovki preserved some of its mystique. When I announced to my Russian friends that I was going to Solovki, they warned me against it as if I were undertaking a journey to the netherworld, complete with fantastical trials and tribulations.

Cherkasov's careful framing of *Solovki* makes sure to stress that this trip is little short of a magical undertaking. The film starts with a panoramic portrait of Moscow. The camera gravitates to the center of Moscow, Lubianka Square, dominated by the headquarters of the secret police. Having brought us into the symbolic center of the Soviet empire, the film proposes we take a trip to its very margin, the Solovki Islands. Nothing is easier for our host: a quick animation tracks a straight line from the headquarters of the secret police to

the intermediary port of Kem'; an inch later we are in Solovki, just in time to
greet the prisoners, who having taken the slower means of transportation, the
boat, arrive after us. The onetime use of animation in a film that otherwise
sports a factual documentary aesthetic strongly highlights the extraordinary
quality of our trip.

Animation is also a literal translation into the medium of film of a leitmotif
of the times, the "living map" (*zhivaia karta*). Cherkasov's map animation was
not original but rather revisited an iconic moment: the first Russian animation
film, Dziga Vertov's *Today* (*Segodnia*, 1923), famously features another map that
comes to life. A couple of years after the making of *Solovki*, this striking image
of the living map was also used to describe the settlement of labor camps and
the inception of the grand projects to be accomplished with convict labor:
"In 1931 it seemed as though the map of Russia had come to life. . . . It was
the map of a whole country born anew, but it was almost as simple to read
as the plan of a city. . . . In Kareliia [the region around Solovki] too, the map
was alive."[29] Both this massive reshaping of the Soviet space and its mapping
were supervised by the OGPU. In the Soviet Union, mapping was under the
strict control of a special department of the secret police.[30] Strategic roads,
factories, camps, and sometimes whole towns never made it onto the map.
Together with such monumental projects as deportations, the introduction
of internal passports, and the building of canals and railroads, the kind of
mapping practiced by the secret police was an integral part of its powerful
drive to reshape and control the country.[31] The seemingly magical manipulation of space achieved in the film was based on real power; the secret police
did not need the tricks of cinematic animation to control space. But what
cinematic animation could do was to transform this manipulation of space
from a painstakingly calculated strategy into eye-catching magic. *Solovki* used
novel cinematic techniques and iconic images, such as the map animation,
together with the veteran of the secret police's bag of tricks—mapping—for
this dramatic reconfiguration of Soviet space.

Once on Solovki, we are taken on a kaleidoscopic tour of the island. As
welcomed guests of the master of the house, the secret police, we are proudly
shown around the key landmarks of its domain: the administrative buildings,
prisoners' living quarters, the dining hall, hospital, and printing press. But it
is immediately apparent that this is not a pious, drawn-out presentation of
Soviet achievements. The island is bustling with people: prisoners play soccer,
dive into the sea, and learn new trades. The film is out to prove that things are
moving on Solovki: with visible fascination, the film inventories all the means
of transportation in Solovki—cars, fleet, train, and to top it all off, Solovki's
own airplane. The film expresses and dares Solovki's mobility with its own

quick cinematic pace. In the spirit of its times, *Solovki* treats movement as a key cinematic spectacle. The movie camera is able to capture movement, and it does. There are practically no shots of static scenes in *Solovki*. According to Gilles Deleuze, "the mobile camera is like a general equivalent of all the means of locomotion that it shows or that it makes use of—airplane, car, boat, bicycle, foot."[32] In *Solovki*, the camera takes its audience for quite a ride around the island. Its electrifying pace entertains and leaves the audience the impression that a lot is happening on Solovki; it also leaves that audience little time to think about what exactly is happening there.

The camera inventories the main occupations of the prisoners: fishing, felling, and agricultural and cultural activities. Work, we are told, is carefully regulated in eight-hour shifts, and the film dwells at length on the remaining leisure time in Solovki. It appears that a great number of prisoners seem to be doing exactly what we are doing, that is, watching a show. Solovki is a society of spectacle. The theater is packed with prisoners, who watch a mixed fare of variety numbers: acrobats form a Soviet star out of their bodies, while heavily painted comedians go for slapstick. When the theater is out, prisoners gather round to watch a burly bare-chested man lift weights and a bear cub do its own tricks. The theater, as Natalia Kuziakina has thoroughly documented, was indeed a strong presence on Solovki.[33] The main company, *Solovetskii 1st Department*, started performing in 1923, the very year the camp was founded, and staged a varied repertory of classical and contemporary plays. Theater activity boomed in 1925 when two other companies appeared on Solovki: *Trash* and *Our Own*. They became extremely popular and controversial by moving away from traditional theater toward variety revues. *Trash* "borrowed some of its dancing numbers from the repertoire of *The Bat* and *Crooked Mirror*, the best pre-Revolutionary cabarets," and combined "mime, short satirical scenes, recitations to musical accompaniment, and topical couplets."[34] *Our Own* relied more on the rich prison folklore and on common prisoners who performed dances, "camp songs, limericks, couplets about everyday life, satire, and polemic."[35] The theater was so popular that tickets became prized possessions not everyone in the camp could afford. Chekists got the bulk of the seats, and what remained rarely sufficed even for the cast of privileged prisoners who had somehow managed to escape hard labor. By 1927, when *Solovki* was shot, censorship and the overall crisis of the camp had stifled much of the theatrical activity, and the regular progression of the shows was repeatedly interrupted by waves of typhus.[36] But while its actual place in the life of the camp was dwindling, the theater became a key image in OGPU-sponsored representations of the camp. Extensively featured in Cherkasov's *Solovki*, the theater made a similarly strong impression on another famous guest of the secret police to Solovki: Maxim Gorky. Written in 1929, Gorky's travelogue also dwells at disproportionate length on the camp's theatrical offerings:

> The concert was very interesting and diverse. A small but very well-coordinated "symphonic ensemble" played the overture of the Barber of Seville, a violinist played Wieniavski's "Mazurka," and Rachmaninoff's "Torrents of Spring"; the prologue to "Clowns" was decently sung, they sang Russian songs, danced "cowboy" and "eccentric" dances, somebody splendidly recited Zharov's "Accordion" to the accompaniment of accordion and piano. The group of acrobats was incredible: five men and one woman made such "tricks" as you cannot see even in a good circus. During the intermission, in the "foyer," a great brass band played Rossini, Verdi, and Beethoven's overture to "Egmont." The conductor was by all means a great talent. The concert itself showed many talented artists. All of them are of course "prisoners," and they must work a lot for the stage and on stage.[37]

Both the filmmakers of *Solovki* and Gorky had ostensibly come to Solovki as "independent outside observers" ready to give the island an objective literary and cinematic representation that would disprove the Western rumors about Soviet camps.[38] But at the Solovki theater, they turn from observers of "life caught unawares" into admiring spectators of carefully staged performances. Rather than a virgin island waiting for its travelers to give it a literary or cinematic representation, Solovki already possesses a wide variety of means of self-presentation: besides the theater, Gorky marvels at the newspaper, magazine, ethnographic society, and the museum that give "the full picture of the variety of SLON's domain" (SLON is the acronym for Solovki camp).[39] The camp's means of representation converge to give such a full picture of the island that there is no need for Gorky or for the filmmakers to fall into "primitive empiricism."[40] They can simply propagate the comprehensive picture that the camp has already put so much work into creating.[41] No wonder Gorky's description of the theater is taken over by a proliferation of seemingly redundant quotation marks: his description is truly a compilation of quotations rather than his own words. As a result, the camp looses its reality and becomes a twice-removed representation, the review of a spectacle. The final result of this description is that the prisoners are framed between quotation marks: the actors "are of course 'prisoners.'" When the camp becomes a spectacle, prisoners are only so-called prisoners, prisoners in quotations marks. As a result, Gorky can focus on the quality of their performance and praise their hard work on stage rather than bother about their actual working and living conditions in the camp.

Gorky pays as much attention to the show as to its reception by the camp audience. He prefaces his description of the theater by announcing that "Seven hundred people fit into the theatre, and it 'was packed.' A 'socially

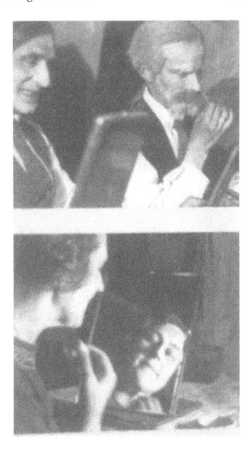

Actors putting on make-up. *Solovki*, 1928, frame enlargement.

dangerous' audience is hungry for spectacles just as any other audience is, and it thanks artists as least as warmly."[42] The film shows the same interest in the audience of Solovki's spectacles, which becomes a spectacle in itself. In a nondescript theater where *Solovki*'s audience could be watching the film, a group of men laugh out loud at the joke on stage. As we watch their amusement, one of them suddenly turns and looks straight at us, as if we were some newcomers just entering the theater. We are invited to the show: in the next shots, we are shown the events on stage unmediated. The film places us in the seats of the local Solovki theater, but not before showing us how an audience is to behave. We see the laughter of the audience before we even see the funny scene; as such, it functions like canned laughter, signaling to us how to react to the joke to come. The film not only carefully stages the camp's presentation but also its reception.

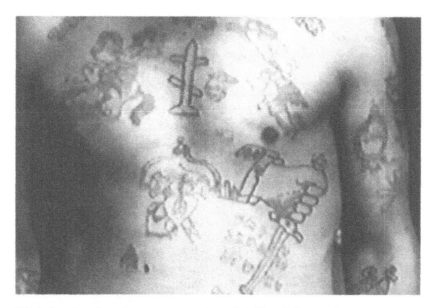

Displaying the prisoners as camp attractions. *Solovki,* 1928, frame enlargement.

The spectators we are shown on-screen are unfailingly entertained and impressed by the spectacle. We are encouraged to follow their example and simply sit back and enjoy the show. One difference between the camp audience and us is that when the lights in their theater go out and their show is over, ours continues uninterrupted. Just in case we might be at a loss as to how to react to the tour of the camp and its historical heritage, the film introduces a group of "tourists" excitedly listening to their guide's presentation of the island. Even when we are outside the theater, the camera continues to frame the prisoners as amusing objects for our entertainment. By so doing, the camera not only encourages its audience to sit back and enjoy the many spectacles that the camp offers, but more importantly, it invites its audience to enjoy the camp as a spectacle. A group of buff male inmates obligingly strip in front of the camera and then comically display their full-body tattoos. Tattoos were used in Soviet camps to announce a complex hierarchy among the common criminals. Outside of the camps, even the uninitiated passer-by probably got their intimidating message. The patronizing eye of the camera silences the violent language of the tattoos, turning their bearers from a threat into an exotic spectacle.

Female prisoners, or at least women the film presents as prisoners, are prime fare of this spectacle. Given how well-fed and content *Solovki's* women look, it seems more likely that they are personnel or Chekists' wives playing the role of prisoners. A prisoner's recollections about the shooting of *Solovki* note that the smartly dressed, beaming prisoners shown on-screen were all "dressed-up Red Army and secret service men."[43] Substituting Chekists' wives for prisoners in camp presentations was also a well-documented practice.[44] In *Solovki*, a woman lasciviously lies on a sofa reading a book and every so often casts inviting glances on the audience. In a similar mood, another woman plays the mandolin smiling flirtatiously at the camera. Since this is a silent film, the audience need not be distracted by her music and can focus instead on her voluptuous figure. The audience is also lured to watch closely various aspects of camp routine. During the roll call, the film focuses on a group of attractive women, ostensibly prisoners, smartly dressed in white silk shirts and dark jackets, heads covered with coquettish hats. Frontally positioned, the camera catches each woman's head movement as she turns from right to left to call out her number. One beautiful face after the other turns to the camera and then away from it. An earring luminously marks the trajectory of the head's movement. The film perversely turns roll call—the moment of pure subjection when one's very gaze is directed by prison routine—into an erotic scene. Provoked by the presence of the camera, one woman looks at the camera and cannot stifle a burst of laughter; the others smile self-consciously. The subject's gaze at the audience is traditionally famed for breaking the spectator's voyeuristic illusion of watching without being seen. Here, the gaze at the audience appears to acquiesce in the camera's invitation to the audience to enjoy this eroticized spectacle.

The roll call, ostensibly a scene of life caught unawares, functions to the same effect as the clearly staged shots of the mandolin player and the reader. The representation of these women prisoners shows how the film collapses the distinction between staged film and "unplayed documentary." At the time, this distinction divided some of the leading figures of Soviet cinema, and as such it was at the heart of the current cinematic scene. Unplayed documentary was famously advocated by Dziga Vertov, whose *Man with a Movie Camera* was partially released the same year as *Solovki*.[45] Revitalized in the West in the 1960s through cinema verité (France) and direct cinema (United States), unplayed documentary was perceived as a reaction against "life in its Sunday best," "official and ritualized."[46] In *Solovki*, shots of life caught unawares and staged shots melt into each other. It is often impossible to tell which is which.[47] The few actual moments of life caught unawares that do exist into the film are fully integrated in the main narrative. The film mixes fictional and documentary scenes as the variety show combines magic tricks with acrobatics. It matters little that magic requires a sleight of hand and creates illusions that deceive the public's eyes, while acrobatics require strong arms and the risk of getting hurt to create an impression. In the variety theater, magic tricks and acrobatic figures coexist as attractions. The shots of life caught unawares and the whole documentary aesthetic of the film simply add excitement to the attraction, like the removal of the security net from under the acrobats. The audience is presented with "the real thing."

Not just a metaphor and not just another attraction of the camp, the variety theater is the prototypical show on which *Solovki* is modeled. The camp as a whole becomes an extended string of variety numbers. *Solovki*'s quick, often quite disconnected succession of eye-catching episodes harkens back to the days when newsreels featuring faraway places were shown in variety theaters, competing with "numbers" for the attention, or rather distraction, of the audience. As in any show of this kind, some numbers, like the parade of camp resources and technological wonders, are meant to inspire the awe of the audience at the craft and power of the performer. Other numbers simply aim to amuse. The ending of the film wraps this kaleidoscope of attractions into a predictable teleological narrative. In the last shots of the film, we come full circle to the port where the prisoners entered Solovki at the beginning of the film. Now the port witnesses the departure of the prisoners before the completion of their term, thanks to good behavior. Harkening back to the beginning of the film, the last scenes frame the whole film as a didactic reeducation narrative.

And yet, despite its upbeat ideological message, *Solovki* was not shielded from censorship. After a high-profile release, the film was banned, resurfacing only after the perestroika. The film was so thoroughly purged that in his *Forward, Soviet!*, Graham Roberts asserts that he has found no reference to *Solovki* "or its maker, in any Russian or English language work" other than in Marina Goldovskaya's film *Solovki Power,* and that "there is no evidence of Cherkasov's film ever being shown to paying audiences."[48] Indeed, it has long been assumed that *Solovki* was shelved without ever being shown to the public. It is Cherkasov's fellow Solovki traveler, Gorky, who provides the hitherto missing evidence of *Solovki*'s public release and gives us a first inkling as to the film's purge. Gorky's travelogue about Solovki starts with a paragraph about Cherkasov's film.[49] Gorky reports that as he was writing, the film was still "shown all over the country," having become the most famous representation of Solovki in the Soviet Union. Gorky, however, seemed hardly impressed. He declared that given the rapid rhythm of change at Solovki, the film already looked outdated. Reports of workers indignant at seeing Solovki inmates enjoy plentiful food and circus when hard-working citizens were experiencing hardship suggest that one thing that was becoming quickly outdated by 1930 was the framing of the camp as a reeducation spa. Gorky, however, clarified his cryptic critique of

Cherkasov's film only five years later, when his coedited volume about the Belomor canal imposed a whole new trend in the representation of the camps, one
that fully superseded *Solovki*. But before we turn to the 1934 Belomor project, let
us explore an intermediary landmark in the collaboration between cinema and
the police, Nikolai Ekk's *Road to Life* (*Putevka v zhizn'*, 1931).

## An OGPU Blockbuster: *Road to Life*

The shelving of *Solovki* did not put an end to the collaboration between
the secret police and cinema. In 1931, Nikolai Ekk's *Road to Life*, a film "made
on the order of the Cheka" (the OGPU), broke all box-office records and
became an instant blockbuster.[50] *Road to Life* was the first major Russian sound
film, and its release was accompanied by a furor that a viewer compared to that
later produced by Gagarin's flight into space.[51] The film also enjoyed immense
international success. At the first Venice Festival, organized under Mussolini's
aegis, the audience referendum declared Ekk the most talented contemporary director, preferring him to René Clair, Frank Capra, Ernst Lubitsch, and
Leni Riefenstahl. Produced in Soviet Russia and welcomed in fascist Italy, the
film provoked a scandal in France, which famously led to the break between
the surrealists and the French Communist Party.[52] The film was immediately
bought by twenty-six countries, and it is still featured as a vintage treat in present-day art theaters.

*Road to Life* is the story of the reeducation of homeless juvenile delinquents in a labor colony run by the secret police. Following the Revolution
and the civil war, millions of children became homeless in the Soviet Union.
For more than a decade, they were not only an eyesore for the new socialist state but also a serious public safety issue. The head of the secret police,
Felix Dzerzhinsky, singled out the problem of homeless children as a top
priority of the secret police, which promptly organized experimental labor
communes where the youth were to be reeducated through labor. Ekk set out
to dramatize the story of one such experiment.[53] As preparation for *Road to
Life*, "Ekk, a student of Meierkhol'd, studied his material thoroughly" at the
GPU labor commune near Moscow, in Liuberets.[54] He also decided to cast the
young orphans from the labor commune in his film. *Road to Life* became not
only the story of an experiment but an experiment in itself. The delinquent
orphans that were transformed by the secret police into communist workers
were also transformed by Ekk into film actors. Besides being the first major
Soviet sound film, *Road to Life* is one of the first feature films whose actors
were in the vast majority prisoners.

The film starts at the scene of a crime—a railway station. The first two characters that we meet are the charismatic gang leader Zhigan, leisurely smoking a cigarette while keeping an eye on the street, and his partner in crime, the glamorous Mazikha. In a corner, a group of street children play cards, dealt by a boy whom the intertitles introduce as "Dandy Mustafa, Zhigan's most apt assistant." As the train unloads its crowd of potential victims, Zhigan's eyes single out a rich lady, comically lost in the bustling street where the gang feels so at home. A minute later her suitcase has disappeared. The camera presents the seamlessly coordinated action of the gang as a slapstick comedy, so that when Zhigan smirks at the lady's pathetic cries, we laugh with him. More noteworthy is the fact that the contemporary public, including women who were so terrorized by the street children that they avoided going into the streets, also laughed with Zhigan and roared with delight as they heard the first thieves' song (*blatnaia pesnia*) that accompanied Zhigan's introduction.[55] Days later, the whole of Moscow was humming these tunes.

The historic first sounds of the film were a train whistle followed by a thieves' song. This film used these forever-memorable moments to present criminality as entertainment for a public that was in real life terrified by it. Enlisting the audience's sympathy for the cunning and glamorous thieves appears no less surprising for a film ordered by the secret police than the salient absence of the police when the criminals leisurely leave with their spoil. Indeed, the particular crime that opens this movie is never solved: the rich lady has lost her luggage for good. The film light-heartedly leaves the railway station and enters the home of a picture-perfect proletarian family, festively dressed up to celebrate the fifteenth birthday of the only son, Kol'ka. The three characters that the subtitles introduce now—Father, Mother, and Kol'ka—are the perfect antithesis of the first three characters: Zhigan, Mazikha, and Mustafa. There seems to be no greater gap than the one separating the criminals' street life from the harmonious life of Kol'ka's family—the father reads the newspaper, the son listens through his earphones, and the mother brushes her hair. Although the scene of hair brushing is prolonged as long as possible through slow motion, there is just so much brushing a woman can do, and in the end, the mother leaves the safe nest. Now the public's worst fears about going out into a city plagued by street children come true: the mother is killed by a street child whom she attempts to stop from stealing an apple. The boundary between the world of the homeless children and the sheltered world of a happy Soviet family has been dramatically crossed; it is in fact Mustafa's craving for the apple that has prompted the mother's death. When Kol'ka flees to the streets to escape the beatings of his now alcoholic father and joins Zhigan's gang, the separation between the two worlds has fully imploded.

The street children's crime is no longer presented as a naughty entertainment for the audience but rather something that can tragically affect anyone's life. The crowd that surrounds the dying mother voices the public anger and preoccupation with the problem of the street children and ventures some solutions, such as "shoot the little bandits." A woman's voice rises over the crowd's clamor saying, "They are not guilty." The next shot, showing the mother's faintly moving lips, might suggest that these are her dying words. And indeed, just as the film presents the street children as a serious threat to the public through the mother's death, it also elicits compassion for the unfortunate children by tracing's Kol'ka's path from a good, happy child to a criminal.

In less than fifteen minutes, the film deftly manipulates the audience's attitude to the street children: it counteracts the disparagement of the young delinquents that the public was wont to bring into the theater by successfully presenting the gang as sympathetic and their first crime as entertainment for spectators that can watch at a safe distance. The public's reassuring distance from the street children is further secured through identification with the sheltered life of a model Soviet family. With the mother's death and Kol'ka's transformation into a street child, the film moves on to present the street children (*besprizorniki*) as a grave problem that could threaten any citizen (or spectator), while at the same time securing sympathy for these dangerous criminals by showing that anyone, like Kol'ka, could end up a *besprizornik*. It is at this moment of profound crisis in the film, when the thin blue line separating order from criminality has been crossed as Kol'ka runs into the street, that the state authoritatively intervenes. The intertitles relay an order that proclaims a special commission convened to solve the problem of the homeless children. Its first action is to arrest hundreds of *besprizorniki*.

## Discipline, Punishment, and a New OGPU Experiment

The next scene would greatly please Michel Foucault. Police, doctors, and social workers come together in the "special commission" to identify, evaluate, and diagnose each street child and find a solution to juvenile delinquency. Old methods, such as physical force, are nowhere in sight. The individual interrogations are demonstratively jolly affairs—the examiners smile indulgently or burst into laughter every time they hear of a crime, past escapes from foster homes, or future plans to escape. The very thought of escape has become preposterous: one can speak softly and laugh loudly when one carries a big stick—except, of course, that this was not the case. The use of force against juvenile delinquents was widespread in the 1920s. The disciplinary gaze of the special commission did not replace older methods such as physical force as much as it covered them up. At first sight, surprisingly, the film suggests as much. Among the various social workers, doctors, policemen, and Chekists are those with stern faces who advocate putting the children into prison. In fact, as the film shows us, they already are in prison: the friendly interrogation room is soon revealed to be housed in a chilling prison, equipped with communal detention rooms where the boys are huddled in no less despondency than in their previous hideouts. As the special commission debates educational principles, the film cuts to the children singing heartbreaking songs in their dismal cell. The social workers and their new ideas have not superseded old disciplinary methods; their talk, even if well intentioned, does little more than distract from the horrible realities of the old prison system.

A burly young Chekist, Sergeev, spells out the problem: neither the prisons nor the orphanages advocated by the social workers and doctors will do. They are two faces of the same bankrupt coin: the failure of both old and new ways of dealing with juvenile delinquency. Instead, Sergeev convinces the commission to allow him to embark on an "unheard of experiment"—the labor colony. Heading a small group of young delinquents, the Chekist dramatically leaves behind the formidable building of the prison. With the same symbolic gesture, he also leaves behind both sides of Foucault's dichotomy between old punishment and new discipline; instead, he sets out to implement the Soviet secret police's unprecedented response to crime.

Sergeev's experiment was based on a real-life phenomenon: the foundation of labor communes for young homeless children by Anton Makarenko, soon to become a leading Soviet pedagogue. Makarenko's account of the communes, titled *Pedagogicheskaia poema*, asserts that he started his first colony in 1920 and developed his methods throughout the early 1920s.[56] Makarenko recounts how in 1921 he spent his first winter in a labor commune, devouring pedagogical literature, "plagued by despair and impotent tension at the difficulty of reeducating his pupils."[57] The revelation of his method came when he finally "broke loose from the chains of his educational training" and flung himself on a disrespectful youth, beating him furiously until the latter asked for forgiveness.[58] Makarenko proudly stuck to his "gendarme method" despite reminders from the "provincial Education Department" that it was "social education they want, not a torture chamber."[59] Despite this criticism, his work won the praise of the OGPU, so that when Felix Dzerzhinsky died in 1926, Makarenko was called on to lead a model commune founded in the late chief's honor.[60] Just like Ekk's *besprizorniki*, Makarenko's pupils first engaged in handicraft-type productions, such as locksmithing, carpentry, shoemaking,

Orphan girl learning to
build cameras in OGPU
colony; one of the first
FEDs to be produced
there. K. Kuznetsov,
*URSS in Construction,*
*no. 4,* 1934, 16" x 11".

and sewing.[61] But by the time Ekk was shooting the film, the commune was
preparing to enter the history of photography: the first portable Soviet 35mm
camera was built in the Dzerzhinsky commune in 1932, and soon it was mass-
produced by the orphans.[62] A knockoff of the German Leica, the camera
was baptized FED, after Dzerzhinsky's initials. Additionally, just so there was
no doubt about who controlled this new means of photographic reproduction in the Soviet Union, the new cameras also featured an engraving of the
new secret police acronym: NKVD. Newsreels of the time also advertised
the NKVD accomplishments in photography and film. *Soiuzkinokhroniki No.*
*64/408* (1931) presents the assembly of photographic cameras in the OGPU
Optical Factory in Leningrad. When a few years later the NKVD initials dis-

appeared from FED cameras, the secret police's proud assertion of its control over Soviet means of photographic and film production continued, with a 1939 newsreel showcasing film projectors produced in an NKVD-run factory.[63] In *Road to Life*, the children build a train instead of cameras, changing the "spectatorial means of transportation," the camera, into a literal means of transportation.

## Film Techniques and Secret Police Tactics

The film was then based on a true story that was extremely familiar to contemporary audiences. From the point of view of those audiences, by the time the film was released, the story had reached a happy ending: the *besprizorniki* who had terrorized the public in the early 1920s had disappeared from the cities and thus no longer posed a danger. But the involvement of the Cheka in the *besprizorniki* problem had created anxiety, such that the press felt compelled to appease the public as to their fate.[64] *Road to Life* presented its audience the hitherto invisible and unsettling side of the story, the actual reeducation of the *besprizorniki* in the labor colonies. Like *Solovki*, *Road to Life* took the audience on a carefully guided tour to an otherwise inaccessible zone of Soviet reality.[65] And also like *Solovki*, *Road to Life* used a documentary aesthetic to secure the audience's trust in what is ultimately a misleading cover-up of its subject. Cherkasov chose a Vertovian "life caught unawares" brand of documentary, claiming to shoot candid snippets of camp life and then loosely putting them together in an entertaining kaleidoscope of attractions. Ekk dropped the pretense of "unplayed film"; instead, he opted for a dramatization couched in a sophisticated realist style with a strong documentary flavor. To create this flavor he used a plethora of temporal markers, citations from contemporary sources, an omniscient voice-over, realistic detail based on arduous on-location research, and the participation of actual *besprizorniki*. The resulting visual style was influential enough that Edgar Morin, the codirector of the first cinema verité documentary, *Chronicle of a Summer* (*Chronique d'un été*, 1961), recently reminisced about the great impact that *Road to Life* had on his formative years.[66] Tellingly, so did Gilles Pontecorvo, the director of *Battle of Algiers* (*La Battaglia di Algeri*, 1965), a fiction film whose use of documentary aesthetics in reconstructing a historical event is so convincing that unsuspecting viewers unfailingly take full sequences for contemporary newsreel footage.[67]

At first sight, unexpectedly, this documentary side of *Road to Life* coexists with an emphatic theatricality. Maya Turovskaya spoke of the incongruity between the high culture–infused theatrical side of *Road to Life*, on the one hand, and "the documentary" and "Chekist sides" of the film, on the other.[68] For her, the clash is epitomized by the choice of Vasilii Kachalov, "the bearer of the most beautiful voice in Soviet theater," to theatrically declaim the last words of the film, which dedicate it to Dzerzhinsky.[69] I believe that the mix between the theatrical and the documentary sides of the film is not a clumsy inconsistency but rather the fitting expression of contemporary "secret police aesthetics." As I have shown in more detail in the first chapter, interrogation as well as trial practices relied on a standard mix of histrionics and reality effect (*effet de réel*).[70] Surveillance reports as well as the massive secret police statistics department provided the plethora of often-fabricated documentary details responsible for the creation of the reality effect. At the same time, both the subjects of interrogations and witnesses to the infamous show trials commonly noticed the exaggerated theatricality that became a secret police hallmark in the 1930s. So it is only fitting that the most theatrical performance in the film is delivered by the leading Chekist, Sergeev. Unlike Makarenko, his historical model, Sergeev never loses his self-control; whenever the situation is desperate, Sergeev represses his dissatisfaction or anger in front of the children. Instead he puts on a manipulative show of trust and optimism that gets unfailingly good results. The audience, however, is let in on the secret: we know that Sergeev puts on an act in front of the children and are aware of his true feelings. This duality defines his acting throughout but is also clearly set up in the very beginning through the use of intertitles. Upon setting out for the labor colony, Sergeev dramatically dismisses the need for guards—why take them along, "since we are going of our own will [*dobrovol'no*]"? He confidently marches in front of the children so that he cannot even watch their actions. But the intertitles relay, in the first person, Sergeev's obsessively recurring thought, "Will they escape?" The suspense peaks as a tram cuts between Sergeev and the group of children, threatening to literalize the famous complicity of the city in hiding the criminal from the police.[71] Trust is clearly not warranted in this situation: the intertitles also tell us that the children had plotted to escape on the way. But Sergeev's act is doubly successful. The children are won over and give up the idea of escaping; furthermore, the film audience is made privy to the Chekist's disguised fears and to the secret information that the police has about the children's escape plan. The intertitles create a complicity between the secret police, the filmmakers, and the audience: we all share a secret. Furthermore, the suspense of this scene viscerally draws us to the side of the secret police. Before we know it, we are sharing Sergeev's anxiety; when he turns his eyes away from the children, we keep on watching them intently, fearing to see them flee.

Sergeev's show of trust is bolstered by a complex arsenal of control tactics. Key among them is secrecy. Sergeev introduces his labor colony idea to the children by conspiratorially saying to them, "My business with you is secret." Of course, his business—the labor colony—is anything but secret: the audience of the film already knows about it, and so does the establishment that had approved it. In classic secret police fashion, the true secret is that there is no secret at all.[72] Instead, the appearance of secrecy is carefully concocted and used as a powerful weapon of intimidation. Sergeev carefully directs the scene of his introduction as to deliberately shroud himself in secrecy and to baffle the children as to his identity. He has them enter a dark room where a strong light singles him out in the far corner. Startled by this uncanny appearance, the children try to guess his identity—they first call him policeman, and then they think he might be a doctor and proceed to undress in front of him. Sergeev's mysterious behavior disproves all of these commonsense hypotheses, but he withholds any information about who he actually is. At a loss, the children call him "fake doctor." In creating this spectacle of secrecy, Sergeev relies mostly on cinematic tricks such as dramatic lighting and character manipulation in the set. Indeed, his role in this scene is surprisingly akin to that of the film director. Even the elements of the scene that are outside of his actual control—most saliently camera movement and editing—work as a seamless continuation of his project. The film and its Chekist protagonist converge in their use of an intimidating poetics of secrecy. Furthermore, the film strengthens its complicit relationship with the audience by letting us in on the real secret, the fact that the colony is no secret at all, and that this fabricated secrecy is just a weapon of persuasion.

This show of complicit trust and secrecy is further secured with carefully administered threats. In response to Sergeev's conspiratorial proposal to join the labor commune, the children break into an explosion of incomprehensible, yet threatening cries. Sergeev, suddenly poker-faced, puts his hand to his chest, as if about to pull out a gun. After a moment of suspense dramatically emphasized by the prolonged close shot, he takes out a box of cigarettes, which he distributes to the children. He has made a point that they will remember: they should accept his friendly offers, like the cigarettes and the labor colony, or else he can always pull out a gun. The camera's protracted close-up emphasizes the ambiguity of his gesture—a kindness lined with a dark threat. This dramatized ambiguity reemerges periodically in the film and functions both as Sergeev's control tactic and as one of the film's defining stylistic devices.[73]

Another quintessentially secret police tactic employed by Sergeev to control the children is to "divide and conquer." From the beginning, Sergeev picks his favorites, Mustafa and, later, Kol'ka. They become the focal points of the reeducated children, and it is through them that Sergeev struggles to control the recalcitrant criminals. Two key challenges to Sergeev's plan—the internal revolt in the labor colony and the brothel—are dealt with in his absence by the reeducated children. As Zhigan, now the brothel boss, observes, "the former criminals—Mustafa and Kol'ka—have become policemen." Of course, this was a key feature of the Soviet camp system: common criminals routinely were put in charge of political prisoners, even becoming guards or camp administrators. They were also responsible for some of the worst abuses to take place in the camps. The film appears completely unaware of the problematic aspects of turning criminals into policemen and instead shows off this transformation as the major accomplishment of the labor colony. Of all the various modes of presentation of secret police methods in the film, this boastful revelation is the most simple-minded. This is sheer self-congratulatory propaganda, as opposed to the insidious work of secrecy, or to the complex playing of ostensible trust against veiled threats. A simple-minded approach to a thorny topic, this boastful self-presentation turns out to be most vulnerable to a subversive reading. For one, it is Zhigan, the charismatic gang leader, who openly comments on the transformation of the criminals into policemen. His comment is meant as an admission of defeat: the craftiness of the secret police is such that even its adversaries have to admit it. But his impact on the audience in this scene could also easily boomerang against the police. After all, Zhigan is one of the strongest and smartest characters in the film. His comments show that he has figured out a police stratagem, one that had been made infamous in Russia since the time of Ivan the Terrible.[74]

Again, Sergeev's policing tactics work hand in hand with the film's poetics. Sergeev's paradoxical selection criterion is that the worst criminals can make for the best cops, for it is the leaders of the wild boys, Mustafa and Kol'ka, the most dangerous of the young criminals, whom he picks as not the least but rather the most promising subjects of reeducation. It is strength, leadership, and not least charisma that distinguish the boys. The film shares the same paradoxical selection criteria—the leaders of the gang, including the older Zhigan, are all extremely charismatic characters, deftly and painstakingly portrayed. They are the stars whom the film works hard to render appealing to the public. The majority of the successfully reeducated boys remain pale presences compared to the gang leaders. Furthermore, it is not the hardened criminals who are one-sided caricatures of evil in the film but the representatives of the old world, such as the rich lady or the *intelligent* who proposes that the children be put into prison.

## Violence and Stylistic Innovation

For the success of his unprecedented experiment, Sergeev puts on an elaborate show that relies on quintessential secret police devices: bafflement, secrecy, and threatening ambiguity. The particular aesthetics and ideology of his show resonate deeply in the film at large. Nowhere is this affinity more visible and revealing than in the representation of violence. Formal innovation in *Road to Life* is primarily concentrated on scenes of violence, which abound in experimentation with fast editing, special effects, and striking sound manipulation. Violence is a major theme of the film, and its representations span a rich spectrum. They go way beyond the simple dialectic of covering up the violence of the police and exposing that of the street children. To start, the two violent climaxes of individual drama in the film—Kol'ka's near death at the hands of his drunken father, and Mustafa's murder—share a very distinct editing style. Extreme close-ups of parts of the human body rapidly succeed one another, to the point that it is hard to see what actually happens. In the scene in which Kol'ka's father repeatedly strikes him, we never see the actual blows. We see Kol'ka's terrorized face as he screams in expectation of the blows, and then the cuts to the father's face. But just before the blow actually falls, the camera abruptly recedes to the back of the father, whose figure thus conceals the event. When Mustafa is attacked by the armed Zhigan, he attempts to blind his opponent by throwing sand in his face. Zhigan still manages to see well enough, but the audience's vision is obstructed. During the fight, we see two hands reaching for a knife and then hear a sob. Instead of actually showing the result of the fight, the film cuts to an image of the rising sun. This source of light replaces rather than shows the image that we would like to see. But here the obstruction of vision is used to different effect. The close-ups plunge the viewer into the middle of the fight, while the hectic movement from shot to shot jars and keeps us from actually seeing the key moments or focusing on a shot long enough to make sense of it. This peculiar editing style ensures that the viewer is never granted the distance to watch the violence as a spectacle. The film does not show violence as much as it subjects the viewer to it. The elision of the climax—the blows that strike Kol'ka or Mustafa's death—is suggestive on multiple counts. These point-of-view shots identify us with the victim so that, just like the dead Mustafa, we can no longer see the actual moment of death. Linked to a reticence to intrude on the moment of death, the obstruction of vision appears as one of the least exploitative and most moving ways of representing violence.

By contrast, the death of Kol'ka's mother is fully exploited for conventional dramatic effect. While the fast editing of fragmentary views again plunges the viewer into the middle of her fight with the street child, the actual denouement of the fight, the mother's death, is emphatically not elided. The film neither asks us to identify with the mother's fading point of view, nor does it hinder us from intruding on the moment of her death. Not missing out on what Edgar Allan Poe declared to be "unquestionably the most poetical topic in the world"—"the death of a beautiful woman," the film turns the mother's death into a melodramatic spectacle.[75] A whole crowd of onlookers dominated by Kol'ka and his father watches this spectacle, while the doctor, and the camera, dramatically single out the very moment of her death.

The decisive fight between the thieves' gang and the reeducated members of the commune is also unambiguously exploited for dramatic effect. Provocatively set in a brothel, the fight is presented as full-fledged visual entertainment. From the very beginning of the fight, the audience is reassured about its outcome. After all, a group of sober young communists armed with revolvers are attacking a group of hysterical prostitutes, their drunken clients, and a pimp. Therefore, the audience can sit back and enjoy the lively spectacle, catching a few glimpses of the prostitutes' bodies as they are uncovered in the fight. The scene starts with an avalanche of special effects illustrating what the drunken thieves see. The heads of their opponents double and triple on the screen. The room starts turning at such a speed that everything becomes a whirl of light, shadow, and sound. The drunks' rude awakening comes with a dramatic cut to an unflinching close-up shot of a revolver that fills the whole screen.

The representation of violence deftly spans distinct genres, from formalist experimentation to austere symbolism, melodrama, and slapstick. The interpellation of the audience is correspondingly complex, as the spectator is asked to occupy a variety of shifting positions relative to the gendered and politicized subjects of the film. The film compellingly elicits the viewer's intimate identification with particular victims of heartrending violence—like Kol'ka and Mustafa—and thus creates the justification for the police's own fierce retaliation. Furthermore, the film glorifies police violence and when necessary covers up its unsavory aspects, minimizing, trivializing, and even presenting it to the audience as an entertaining spectacle. Fully harnessed in the service of the police, the film's sophisticated poetics also offer a complex prism into the secret police's "unprecedented experiment."

One can hardly find a more sensitive topic in the Soviet Union of the 1930s than its system of confinement. *Road to Life* is arguably the most sophisticated visual representation of this thorny topic to come out of this period. The film deftly walks dazzlingly thin lines between covering up the unseemly realities of the Soviet confinement system, bragging about its innovations and power,

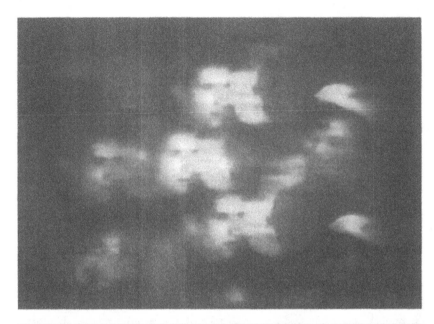

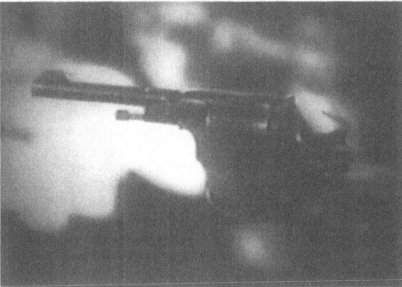

The orgy of visual effects in this brothel scene multiplies and obscures the heads of prostitutes and their clients; the scene ends dramatically with a long close-up of a revolver. *Road to Life,* 1931, frame enlargements.

and delivering more or less veiled threats to those who might resist it. This is
no simple-minded cover-up; rather, the film is an extremely intricate concoction of propaganda, innuendos, misinformation, and carefully framed revelations, all peppered with the occasional Freudian slip.

## Interpellating a Dubious Public: The Belomor Project

Maxim Gorky's dismissal of Cherkasov's *Solovki* might appear as surprising
as the film's banning. After all, Cherkasov, Gorky, and the OGPU all shared
the same project: to dispel unseemly rumors about Soviet camps through
"objective accounts" of the camps registered by independent observers.
Indeed, both Cherkasov and Gorky represented a new trend in the representation of the camps that emerged in the late 1920s and lasted for almost a
decade. As Dariusz Tolczyk has shown, this new trend opposed the glorifica-
tion of revolutionary violence that suffused the literature of the early 1920s
and created the fiction of objective, impartial, factual observation.[76] Thus,
travelogues, statistics-filled reportages, and documentary films gained undeniable precedence over the fictionalized accounts of the early 1920s. And still
there was enough variation within this general trend for *Solovki* to be banned
as an outcast while Gorky's grand coedited opus about the camps, *Belomor: An
Account of the Construction of the New Canal Between the White Sea and the Baltic Sea*
(*Belomorsko-Baltiiskii kanal imeni Stalina: istoriia stroitel'stva*, 1934), was hailed as a
model for Soviet art.[77]

Even a first glance at *Belomorsko* shows that while the collaboration between
artists and the secret police continued after *Solovki*, its character and outcomes
were rapidly changing. Gorky coedited this volume about the Belomor labor
camp with the OGPU camp commander, Semen Firin.[78] The OGPU was
no longer just collaborating with the arts but visibly advertised its authorship. Besides Firin's editorial work, the OGPU contributed its own texts and
illustrations, such as statistics, plans, and prisoners' personal files and photographs, which are dutifully acknowledged in the body of the text and whose
presence is emphasized in the striking bibliography, where the OGPU is the
most cited author.[79]

Furthermore, the utter breadth of the Belomor project was unprecedented.
The editors coordinated the work of a whole army of artists and secret police
agents. Around 120 leading Soviet writers visited the far north to document the
construction of the White Sea Canal by thousands of camp inmates during a
trip carefully orchestrated by the OGPU in August 1933.[80] Among the popular writers who took the trip were Valentin Kataev, Il'ia Il'f, Evgenii Petrov,

Artists on their visit to the Belomor camp. A. Rodchenko, *URSS in Construction*, *no. 12*, 1933, 8" x 11".

Aleksei Tolstoi, and Mikhail Zoshchenko. In the end, thirty-six writers were credited for contributing to the ensuing 613-page opus. The Belomor project did not limit itself to rallying literary establishment and token fellow travelers but vigorously enlisted the support of the visual arts. This monumental volume was richly illustrated by a collective of artists that included Alexander Rodchenko and film director Alexander Lemberg. Rodchenko's contribution to the volume was selected from the over three thousand photographs that he took while visiting the camp.[81] In addition to his work on the book, Lemberg also produced both silent and sound documentary shorts about Belomor. Lemberg had strong credentials for this work: as a cameraman for Dziga Vertov's film about the Socialist Revolutionaries trial, he was a veteran at filming political prisoners.[82] The longest of Lemberg's Belomor documentaries, *Belomor-Baltic Canal (Belomorsko-Baltiiskii vodnyi put')*, was based on a screenplay by two of the writers of *Belomorsko*, Viktor Shklovsky and Vera Inber. Closely interconnected, the films, photographs, drawings, and texts about Belomor compose a multimedia representation of the camps, to which I will refer as the Belomor project. An examination of this project reveals the new terms of the collaboration between the secret police and the arts. My analysis will draw attention to the previously ignored role of cinema in the Belomor project; furthermore, we will consider cinema's position vis-à-vis other means of representation employed by the secret police, such as photography, painting, and most emphatically, literature.[83]

Before the public even got to read *Belomorsko*, its reception was already carefully orchestrated. The introduction to the English edition informs us how we are going to react to this reading: "the reader will echo the laughter that shook the camp when some of these stories were told . . . [these stories] are all extremely diverting where they are not exciting."[84] The emphasis on a model audience whose reactions we should echo is also salient in the presentation of the Soviet edition. Before the book became available, the Soviet press publicized the writers' reactions to their camp subject: "the literati were 'beaming' while listening to the prisoner stories," and "could hardly 'hold their notebooks'" as "their fingers were shaking from astonishment."[85] The first printed copies were delivered in January 1934 directly to the Seventeenth Congress of the Communist Party where, the press announced, "the book was seen in the hands of nearly every delegate," and "2,500 copies were supposedly sold at the Congress's bookstands."[86] Potential readers were carefully shown how the cultural and political establishment received the book. This establishment was decidedly not an abstract entity but rather a collection of individuals: the cultural and political representatives of the Soviet masses, who joined their shaking hands to hold up the book for all to see from the right angle. The reader was presented with a relatively rich choice of literati to identify with in his new role as camp spectator. This variety of points of view was mere show, as the individual voices of the writers melted in the collective authorship of each article. The book presented two exceptions that were carefully orchestrated to prove the rule. The first was Maxim Gorky, the ultimate authority figure, who signed the introduction and conclusion of the book. More striking is the second exception, personified by Mikhail Zoshchenko, who signed "The Story of a Reforging" ("Istoriia odnoi perekovki").

Zoshchenko was a fellow traveler whom the Soviet regime treated with suspicion and later subjected to persecution. His name on the list of authors of *Belomorsko* thus still surprises admirers; given his literary persona they would have likely expected Zoshchenko to have kept his distance from such a problematic eulogy to the regime.[87] In *Belomorsko*, Zoshchenko's relative independence from the literary establishment was not brushed under the communal carpet but rather emphasized and craftily used to bestow authority upon the official narrative. Not only did Zoshchenko stand conspicuously apart from the community of writers busily working together on coauthored articles; he started his article by confessing that on arrival to the camp he approached Belomor's holy

of holies, "reeducation, skeptically": "I imagined that this celebrated reforging of people simply arose out of a single fundamental motive—the desire
. . . to obtain an earlier release and better conditions."[88] As a result, he turned
his attention to the worst criminals in order "to discern the authentic, perhaps
hidden, feelings, desires and intentions of people like these."[89] "The Story of a
Reforging" focuses on just such a criminal, Abram Isaakovich Rottenburg. In
the course of presenting the story of Rottenburg's conversion from a recidi-
vist criminal into a camp chief, Zoshchenko himself undergoes a conversion,
which he announces in the penitent confessional mode of the times: "I must
admit that on the whole I was greatly mistaken, and that I actually saw this
reconstruction of consciousness."[90] The trope of the Belomorstroi camp as a
conversion and reconstruction site for the artist as well as for the prisoners also
took center stage in Alexander Rodchenko's 1936 article "The Reconstruction
of the Artist" ("Perestroika khudozhnika"). There Rodchenko described the
over three thousand photographs he took at Belomorstroi as a turning point
in his career, more precisely a turning point away from the formalism that
he had been aggressively denounced for: "Gigantic will brought the outcasts
from the past here to the canal. . . . I was lost and amazed. I was taken by this
enthusiasm. I forgot about all my creative upsets. I was simply photographing.
I did not think about formalism. I was shocked by the sensitivity and wisdom
that had been brought to bear in reeducating people."[91]

In his own conversion narrative, Zoshchenko the independent skeptic
addresses the potential like-minded skeptics among *Belomorsko*'s readers: "A
skeptic who was accustomed to doubt human emotions, might feel dubious
on three accounts."[92] Zoshchenko's words allow for the possibility of a divide
in the audience of *Belomorsko*'s readers, and for the existence of dubious readers who might have given previous consideration to the topic and built arguments that subject Soviet dogma to rational questioning. Zoshchenko thus
exploits his literary persona to persuade this skeptical audience:

> I have placed these three theories in the scales of my professional capacity for
> understanding people. And I conclude that . . . Rottenburg . . . changed his psyche
> and reeducated his consciousness. . . . I am as certain of this as I am of myself.
> Otherwise I am but a naïve fellow, a dreamer, and a simpleton—sins that I have
> never suffered of in my life.[93]

In Zoshchenko's conclusion, loudly trumpeted claims to authority supersede
the rational argumentation of the skeptic's pedantically numbered theories.
The triumphant tone of this grand finale proclaims the dissolution of skepticism under the blow of rhetorical force. The figure of a skeptical observer
crushed by the achievements of Soviet camps was already well in place in a
1932 eulogy to the Dnieprostroi dam.[94] Here the "doubting Thomas" was H.

G. Wells, "who [could] call forth nothing but skepticism and a condescending smile" when Lenin showed him the plans for Dnieprostroi: "'Was it not stark madness to speak of electric suns, electric trains and ploughs . . . at a meeting illuminated . . . by smoking kerosene lamps and candle-light?' Thus reasoned Wells. This doubting Thomas, this professional dreamer and fantast, refused to give credence to the fiery oratory forecasting our electrified tomorrow."[95] Again, the skeptic's reasonable arguments are crushed by prophetic rhetoric. The question obsessively repeated over two pages in *Dnieprostroi* is "what would Mr. H. G. Wells, professional utopian, romanticist and fantast, have said [ten years later], after viewing the thousands of electric suns which flashed up today on the map?"[96] Since Wells is not available, the writer gives two alternatives: "he would smile as condescendingly as ten years ago" or "he might throw his paper Utopias into the stove and burn them up."[97] Wells's conversion remains up in the air, as his elusive silence defies and provokes the artillery of furiously impotent questioning. Instead, Zoshchenko the skeptic undergoes a swift and dramatic conversion, but not before making a show of the freedom allowed him to express his skepticism. The skeptical readers inclined to identify with him had better take notice. For the book also informs us of the fate of those skeptics who unlike Wells were not out of reach, and unlike Zoshchenko did not overcome their skepticism in the space of a page.

> But there were still enemies within the new world. The Soviet Press of the year 1931 recorded accidents and delays. . . . In scientific journals and treatises (as later findings proved), "essentially unscientific and untrue hypotheses" were propounded in order to impede and obstruct the nation's progress. . . . They are no longer armed men but engineers, professors, members of the press, who give a bad name or wreck the new plans. The G.P.U. carried mass arrests among the wreckers, for if they were allowed to continue their activities the Plan might be a failure. Thousands of those who were arrested were sent to labor camps.[98]

*Belomorsko* thus offered not only positive models of camp reception—the beaming literati and the delegates—but also thousands of negative examples such as the scholars, who were without hesitation equated with saboteurs for giving the camp a bad name. For the skeptical reader, this is a barely veiled threat: one's skepticism should be overcome in record time, or else one may well do time. If *Belomorsko* feigns to allow a modicum of critical thinking and argumentation, it quickly drowns it under a forceful rhetoric that combines loud claims to authority and oblique threats.

In his comparison of early 1920s representations of the camps with their immediate successors, Dariusz Tolczyk has argued that "a strategy of assault and moral challenge gives way to a manipulative assumption of ethical unanimity between author(ities) and the reader (society)."[99] This general trend certainly occurred. At the same time, the second term of this comparison (the late 1920s and early 1930s) did not present a univocal or static interpellation of the public. Belomor's projection of a partly dubious readership to be drawn into consensus by detailed case studies and aggressive rhetoric was significantly different from *Solovki*'s projection of an open-eyed public to be awed by the camp as a kaleidoscope of attractions.

## Multimedia Portraits of the Camp Inmate

The portrait of the camp inmate has also undergone significant changes. If in *Solovki* the prisoners were seen as exotic others easily reeducated in the course of a summer, the Belomor prisoners are hardened evildoers who pose serious challenges to the state. The introduction of the prisoners in the two films underscores this contrast: *Solovki*'s prisoners meet our eyes as a group of regularly dressed men and women leisurely disembarking in the Solovki port; there are no obvious markers of their prisoner status, so that an unsuspecting viewer might confuse them with the tourist group shown later in the film. There is no mistaking the prisoners in Lemberg's *Belomor-Baltic Canal*: here they are introduced through a succession of police mug shots. In the book, drawn-out prisoner biographies all structured as conversion narratives detail grisly past crimes, the long and stubborn resistance to reeducation, and the final, almost miraculous conversion to its truth. It is notable that Zoshchenko's skepticism toward reeducation does not question the whole show of the camp as a benevolent school of labor but rather the ability of hardened evildoers to change for the better. Even the positive heroes of reeducation are shown as recalcitrant criminals; furthermore, there are lost cases of irremediably corrupt inmates.[100] The reeducation of such hostile elements justifies tough measures. After all—the book explains for an audience that might have thought otherwise after viewing *Solovki*—the prisoners are not at a "summer resort" but rather in a hard labor camp.[101] On the same page, the image of a guard pointing his intimidating gun toward the camp drives the point home.

The differences between *Solovki* and the Belomor project's understanding of the inmate, the camp system, and the role of the secret police correspond to historic changes in Soviet criminological dogma. *Solovki* illustrates the 1920s dogma that criminals were remainders of the old order fated to disappear in the new socialist state; its criminals appear as exotic specimens easily reeducated in the course of a summer through participation in enlightening and entertaining cultural activities. Chekists have little to do in the camp other than taste the communal soup and otherwise check the well-being of the prisoners. The dogma of the 1930s no longer proclaimed that criminals were on their way out from Soviet society: on the contrary, they were threatening the new order from every corner, often in their most menacing incarnation as state enemies. Accordingly, in Belomor we are given the impression that Chekists hardly ever sleep, given how busy they are conducting thousands of arrests, managing a monumental construction site, and reeducating inmates. This change in criminological dogma is also made manifest in the different comparisons of Soviet and Western approaches to crime drawn in Maxim Gorky's 1929 article "Solovki" and in his 1934 edited volume on Belomor. In "Solovki" Gorky views common criminals in early Soviet fashion, as remainders and helpless victims of the old social order.[102] *Belomor* also draws a comparison between capitalist and Soviet criminology, complete with a gory, if encyclopedic, catalog of prison abuses in capitalist countries. But here the criminals are no longer sympathetic or helpless; they are fearsome enemies. Indeed, the comparison with Western criminology is subsumed in a chapter titled "The Country and Its Enemies," which reads like a paranoid inventory of kulaks, Mensheviks, ill-wishing foreigners, engineer-saboteurs, spies, and common thieves. Giving the lie to early promises, *Belomorsko* makes it clear that criminality has not been abolished and is indeed rife: "The new world is on the offensive, but there are still very many inimical people. Their resistance is varied."[103]

## Belomor's Femininity: The Prostitute and the Shock Worker

The presentation of Belomor's women prisoners underscores these changes in the overall portrait of the inmate. Instead of *Solovki*'s tantalizing and decontextualized portraits of beautiful women, Belomor presents unsavory biographies of individual inmates and their subsequent conversion into camp "shock workers" [udarniki], model workers who achieved results over and above their allocated quotas. One such case study follows the biography of Pavlova, a former Solovki prisoner now transferred to Belomor: an orphan, she was pushed into theft, prostitution, and murder by an abusive environment. In the camp, she was one of the most recalcitrant criminals, mocking or violently rejecting all her comrades' attempts to reeducate her, until one day, trusted with organizing a women's brigade, she made the switch to shock worker. The filmic representation of women in *Solovki* and in *Belomor-Baltic Canal* differs along the same lines, as becomes apparent in their respective treatment of the women prisoners' identification. In *Solovki*, the prisoners' identification during roll call was eclipsed by the eroticized presen-

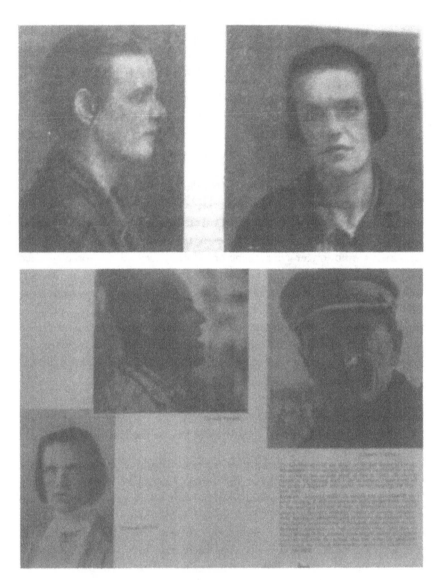

Pavlova's mug shots; collage honoring her as a shock worker. *Belomorsko-Baltiiskii kanal imeni Stalina,* 1934, 3" x 1/2", p. 305; and A. Rodchenko, *URSS in Construction,* no. *12,* 1933, 8" x 11".

Mug shots introducing the prisoners. *The Belomor-Baltic Canal*, 1935(?), frame enlargement.

tation. In Lemberg's *Belomor-Baltic Canal*, mug shots of women present the same moment of identification but in a radically different manner. The mug shot conserves the profile and frontal image of the face, but the graceful turning of the head from left to right has disappeared and so have the earrings that marked its trajectory. The mug shots cut to the point: these women are criminals and their pictures are to identify them as such. In *Belomorsko*, only one woman resembles the *Solovki* prisoners as a traditional object of desire. She is Rottenburg's lover, a beautiful and elegant thief who having fled Soviet Russia, has missed her chance at reeducation. Judging from the other images of women, her type of femininity is already extinct in Belomor. Dug out of police archives, her tantalizing image is offered to the proletarian reader as a vintage frill.

While relegating *Solovki*'s depiction of femininity to the past, the Belomor project creates a new, and sharply polarized representation of women: on one hand stands the woman criminal; on the other, the woman shock worker. *Belomorsko* carefully preserved sexual difference in its representation of women, while at the same time loudly proclaiming women to be equal to men both in their achievements and in their crimes. The fact that women can outdo men at what is traditionally considered men's work is a leitmotif of the book.[104] At the same time, we are told that "women were no easier material [for reeducation] than the men," and there is always the danger that they would go back to "their lives of thieving, drunkenness, and prostitution." Women are shown to commit all the crimes and misdemeanors that men commit, plus one: prostitution. Prostitutes are no doubt overrepresented in the Belomor project. Furthermore, few other women prisoners escape the exposure of their improper sexual past, unlike the male criminals, whose biographies mostly ignore their sex life. The Belomor female inmate is sexually delinquent, and as such her reeducation presupposes an extra step that men are not required to take: the acquisition of modesty (*stydlivost'*). This is serious business, regulated by the camp commander himself in an order circulated among both women and men.[105] *Belomorsko* tells us that the order made a great impression on the women, who like "Natal'ia Krivoruchko, former prostitute and thief," "for the first time in life . . . found out that they have modesty. And finding out about it, they in truth felt it."[106] "This order spread throughout the camp" and reached our acquaintance Pavlova, who exclaimed, "Modesty . . . I even forgot that word."[107] Invoking the new feminine ideal immediately calls it into being. The last chapter of the book gives proof of this transfiguration, as it presents us with the ultimate portrait of the reeducated woman, embodied by shock worker Iankovskaia:

> She came out in a poppy-red sweater; she was pale; about her mouth was a network of young wrinkles, such as come from frequent weeping. And that's no wonder. She was only twenty-four, but she experienced enough for fifty. The hall applauded her as soon as she appeared, and she was so confused that she also applauded. Humming loudly, the cameras were immediately trained on her.
> And that was fine.
> It is fine that film archives preserve a living image of this woman.[108]

Little matter what Iankovskaia has to say in her speech: we never hear a word. Instead, what concerns the authors is her appearance, which indeed speaks volumes. The poppy-red sweater advantageously brings out both her paleness and her ideology, and on top of it all, it catches the eye of the crowd and glues it to the speaker. Iankovskaia is the poster child of the new ideologically correct and useful sex appeal. If she is fittingly modest to the point of confusion, our narrator is not. He does not keep the distance of the crowd from Iankovskaia's podium. Well acquainted with her life story, he gets close enough to notice the particulars of her fine wrinkles. Throughout the book, the writers pride themselves as particularly attuned to what prisoners' faces hide. Iankovskaia's wrinkles, folding parts of her face out of view, are of particular interest. The narrator's emphasis on the unflattering signs of aging that mark the face of his female subject goes against the most basic principles of conventional portraiture; instead, it makes perfect sense in another representational system, that of police portraiture. One of the earliest experts on police photography, Alphonse Bertillon, explicitly warned against the portrait photographer's custom of softening or erasing wrinkles, and instead recommended the use of strong direct lighting in order to accentuate them so that the police could take advantage of the wrinkles' great potential as identifying characteristics.[109] In Iankovskaia's idealized image as a reeducated inmate, the emphatic presence of wrinkles functions as a reminder not only of her difficult criminal past but also of her portraitist's knack for turning a peculiarly searching gaze on his subject. On close inspection, Iankovskaia's wrinkles are declared clean, washed by her tears of suffering and contrition.

## The Place of the Arts in the Belomor Project

Both the writers and the camera sanction Iankovskaia's status as the iconic figure of the reeducated woman and proceed to immortalize her portrait. These new images of shock workers are typically contrasted with the old portraits of the criminal. Another woman delegate, Iurtseva, who makes a speech in front of the prisoners, "is called into a separate room, where there were two artists. They drew two pictures of me, and gave me one. Perhaps, on receiving her portrait, Iurtseva thought about the change in her life. The old Iurtseva, photographed 15 times by detectives, and the Udarnik Iurtseva being drawn twice by an artist.[110] In the camp, the official function of art, whether photography, writing, filmmaking, or drawing, is to provide iconic representations of the prisoners that foreground the reeducation narrative to the world and to themselves. But there is a clear hierarchy between the arts. Photography, the prime medium used by the state to record criminals like Iurtseva, is usually replaced with drawing and painting when it comes to creating the ceremonial portrait of the reeducated worker. These portrait drawings, however, are often based on photographs, whose indexical quality is thus altered for the sake of idealization.

Beyond carefully selecting the iconic moment (Iankovskaia pale in her red sweater), the artist also programmatically transfigures it into a larger-than-life image. Before hearing one another's speeches,

> [Prisoners] walk about in the hall and the club rooms, looking at the photographs and portraits on the walls. The photographs are of the same people. The rock worker . . . .and the concrete worker look with respect at their own portraits. The portraits show huge, heroic, sharply lighted faces, in proud foreshortening. The rock worker and the concrete worker wink meaningfully at each other. Self-respect is a new, unusual thing to them.[111]

This socialist realist art is a mirror stage for adults, where the former criminals see larger-than-life, two-dimensional portraits of themselves. Unlike in Lacan's mirror stage, the subject does not admire her own, however distorted, vision of herself, but the regime's: the socialist mirror stage replaces old-fashioned mirrors with paintings. These carefully crafted portraits weave ideology into the subject's body and facial features, enlarging and foreshortening them. And like the good-cop version of Dorian Gray's portrait, these idealized paintings are declared able to change their models. Just as the invocation of the word "modesty" is claimed to make the women prisoners "in fact feel modesty for the first time in their lives," the idealized portraits change the prisoners: they instill self-consciousness, self-respect, and they trace individualized trajectories of reeducation, spelling it out as the meaning of one's camp experience.

Surveying the halls, our narrator notes:

> A superficial physiognomist would characterize these people swiftly: a criminal type; an intellectual; a typical Kulak. But we look attentively for *the long stratification of their biographies* [*naplastovaniia biografii*], *which has eaten into their skin and muscles*, we can distinguish something new and different—something characteristic of the Belomorstroi people. . . .[112]
>
> The biographies of these people have been revised, cleaned, supplemented [*ispravleny, ochishcheny, dopolneny*]. (emphasis mine)[113]

The word biography (life writing) is hardly used at random. It is not only the prisoners' life in the camps that has changed their faces but also the representation of those lives. Zoshchenko's rewriting of Rottenburg's autobiography is one such revision, "the strange life-story written by the man himself, but with the lines drawn more firmly, as it were, by me."[114] Zoshchenko justified his changes by explaining that in Rottenburg's autobiography "the composition was complicated and confused and the reader would find it difficult to follow the course of events. There were dead tissues that needed to be revived with the breath of literature."[115] What is even stranger than Rottenburg's life story is Zoshchenko's rhetoric. The (auto)biography has "dead tissues," a metaphor that he reiterates in his conclusion: "So that is the end of our interesting story. Now we'll have to scrape the superficial tissues a little, as they say, with a surgeon's knife."[116] Just like Iankovskaia's "living" film image, Zoshchenko's representation of Rottenburg is declared alive, and also superior to Rottenburg's life and autobiography, less confusing, complicated, and open to interpretation. Whenever the prisoner's life threatened to overwhelm the biography obligingly "cleaned, revised, and supplemented" for her by the state, she was in danger of being cut to fit this scenario "with a surgeon's knife." Or else camp life could be relied on to eat her skin and muscles down to the correct profile. In the process, the camps reduced many of their prisoners to dead tissue, while their oversized representations "lived on" unchallenged. This art was intimately implicated into the central utopia of the camps—reeducation—and complicit in the abuses that underlined it.

In redefining the lines of prisoner biographies, art also redefines its own boundaries. Unlike in *Solovki*, at Belomorstroi art does not function as diversion; instead, art is instrumental to the camp project. This shift is poignantly represented in a photograph of a prisoners' orchestra playing on the construction site while prisoners work in the background. Harnessed to the great construction project, the orchestra is not even allowed the modicum of artistic autonomy conferred by the physical confines of the theater. The theater—*Solovki*'s privileged space, the prisoners' escapist haven from the harsh realities of camp life—has lost its privileged place in *Belomorsko*. When prisoners meet to watch each other perform on stage, there is no music, acrobatics, theater, or dance. Instead, one after the other, prisoners take the stage at the Worker's Club and tell their own life stories. The speeches delivered at the final meeting of Belomorstroi represent the culmination of the new art of self-presentation that replaces traditional performing arts. We have seen the prisoners rehearse this self-performance over and over during the narrative when they share their life stories with one another and with the writers. The artists are at hand to assist with this self-presentation by selecting the iconic moments and retouching any blemishes. Furthermore, their role is to propagate the prisoners' stories to audiences outside of the camp.

Like the prisoners, these outside audiences are not just presented with the "diverting" and "exciting" stories that the introduction to the English edition promised its readers.[117] The representation of Belomorstroi is neither meant to entertain nor to fully cover up the unpleasant realities of the camp. As a Chekist tells a prisoner, life in the camps cannot be too rosy or people might volunteer to come live in the camps. Less euphemistically, the audience is presented with a stark image of the camp that should deter them from any actions that might land them there. At least for Soviet audiences, the advertisement of the book as "diverting" turns out to be either anachronistic rhetoric left over from earlier presentations of the camps, or a lure tempting the audience to read a book meant in fact to make their "fingers shake"—less "from excitement" than from apprehension. The films as well as *Belomorsko* are significantly more informative than *Solovki* about the realities of camp, which is presented neither as a summer resort nor as a variety theater but as a construction site. Belomor is a "school of labor" populated with hardened criminals—sometimes incorrigible, and sometimes convertible into heroic shock workers. Rather than framing the prisoner as the audience's exotic other, the artistic representations of the camp now show him as the protagonist of the most common socialist realist narrative of conversion.[118] The contemplation of this narrative is not meant to entertain the audience as much as to inform and, in the case of a dubious spectator, to provide models for his own conversion story. In case the audience is slow to pick up on the lesson so carefully laid out for them, its members are threatened with becoming prisoners themselves. The boundary between audience and its show—the prisoners—is collapsed; the audience finds itself on shifting ground as art breaks the fourth wall and imposes itself as a living art of prescribed self-fashioning.

In the years immediately following the Revolution, the secret police appeared too busy nationalizing and policing the cinema to actually enlist it for its own purposes. This attitude visibly changed with the creation of the ODSK in 1925 and with the secret police's involvement in large-scale cinematic projects starting with the 1927 *Solovki* through *Road to Life* and the Belomor documentaries. Cinema was charged with a most sensitive mission, the public presentation of the Gulag. All films analyzed in this chapter took their viewers on carefully guided tours of this infamous zone of Soviet reality, but their travel packages differed significantly. *Road to Life* was both the most popular and the most sophisticated offering. It mixed the traditional appeal of melodrama with the latest technological innovation—sound—and topped the bill by using real delinquent children as actors. Beyond such irresistible crowd lures, the film also offered a consummate realist style punctuated by undeniable moments of formal experimentation. On close examination, the film's poetics and its complex manipulation of the audience appeared to go hand in hand with its secret police protagonist's policing tactics, such as bafflement, intimidation, secrecy, and deft control over his child subjects' emotions and subversive impulses. If *Road to Life* was a doubly successful secret police venture into cinema and cinematic venture into the Gulag, it was, as we have seen, neither the first nor the last joint venture of this nature. Already in 1928 *Solovki* framed the camp as an entertaining spectacle, casting its prisoners as exotic others for an audience that was presumed innocent. This presumption, together with the exoticized border between audience and prisoners, disappeared in the growingly paranoid atmosphere of the 1930s. The 1934 Belomor project is thus haunted by the figure of the dubious spectator, one that doubts the image of the camp and who is in turn to be doubted as a potential suspect. Luring with the promise of an entertaining spectacle of criminality, kino police gradually turned on its spectators, finally casting them as the main target of its increasingly suspicious gaze.

## CHAPTER FIVE

# Literary Theory and the Secret Police

## *Writing and Estranging the Self*

The foremost theorists of literary estrangement, Bertolt Brecht and Viktor Shklovsky, shared a preoccupation with being interrogated.

> I often imagine being interrogated by a tribunal.
> "Now tell us, Mr. Brecht, are you really in earnest?"[1]

> I give my deposition [*pokazaniie*]. I declare. I lived through the revolution honestly.[2]

Brecht's and Shklovsky's conversations with imaginary interrogators seem to echo each other, as if Shklovsky were answering the question that Brecht feared his interrogator might ask. In fact, Brecht was conversing with Walter Benjamin, who preserved Brecht's words in a diary entry from July 6, 1934, together with a possible clue to this puzzling fascination with interrogations. Benjamin laconically noted that in the same conversation, Brecht asserted that "the methods of the GPU" were based on "certain kinds of estrangement" (*Entfremdung*).[3] In the same passage, Brecht used the same word, *Entfremdung*, to describe Kafka's fiction. Brecht's words assume that there are different kinds of estrangement, such as secret police estrangement and artistic estrangement.[4] His provocative musings, however, point to a question he left unanswered: What is the relationship between artistic estrangement and GPU estrangement? Could the fascination that the two theorists of artistic estrangement showed for interrogations have something to do with these "certain kinds of estrangement" practiced by the secret police? We have already seen the secret police meddle in and influence questions that one would usually believe to be the province of literary theory, such as omniscient or unreliable narration; or the relationship between word, image, and their human referents; or the boundaries between literature and extraliterary genres such as the police file. But could it be that the shadow of the secret police reached as far as estrangement, the foundational concept of Russian Formalism, the school of literary theory long faulted as apolitical for its support of the autonomy of art?

To grapple with these questions, I will first turn to the work of Viktor Shklovsky, a leading Formalist who had firsthand knowledge of the methods of the Soviet secret police, having himself undergone a number of interrogations. The connections between the politics and aesthetics of estrangement in the context of Shklovsky's work have been long overlooked or denied, even though they have been thoroughly analyzed in the context of Brecht's work. Thus, Fredric Jameson argued that the "purpose" of Brecht's estrangement is "political in the most thoroughgoing sense of the word; it is, as Brecht insisted over and over, to make you aware that the objects and institutions you thought to be natural were really only historical: the result of change, they themselves henceforth became in their turn changeable."[5] By contrast, Jameson charges, Shklovsky's theory of estrangement, which argues that the goal of art is to defamiliarize, make strange, or present the world from unusual angles and thus refresh our routine-dulled perception, suffers from ahistoricity and essentialism, since it is based on the belief that objects exist in a "unitary, atemporal way" prior to being temporarily made strange by the artist.[6] These charges against estrangement are part of a larger critique of Shklovsky's Formalist school for what has been long seen as its championing of an autonomous art divorced from life, history, and politics. This critique was already well in place in the 1920s, and ranged from serious studies by major figures such as Lev Trotsky (1924) and Mikhail Bakhtin (1928) to inflammatory denunciations in the press proclaiming that "more promising members [of the Formalist school] will have to undergo a thorough reeducation in the tough elementary school of marxism . . . they will have to go to an ideological canossa . . . we ought to send [them] to forced labor under good surveillance."[7] The more judicious of these critics at best recognized that by the late 1920s, Formalism had evolved toward a more politically aware sociological criticism.[8] Shklovsky, however, was seen as a retrograde exception and was accused of sticking to his own version of "canned Formalism."[9] As the cornerstone of his literary theory, estrangement bore the brunt of this accusation. However, it is not clear whether it is estrangement that is ahistorical or the critics' account of it. Noting that Shklovsky's prolific work has been a set of variations on the theme of estrangement, most studies nevertheless neglect the differences among these variations or their development over time; instead, they narrowly focus on "Art as Device," ("Iskusstvo kak priem"), an article published by Shklovsky in 1917, at the age of twenty. In this chapter, I will argue that in the decade following "Art as Device," Shklovsky's estrangement underwent profound transformations that were intricately bound up with the major political events of his time—the Revolution, the civil war, the ascendancy of the secret police, and the first major Soviet show trial, the 1922 trial of the Socialist Revolutionaries.

A number of critics have previously challenged the common charge against estrangement as a device of art for art's sake. Thus, Viktor Erlich argued that "as opposed to a pure art for art's sake doctrine, Shklovsky came to define poetry not in terms of what it is but in terms of what it is for. [Shklovsky showed a] rather unexpected preoccupation with the uses of poetry and therapeutic value of creative deformation" on our routine-dulled perception of the world.[10] Jurij Striedter further expanded our understanding of estrangement by arguing that the first aspect of estrangement, "unmistakable in the passages from Tolstoy discussed by Shklovsky" was "ethical—and directed toward cognition of the world."[11] Estrangement "corrects the reader's relationship to the world around him" by "impeding the kind of perception automatized by linguistic and social conventions, forcing the reader to see things anew."[12] Svetlana Boym's study "Estrangement as a Lifestyle: Shklovsky and Brodsky" further challenged the notion of estrangement as an apolitical artistic device through an analysis of estrangement "as a way of life" singularly fitted to the experience of exile and political dissent.[13] And Galin Tikhanov convincingly showed the impact of World War I on Shklovsky's early understanding of estrangement.[14]

What has remained so far in the shadows is the dark side of estrangement, its entanglements with revolutionary and police state politics. This chapter throws light on this Mr. Hyde of estrangement, while also addressing its encounters with artistic estrangement. I trace the conflicted relationship between the politics and aesthetics of these different kinds of estrangements and their development through Shklovsky's oeuvre and beyond, in the work of Nicolae Steinhardt, and also in police interrogation and reeducation practices. If artistic estrangement was first theorized in a scholarly article, its significant reworkings took place mostly in autobiographical writings. This chapter addresses this choice of memoir as well as the explicit evocations of first-person narratives standardly found in secret police files, such as confessions, trial and interrogation depositions, autobiographies, and letters to the government.

## Two Masters of Estrangement:
## Lev Tolstoy and Ivan the Terrible

Shklovsky coined the term *ostranenie* (estrangement) in his 1917 "Art as Device," a short essay that thus became the birth certificate of artistic estrangement. There he argued that our perception of the world was so dulled by routine that we do not fully see objects around us but merely recognize them. "If we examine the general laws of perception, we see that as it becomes habitual, it also becomes automatic. If someone compared the sensation of holding a pen or speaking a foreign language for the first time, with the sensation of performing this same operation for the ten thousandth time, he would agree with us."[15] In the striking language that characterized him, Shklovsky went on to denounce this stultifying effect of automatization on our perception of things and people: "Automatization devours works, clothes, furniture, one's wife, and the fear of war. . . . And so life is reckoned as nothing."[16] Artistic estrangement was his antidote for this automatization. As stated earlier, Shklovsky believed that the role of the writer was to jolt readers out of their routine-dulled lives by making the familiar appear strange, offering different angles on life and thus restoring fresh perception. As Benjamin Sher concisely put it, "*ostranenie* is a process or act that endows an object or image with 'strangeness'" by "removing it from the network of conventional, formulaic, and stereotypical perceptions and linguistic expressions."[17] According to Shklovsky, artists use a variety of techniques to estrange their material. His favorite examples of such techniques are: calling attention to language and "complicating form," thus making "perception long and 'laborious'" instead of automatic[18]; presenting familiar material from the point of view of an outsider, such as an animal, a child, or a foreigner; and foregoing the conventional names for things, describing them as if seen for the first time. These estrangement techniques present objects in a new light and "intensify the sensation of things."[19] As a result, "the stone feels stony," one's wife more lovable, and war more terrifying.[20]

Shklovsky's discussion of estrangement in "Art as Device" relies heavily on examples, mostly taken from the works of Lev Tolstoy. But while estrangement is an artistic device, its objects appear to be invariably political. Thus a horse's point of view estranges "the institution of private property."[21] Shklovsky also dwells on Tolstoy's estrangement of flogging, a then common form of torture that Tolstoy "made strange" by placing it in comparison with unusual torture techniques. Shklovsky chose the following quote from Tolstoy: "Just why this stupid, savage manner of inflicting pain and no other: such as pricking the shoulder or some other such part of the body with needles, squeezing someone's hands or feet in a vise, etc."[22] Besides torture, estrangement in Tolstoy, as Shklovsky's examples demonstrate, similarly debunked conventional views on marriage, church rituals, bourgeois art, and war—all hot topics of political controversy in 1917. Indeed, the examples were so weighted toward political criticism that Shklovsky felt obliged to "apologize for the harshness of [his] examples" and to warn writers not to defamiliarize only those things they "sneered at."[23] However, despite this brief theoretical disclaimer, he went on amassing jarring, violent examples of an estrangement that he believed Tolstoy devised in order to "get to the conscience."[24] His only other prose examples of estrangement came from graphic erotic riddles. Cited at the very end of the article, they read like a last gesture of épater les bourgeois after pricking their consciences.

In "The Structure of Fiction" (1920), published three years after "Art as Device," Shklovsky's explanation of artistic estrangement is brought even closer to the realm of politics: "In order to transform an object into a fact of art, it is necessary first to withdraw it from the domain of life. To do this, we must first and foremost 'shake up the object,' as Ivan the Terrible 'sorted out' his men. . . . An artist always incited insurrections among things. Things are always in a state of revolt with poets."[25] Shklovsky chose the vocabulary of political turmoil—insurrections, revolt, and tyranny—in order to explain artistic estrangement. He matter-of-factly enlisted the defamiliarizing effect of political violence to clarify a more obscure phenomenon, artistic estrangement. Aspiring estrangement artists were given the model of Ivan the Terrible in addition to that of Tolstoy.

## Revolutionary Estrangement and the Explosion of the Self

To understand Shklovsky's shift toward a more politicized description of estrangement, it is instructive to consider his *Sentimental Journey* (*Sentimental'noe puteshestvie*, 1923), a book of memoirs that covers the period from 1917—the year of both "Art as Device" and the October Revolution—to 1922. The 1917 article left us with the image of an iconoclastic youth, who used estrangement as his versatile weapon against stale literary criticism, bourgeois politics, and routine. Six years later, we find a radically different author and a radically different estrangement. Since in the wake of the Revolution "there was no regular life of any kind" (*byta nikakogo*), the writer was no longer needed to estrange routine.[26] The theorist of artistic estrangement was reduced to confessing, "I can't put together all the strange things (*vse to strannoe*) I have seen in Russia."[27] The helpless exclamation "it is strange" (*stranno*) punctuates the narrative. This "strangeness" has the same effect as artistic estrangement: it heightens perception. Shklovsky approvingly quotes from Boris Eikhenbaum, "The difference between revolutionary life and ordinary life is that now everything is felt."[28] The corollary is that "life became art" (*zhizn' stala iskusstvom*).[29] The Revolution has turned life into art in the same way that the artist hitherto used to turn her material into art—by making it strange and thus capable of intensifying sensation. This strangeness comes to define revolutionary Russia for Shklovsky, who concludes his contemporary collection of articles, *The Move of the Knight* (*Khod konia*, 1923), thus: "What a strange country [*strannaia strana*]. . . . The country of electrification and Robinson Crusoes."[30]

The narrator of *Sentimental Journey* is reduced to registering the effects of this revolutionary brand of estrangement on the ravaged landscape and on people. The prose is often limited to laconic narration:

> After the explosion, our soldiers, surrounded by enemies, were waiting for a train to come for them; while waiting, they busied themselves by picking up and putting together the shattered pieces of their comrades' bodies.
>
> They picked up pieces for a long time.
>
> Naturally, some of the pieces got mixed up.
>
> One officer went up to the long row of corpses.
>
> The last body had been put together out of the leftover pieces.
>
> It had the torso of a large man. Someone had added a small head; on the chest were small arms of different sizes, both left.
>
> The officer looked for a rather long time; then he sat on the ground and burst out laughing . . . laughing . . . laughing . . .
>
> In Tiflis—I am returning to my trip—a crime was committed.[31]

In this scene, the terms of Shklovsky's 1920 description of estrangement are sinisterly literalized. "The object"—the human body—is shaken up to the point where it is permanently "withdrawn from the domain of life." The human body parts are thrown into a strikingly new configuration. While pathetically trying to restore the old order of things, the soldiers only top the horror by assembling an incongruous human collage. The officer's laughter at the horror of the dismembered body is proof that the ultimate end of artistic estrangement, the alteration of habitual perception, has also been outdone.

While registering the effects of revolutionary estrangement on other people, Shklovsky himself was hardly spared its effect. He too became literally pulverized, twisted, and disjointed by an explosion described at length.[32] His body not only looked unrecognizably strange; it was literally shot through with foreign bodies—little shrapnel fragments that jutted out through his underwear for months after. *Sentimental Journey* is a blowup of this explosion scene. Throughout this text, Shklovsky uses explosions as his metaphor for the Revolution: "I didn't see the October Revolution [in Petersburg]; I didn't see the explosion [*vzryva*], if there was an explosion."[33] A couple of pages later, he rebukes his own doubts and reiterates the explosion metaphor: "If you don't believe that there was a revolution, go put your hand in [Russia's] wound. It's wide. The hole was pierced by a three-inch shell."[34] As a book of memoirs, *Sentimental Journey* registers the effects of the big explosion—the Revolution and the civil war—not only on landscape and on people but first and foremost on the self.

Finished during Shklovsky's 1922–23 exile in Berlin, the memoirs follow his hectic trajectory through various countries ravaged by war and revolution. The impetus for the last portion of Shklovsky's "sentimental journey" was provided by the Bolshevik secret police, the Cheka, as Shklovsky fled Saint Petersburg fearing that he would be arrested together with other prominent Socialist Revolutionaries. As a Socialist Revolutionary (SR), Shklovsky had joined an underground organization plotting to restore the Constituent Assembly, recently dispersed by the Bolsheviks.[35] In *Sentimental Journey* Shklovsky repeatedly reminds us of his dramatic involvement with politics. Thus he proudly recounts the shock of a rival Marxist critic at seeing him in the midst of a civil war street fight. *Sentimental Journey* revels in reproducing that shock, while directing it at its readers. A far cry from the hackneyed portrait of the apolitical Formalist critic, we discover Shklovsky the armored car commander, then a wanted fugitive. We follow him as he was constantly hounded by the Cheka, narrowly escaping arrests by jumping off trains, and hiding his identity under various fake passports. The disintegration of the self, experienced firsthand in the explosion, is developed into the leitmotif of the memoir: "Life flows in staccato pieces belonging to different systems. Only our clothing, not the body, joins together the disparate moments of life."[36] In the course of his travels, Shklovsky lost even that last shell of identity, his clothes. They got stolen, or he shed them for more or less successful disguises.

## Self-Estrangement and Self-Effacement

In his quest for survival, Shklovsky engaged in various experiments in self-presentation: he put on masks and forever devised camouflages. Sometimes, these experiments went awry. Although trying to make himself inconspicuous, he once ended up with violet dyed hair and an outfit that "begged for arrest": "I was absurdly dressed. In a poncho, a sailor's shirt and a Red Army soldier's hat."[37] When he finally did get arrested, it was his literary talent that saved him: "They let me out. I am a professional raconteur."[38] This concoction of fake identities is a half artistic, half criminal endeavor. It appropriates the lesson of revolutionary estrangement—the self's fragmentation, strangeness, and plasticity—and turns it to one's own advantage. Shklovsky assumed the revolutionary estrangement of the self and moved beyond it toward a voluntary, controlled, and creative self-estrangement. In concocting this new kind of self-estrangement, Shklovsky used his literary talents for political purposes.

This hybrid self-estrangement secured his survival and offered mischievous pleasures. However, Shklovsky openly abandoned it in *Sentimental Journey*:

According to my [fake] passport, I was a technician. [The Cheka] questioned me about my specialty. . . . I held my own very convincingly. It's pleasant to lose oneself. To forget your name, slip out of your old habits. To think up some other man and consider yourself him. If it had not been for my writing desk, for my work, I would have never become Viktor Shklovsky again. I was writing a book, *Plot as a Manifestation of Style*.[39]

The imposed self-fashioning of a runaway is often restricted to camouflage, and its closeness to self-effacement haunts the memoirs. Soon after he was released from the Cheka interrogation, Shklovsky inspected his fake passport only to be spooked by the discovery that the technician had been dead for some time. He ended the story with a firm return to his literary persona, which he presented here as the last haven of his endangered identity. However, this is hardly a happy ending to Shklovsky's experience of revolutionary estrangement. For despite this determination to become once again the critic Viktor Shklovsky, there could hardly be a more dramatic difference between the iconoclastic critic of "Art as Device" and the narrator of *Sentimental Journey*. The former, the theorist and practitioner of estrangement, self-confidently put the whole world under iconoclastic question marks. The latter relinquished his right to comment upon the world in favor of self-presentation. He set the tone of his memoirs by declaring, "I don't want to be a critic of events: I only want to leave material for the critics . . . I am making of myself a case study for posterity [*prigotovliaiu iz sebia dlia potomstva preparat*]."[40] Rather than teaching us "How Don Quixote Is Made," *Sentimental Journey* confesses how Viktor Shklovsky is made.[41]

The first admission is that Viktor Shklovsky is not self-made:

The forces moving me were external to me.
The forces moving others were external to them.
I am only a falling stone.
A stone that falls and can, at the same time, light a lantern to observe its own course.[42]

. . . . . . . . . . . . . . . . . . . . . . . . . . . . . . . . . . . . . . . . . . . . . . . . . . . . . . . . . . . . . . . . . . . . . . . . . . . . . . . . . . . . . . . . . . . . . . . . . . . . . . . . . .

I've gone off a tangent, but everything that organizes the individual is external to him. He is only the point where lines of force intersect.[43]

In "Art as Device" "the stone made stony" was Shklovsky's memorable example of an estranged object. Here it is Shklovsky himself who has been turned into a stone; in other words, the theoretician of estrangement has become an object of estrangement. While this self/stone does not have even the freedom of a free fall, writing seems to preserve a last margin of freedom, that of recording a fall that the self cannot stop or of going off on a tangent. How-

ever, the image of the stone that can light a lantern and record its own fall is
painfully improbable. This strain is visible in another image of the effects of
the Revolution on Saint Petersburg's inhabitants, which fits well the author of
*Sentimental Journey*: "a man whose insides [*vnutrennost'*] have been torn out by
an explosion, but he keeps on talking."[44] As these images suggest, Shklovsky's
autobiographical persona is singularly disconcerting in *Sentimental Journey*. This
is not, as Marxist critics have commonly accused the Formalists, because he
is hiding behind his devices and carefully constructed persona.[45] Even as he
reveled in the ingenuity of his disguises, Shklovsky was de facto divulging the
well-kept secrets of his fake personas. In *Sentimental Journey* he took his masks
off, one by one, abandoned his fake passports, and signed his own name. As
much as a travelogue or a collection of impressions and bons mots, Shklovsky's
memoirs recall a trial deposition.

## Deposition and Autobiography: An Estranging Encounter

In his introduction to *Sentimental Journey*, Sidney Monas briefly suggested
that "there is, in Shklovsky's statement about the war, something that suggests
he is preparing a case before an imagined revolutionary tribunal, exculpating
himself from the charges of chauvinism."[46] Monas did not pursue the idea,
deeming "the other 'case' he [Shklovsky] also prepares, the case study for
posterity," "more interesting."[47] I disagree. While the address to posterity is a
commonplace of memoirs across time, the address to the Bolshevik tribunal
distinguishes Shklovsky's brand of autobiographical writing. Shklovsky himself repeatedly proposed the trial as a motivation for writing the book: "And
all this [writing] because I cannot forget about the trial, the trial that begins in
Moscow tomorrow. . . . And at this moment, with my life in fragments, I stand
before the ordered consciousness of the communists."[48] Shklovsky refers here
to the infamous trial of the SRs that took place in the summer of 1922, at the
time when he was writing *Sentimental Journey* in Berlin. The ten men and two
women who stood trial received death sentences, which were then commuted
to life imprisonment under the pressure of the international socialist movement.[49] Shklovsky understandably treats their trial as his own; the pamphlet
that denounced the SRs implicated Shklovsky, and this prompted him to flee
abroad, barely escaping the tribunal's draconian judgment.[50]

In the historical context of Shklovsky's writings, a trial deposition is not
a surprising model for autobiographical writing. Indeed, a Soviet observer
of the Shakhty affair, another famous trial of the 1920s closely modeled on
the SR trial, noted the prevalence of autobiography in the depositions: "The

following routine has been worked out. Each of the accused . . . starts his
testimony with an autobiographical sketch."[51] As I showed in the first chapter,
Soviet interrogations and trial depositions were set apart by the adoption of
an (auto)biographical model. As a result, autobiography became the standard
starting point of any secret police interrogation, like the ones that Shklovsky
described being subjected to[52]:

> Sometimes I was summoned to the local Cheka, which checked all newcomers prac-
> tically every day. They would question me item by item: who are you, what did you
> do before the war, during the war, between February and October, and so on.[53]

The use of autobiography as defense in a trial is not new. Indeed, it goes back
to Rousseau's self-conscious inauguration of the genre on the first page of *Les
confessions*: "Let the trumpet of the Last Judgment sound when it pleases; I will
come, this book in hand, and present myself in front of the sovereign judge."[54]
If Rousseau wrote his autobiography for God's last judgment, many Soviet
citizens wrote their autobiographies for the investigator's judgment. Giving
an account of oneself in these peculiar conditions and for this peculiar audience certainly molded that account. In regard to the "problem of confession
for cases being investigated for trial . . . the role of the other in formulating
discourse" is, as Mikhail Bakhtin tersely noticed in the 1930s, constitutive of
the resulting texts.[55] This jarring intrusion of the deposition into autobiography recalls the little shrapnel fragments that jut out of Shklovsky's underwear,
continuously reminding him of his own, literal estrangement. Louis Althusser's
model of interpellation seems particularly apt in describing these forced autobiographies.[56] These texts were certainly not as much expressing a subject
that was always already there as they were interpellating one into existence.[57]
However, while interrogated suspects were not free to express who they were
but rather were shaped by the interpellation, they certainly had some flexibility
in manipulating their image. Shklovsky's fake autobiographies, composed in
answer to the investigator's questions, offer a concrete example.

Shklovsky used his art to concoct his actual depositions, and used the model
of the deposition when he wrote his memoirs. This mixture of genres is certainly troubling and raises questions about any clear-cut separation between
aesthetics and politics, as well as between subversion and surrender. It is a testimony to the power and fascination that the new Soviet genres exerted over
Shklovsky that even after he had been freed from interrogation, he chose the
deposition as a model for his memoirs. At the same time, practicing this genre
outside of its confining context allowed the writer to take certain freedoms—
irony, paradox, and double entendre—that undermine this genre from within.
Also, as Julie Cassiday reminds us, trial depositions in the 1920s differed from
the fully scripted self-denigrating confessions made infamous by the 1930s

Stalinist show trials.[58] Significantly, the defendants in the 1922 SR trial did not confess to their alleged crimes; instead, they "used the trial as a platform for condemning Soviet excesses and preaching their own brand of socialism."[59] Therefore, Shklovsky's appropriation of the genre of trial deposition is far from a univocal gesture of surrender.

This estranging presence of official Soviet genres in the intimate genre of autobiography is first visible in *Sentimental Journey* but is not limited to it. Written in quick succession, both of Shklovsky's next two autobiographical texts, *Zoo, or Letters Not About Love* (*Zoo, ili pis'ma ne o liubvi*, 1923) and *Third Factory* (*Tret'ia fabrika*, 1926), are defined by similarly incongruous mixtures between the private and the public, the literary and the political. At first sight, *Zoo* appears to have rid itself of the sinister shadow of the state-appointed reader. It starts as a collage of intimate letters to and from Elsa Triolet, an émigré with whom the narrator was in love during his exile in Berlin. The text's surprise comes at the very end: the narrator abruptly shifts from addressing his lover to addressing the All Russian Central Executive Committee, begging for permission to return to Russia.[60] Shklovsky's epistolary style does not change significantly: it remains wry, outspoken, and intimate, as he pours his heart out to his new readers, confessing the pain of exile and the secrets of his love affair. His strangely intimate letters to the government deny both the basic distance from oneself that is common in an official self-presentation, and the common distance from the establishment itself. As such, they take the paradoxical form of raw confessions running over the blanks of a government form.

If *Zoo* starts as a collection of love letters and ends as a letter to the establishment, *Third Factory* starts as a capitulation to the Soviet establishment but ends up as an unwelcome subversion.

> After *Zoo*, I wrote *Third Factory*, a book completely incomprehensible to me. In that book I wanted to capitulate to the time—not only capitulate, but take my troops to the other side. I wanted to come to terms with the present. As it turned out, however, I had no say in the matter. But the material on the village and the material on my own disordered state in life, included in the book, got out of hand and acquired a shape contrary to my original plan, so the book was resented. On the whole, however, books are not written to please; in fact, sometimes books are not written: they emerge, they happen. I write this not to vindicate myself but to present a fact.[61]

Here, Shklovsky attributes the main contradiction between his autobiography's intent and its final result to the opposing pulls of two external forces— "the times" and the literary process by which books emerge. Richard Sheldon has identified contradiction as the subversive hallmark of Shklovsky's style.[62]

If we follow Shklovsky's own account, however, his contradictions are less willful subversions than traces of contradictory external forces that the self registers. This determinism could itself be taken for a declaration of surrender. But again, a closer look at the historical context denies such easy verdicts. Igal Halfin showed that the battle between the determinist and the voluntarist view defined the Soviet discourse on the self in the 1920s and early 1930s.[63] In the early 1920s, the behaviorist-deterministic view held that "[m]an might have known the forces operating within him, but he could do little by way of controlling them."[64] This view, so close in its formulation to Shklovsky's description of the self as a "point where lines of force intersect," was replaced in the late 1920s by a voluntarist doctrine whereby "man was being called out to become his own master, a subject of history and not its object."[65] The early 1930s took this belief in the plasticity of human nature to an extreme, as "Soviet men and women were expected to reforge themselves."[66] As the establishment forcefully moved toward a voluntarist view of the self, declaring determinism to be an attack on the idea of revolution and its new man, Shklovsky's view became all the more deterministic. In *Sentimental Journey,* he expressed his distrust of the Bolshevik reforging of the new man:

> The Bolsheviks believe in miracles.
>
> They even perform miracles, but miracles are performed poorly.
>
> You remember the folk tale about the devil who could make an old man young again? First he consumes the man in fire; then he restores him to life rejuvenated. Then the devil's apprentice tries to perform the miracle. He's able to consume the man in fire, but he can't rejuvenate him.[67]

Shklovsky's criticism of the holy of holies of Soviet utopia—the reeducation or reforging of the new man (*perekovka*)—added insult to injury by describing the communist project in the language of religious parable. However, the view of the self that challenged Soviet orthodoxy also questions the possibility of agency and thus of subversion.

*Third Factory* took this deterministic view to an extreme as Shklovsky started speaking in the "voice of a half-processed commodity" (*golos polufabrikata*).[68] He divided his life into three periods, united through the leitmotif of the factories that had processed him: "The first factory was my family and school. The second was *Opoiaz* [the Formalist research group to which Shklovsky belonged]. And the third [the film factory where he was currently working] is processing [*obrabatyvaet*] me at the very moment."[69] In Shklovsky's self-portrait as a commodity, the terms of Marxist alienation have been self-consciously revisited. If Marxism deplores the alienation of the worker from the commodified object of his or her labor, Shklovsky shows that in the Soviet Union this gap is bridged by turning the individual into an alienated commodity. At the end of his critique of "The Fetishism of Commodities," Marx imagined the commodities obnoxiously boasting about their "natural" exchange value.[70] Shklovsky's commodity, or Shklovsky as commodity, speaks of his own alienation, of just how unnatural he feels. This distressing image of the self as a commodity is the culmination of a long process of estrangement of the self. While revolutionary estrangement dramatically exploded the self, this everyday estrangement "deformed the material" in quieter if relentless fashion.

Shklovsky's theoretical and autobiographical work throws some rare light on these other "kinds of estrangement." He rarely offers solutions, however, except briefly in the *Sentimental Journey* account of his interrogations. His response there is self-estrangement—the half-criminal, half-artistic concoction of fake identities and biographies that secured his survival. Although openly abandoned when the fugitive decides to become again the critic Viktor Shklovsky, this self-estrangement later developed into a powerful art of survival in the work of Nicolae Steinhardt and Joseph Brodsky.

## "*This* is surrealism": Estrangement in the Interrogation Room

For a Romanian, Nicolae Steinhardt's name is associated with a legendary generation of intellectuals who shaped the Romanian cultural scene between the two world wars, intellectuals such as Emil Cioran, Dinu Pillat, Eugen Ionescu, Mircea Eliade, Constantin Noica, and Petre Țuțea. This loose group is credited with an unprecedented effervescence of intellectual life and discredited for extremist right-wing leanings. Some of them chose to emigrate—they are the ones whose names are easily recognizable abroad; others stayed behind, writing for the drawer or for a close group of friends. In 1960, over twenty of those who stayed were put on trial and condemned to prison terms that ranged from six to twenty-five years, partly for reading and disseminating the books of their émigré friends.[71] One of the defendants in this intellectual show trial, Steinhardt was condemned largely for refusing to testify against his friends.

Steinhardt's prison experience became the subject of his main work, *Happiness Journal (Jurnalul fericirii)*, an extraordinary memoir written in experimental prose. The book was a cause célèbre decades before it was published. Steinhardt's voluminous secret police file tells this story in characteristic detail.[72] In 1972, as Steinhardt was composing his manuscript, the secret police placed him under continuous surveillance. Having bugged his apartment, they noted every gesture, from breakfast to dinner; but for long periods of time, the transcriber was reduced to noting, "the scratch of a pen on paper." Soon intrigued by this writing, a couple of agents broke into Steinhardt's apartment, took a look at the *Happiness Journal* manuscript, and photographed it for the reading pleasure of their superiors. Having convinced themselves of its subversive intent, the police fabricated an anonymous denunciation accusing Steinhardt of homosexuality and of possession of foreign currency and used it as a justification for a search of his apartment.[73] During the search, conducted on December 14, 1972, they found the manuscript, "as if by chance" and confiscated it.[74] After pressure from the Writers' Union, the manuscript was returned in 1975, only to be confiscated again in 1984. In the late 1980s, Radio Free Europe broadcast fragments of *Happiness Journal*, to which people listened despite the government's interdiction and despite the static, which always seemed to grow thicker when one most wanted to hear. Steinhardt died soon thereafter, in March 1989, a few months before the revolution that made the publication of his book finally possible. In 1991, just as I was starting to forget the feeling of waiting in line for hours in the hope of getting some elusive food item, such as bread, milk, or bananas, I gleefully positioned myself in a line winding around my hometown's main bookstore. It was the first time that I saw people queuing in a festive mood: *Happiness Journal* was on sale.

Steinhardt's book starts with a seemingly banal conversation between unnamed speakers. It will soon turn out that this conversation is Steinhardt's interrogation, and that one of the speakers is a close friend turned collaborator of the secret police. But the first page keeps all this information from the reader: the interrogation room and the arrest are not named, so that we are abruptly ushered into a disorienting text. Our confusion is in fact carefully staged to mirror that of the narrator, who finds himself in an "unreal and subtle décor, carefully concocted":

> I am looking at her [the friend turned collaborator]—it is she, but as if in a dream, she does unexpected things, she speaks *otherly* [*altfel*]; and synchronous with her, the world is also *other* [*alta*], it is surrealist. See, *this* is surrealism: objects, the same objects, have an other order, an other finality. *So this is also possible.* Now, yes, the teapot is also a woman, the stove is an elephant . . . Max Ernst, Dali, Duchamp. . . . But also Munch's *Scream*, I want to scream, to wake up from the nightmare, to come back to our old earth, good and gentle, where, obedient, things are what we know they are and answer the meanings that we always gave them. . . . I would like to get out of this unsettling town by Delvaux, from this Tanguy field, with severed members, soft and rejoined according to bizarre affinities, through *different* couplings than those we are accustomed to. *Home,* on earth. . . . This cannot be the earth. This is not she. (original emphasis)[75]

Steinhardt's striking exclamation regarding the interrogation room—"*this* is surrealism"—might come as a surprise to readers of John Bender's classic account of the origins of modern confinement, *Imagining the Penitentiary*. Bender's thorough assessment of the emergence of this modern institution in the eighteenth century could be summarized thus: this is realism. Indeed, Bender shows how the modern European prison was built on the premises of the realist novel, and in particular on the realist belief in the changing nature of human character. Thus the realist interest in the influence of the environment on the development of the individual was translated into the modern prison's emphasis on psychology and the reformation of the prisoner in the carefully designed environment of the prison. Bender believes that like the realist novel, which tried to hide its fictional devices and pass for unmediated reality, the emerging modern prison tried to gain legitimacy by passing itself off as the natural order of things.[76] Bender endeavors to oppose this naturalizing and essentializing claim of the modern penitentiary by historicizing its creation and revealing its roots in literary realism. And indeed, it takes all the insight of Bender's analysis to bare these fictional roots: he repeatedly undermines deeply entrenched commonplaces and painstakingly builds an intricate argument. In contrast, Steinhardt's exclamation *"this* is surrealism" was instantaneous, as his penitentiary's fictional devices were histrionically flaunted. The difference could not be starker: while the realist aesthetic of the early modern penitentiary aimed to naturalize, the surrealist aesthetic of Steinhardt's post–World War II interrogation room aimed to estrange.

Indeed, Steinhardt's conflation of the interrogation room with surrealism (*"this* is surrealism"*) recalls Shklovsky's observation that during the Revolution "life became art." An erudite literary critic, Steinhardt chooses a particular kind of art to stand for the interrogation room: surrealism. For Steinhardt, surrealism is defined first of all by its difference from the familiar, everyday world, an opposition that he insistently emphasizes through both repetition and italics. This interrogation room surrealism is further based on a divorce between "things" and the "meanings we always gave them." Roman Jakobson argued that "to point out that the sign is not identical with the referent" is the very basis of estrangement since otherwise "the object becomes automatized and the perception of reality withers away."[77] According to Viktor Erlich, even though the French surrealists were unaware of Shklovsky's work, and he was unaware of theirs, their particular understanding of artistic estrangement was "strikingly similar" to Shklovsky's, to the point of a "virtual identity of formulation."[78] And indeed, what qualifies the interrogation room as surreal for Steinhardt is precisely its ability to present the world in a radically different light and alter normal perception, or in Shklovsky's ideolect, to estrange. Steinhardt's description of the interrogation room indirectly meets Shklovsky's estrangement through the French surrealist connection.

Like Shklovsky, Steinhardt soon realizes that there are also crucial differences between artistic—in this case surrealist—estrangement and secret police estrangement. The reader's temporary excursion through literature estranges by offering different angles on the world, so that on returning, one finds the stone stonier, and one's wife more lovable. Secret police estrangement offers a one-way ride to a radically different world, with no return ticket. No matter how much he wants to get out of the surrealist decor of the interrogation room, Steinhardt has no way out: the world of everyday reality has become as inaccessible to him as an escapist fiction. Steinhardt soon realizes that he resembles less a reader of surrealist literature, who can enter and exit his surrealist text at will by simply opening and closing a book, than a character in a fiction experimenting with the death of its characters:

> now everything is the same to me, everything is gray and the same. I step into the world of the nouveau roman and of a literature without characters . . . where the SELF disappears confused in an undifferentiated crowd. Personality (what's that?) is fragmented, passed through the sieve to the last smidgen. No matter what I do, I'm lost. You're lost, you're lost. (original emphasis)[79]

That initial reading of the interrogation room, as surrealism, revolved around one key word, italicized by Steinhardt—"*other*." In his revised reading, the key term is "same" or "undifferentiated." This complete reversal gets to the very core of the distinction between artistic and interrogation room estrangement. Both divorce things from the meanings we usually give them and insert them in "an other order." But unlike a surrealist text, "the other order" of the interrogation room is soon revealed to forcefully bar its captive's access to any other order of things. It thus annuls the very possibility of difference, which crumbles into oppressive, undifferentiated sameness. The teapot is not like a woman; "the teapot is a woman." The face of his friend is not like the face of a collaborator; it is the face of a collaborator.

It is not just familiar objects like a teapot or the stove that, severed from their usual associations with the home, "have an other finality" in the interrogation room.[80] It it first and foremost the self that has been violently severed from the world as he knows it and inserted in "this other order," where the central elements of his identity, "jew, intellectual, cityman," take on a whole new meaning—enemy.[81] The defining twist of interrogation room estrangement is that its object par excellence is the self. As we have seen, this was also true of the revolutionary estrangement described by Shklovsky in *Sentimental Journey*; there the culmination of that revolutionary estrangement was his, and the other soldiers', explosions, and then the incongruous collage of body parts on an anonymous battlefield. Steinhardt's description of the "Tanguy field, with severed members, soft and rejoined according to bizarre affinities, through different couplings than those we are accustomed to" expresses this radical estrangement of the human body in uncannily similar terms.

There are also significant differences. In Shklovsky's description, estrangement is a side effect of revolutionary or civil war violence. Steinhardt's estrangement is carefully orchestrated by his interrogators. This is no accidental explosion but rather a prolonged process of breaking the suspect that combines a carefully designed regimen of physical torture and psychological abuse. Steinhardt believes that the estranging surrealist decor is deliberately designed by his interrogators: "Oh, you [the interrogators] wish that I would let myself be wrapped up in the magic of semi-dreaming, in the dizzying smoke of a surrealist scenography."[82] For Steinhardt, the investigators' performance is certainly no art for art's sake; instead, it has a clear purpose: "everything in this unreal and subtle décor, carefully concocted, pushes me to take refuge in confusion and get lost/lose myself [să mă pierd] in the haze."[83] The common meanings of the Romanian mă pierd are "I am getting lost" as well as "I am losing my cool"; its literal meaning, however, is "I lose myself." Steinhardt plays on this ambiguity to show how the carefully manipulated feeling of spatial disorientation leads to psychological confusion and finally to the confession that amounts to self-destruction: "I am getting lost in the smoke of confusion, I stray in forgetting, I let myself pray to the sweet delirium of evanescence, and then I confess, I confess. . . . No matter what I do, I'm lost."[84]

Steinhardt's reading of the interrogation room as an artfully estranged surrealist decor designed to sever his ties to the outside world, produce confusion, and finally elicit confession is hardly a literary critic's far-fetched interpretation of his prison experience; nor is its validity limited to Eastern Europe. The *Kubark Counterintelligence Interrogation* was written in 1963 and functioned as the leading CIA manual on interrogation until 1983, when it was revised and retitled *Human Resource Exploitation Training Manual*.[85] The *Kubark* offers investigators a catalog of interrogation principles and techniques; it also proposes a general course of action that can then be adapted to the particular profile of each suspect. According to the *Kubark*, the first goal of interrogation is to cut the suspect's ties to the outside world. While arrest and incarceration forcefully sever the suspect from his own environment, the *Kubark* suggests additional techniques to enhance the feeling of isolation; thus, on arrest, the clothes of the suspect should be immediately taken away and replaced with new, preferably ill-fitting garb. "The point [of this] is that man's sense of identity depends upon a continuity in surroundings, habits, appearance, actions, relations with others, etc. Detention permits the interrogator to cut through these links and throw the interrogatee back upon his own unaided internal resources."[86] The *Kubark* recommends that this feeling of isolation be cultivated throughout the interrogation: "there should not be a telephone in the [interrogation] room . . . it is a visible link to the outside; its presence makes a subject feel less cut off, better able to resist."[87] The *Kubark* notes that the feeling of isolation can be exacerbated through carefully designed solitary confinement and "deprivation of sensory stimuli" to lead progressively to anxiety, unbearable stress, confusion, "delusions, hallucinations, and other pathological effects."[88]

These techniques are designed "to enhance within the subject his feelings of being cut off from the known and the reasssuring, and of being *plunged into the strange.*" (my emphasis)[89] The *Kubark* insists that the interrogator should not just "make the subject's world [the interrogation environment] unlike the world to which he has been accustomed but also *strange in itself*" (my emphasis).[90] It goes on to warn that "little is gained by replacing one routine [the free man's] with another [the prisoner's]."[91] What should define the new world of the interrogation are "constant disruptions of patterns," a constant undermining of all "familiarity" and "routine."[92] The description of a key technique designed "to plunge the subject into the strange" merits full quotation:

> The aim of the Alice in Wonderland or confusion technique is to confound the expectations and conditioned reactions of the interrogatee. He is accustomed to a world that makes some sense, at least to him: a world of continuity and logic, a predictable world. He clings to this world to reinforce his identity and powers of resistance.
>
> The confusion technique is designed not only to *obliterate the familiar* but to replace it with *the weird.* . . . Pitch, tone, and volume of the interrogators' voices are unrelated to the import of the questions. . . . In this *strange atmosphere* the subject finds that the pattern of speech and thought which he had learned to consider *normal* have been replaced by an *eerie* meaninglessness. (my emphasis)[93]

Subjected to this technique, the suspect may well feel, like Steinhardt, that she was plunged into the midst of a strange text. The name "Alice in Wonderland" shows that this is a carefully staged impression; it also provides specificity and added accuracy concerning the position of the interrogatee. Alice's fall into the underworld lands her at the center of an absurd interrogation and trial. Unlike a reader of surrealist literature, Alice has little control over her sojourn in Wonderland: she cannot enter or exit at will. "Alice in Wonderland" was only one of the interrogation techniques aimed at "obliterating the familiar" and creating a "strange atmosphere." The *Kubark* suggests a number of techniques to be used to this end, neatly summarized by its successor manual: persistent manipulation of time, the use of retarding and advancing clocks, serving meals at odd times, disrupting sleep schedules, and disorientation regarding day and night.[94]

As such, estrangement, or the deliberate and crafted replacement of the "familiar" with the "strange," appears as a key interrogation device:

> The effectiveness of most of the non-coercive techniques depends upon their unsettling effect. The interrogation situation is in itself disturbing to most people encountering it for the first time. The aim is to enhance this effect, to disrupt radically the familiar emotional and psychological associations of the subject. When this aim is achieved, resistance is seriously impaired. There is an interval—which may be extremely brief—of suspended animation, a kind of psychological shock or paralysis. It is caused by a traumatic or sub-traumatic experience which explodes, as it were, the world that is familiar to the subject as well as his image of himself within that world. Experienced interrogators recognize this effect when it appears and know that at this moment the source is far more open to suggestion, far likelier to comply than he was just before he experienced the shock.[95]

This explosion is the climactic moment toward which the whole manual has worked. When it finally reaches this moment, its usually composed, didactic language is itself unsettled—subordinate clauses are crammed within dashes, interrupting the usually trim syntax. Unable to find the exact word, the author resorts to approximations ("a kind of psychological shock or paralysis") and figurative language ("explodes, as it were"). Capturing the climactic moment of exploding the subject's familiar world and "image of himself" tests the limits of the *Kubark*'s rhetoric; taking up the challenge, the manual repeatedly revisits this moment, unpacking the process of "breaking the suspect" so dramatically compressed in the explosion metaphor.[96] Thus we learn that "the capacity for resistance is diminished by the disorientation" and confusion caused by severing the links of the suspect with his environment and plunging him into a strange environment.[97] As a result, the subject enters a state of "suggestibility" and even "loss of autonomy," at which point he is likely to comply with the demands made by the interrogator.[98] All of this, the *Kubark* explains, can be achieved through the "non-coercive techniques" summarized earlier. "Non-coercive interrogation is not conducted without pressure. On the contrary, the goal is to generate maximum pressure inside the interrogatee. His resistance is sapped, his urge to yield is fortified, until in the end he defeats himself."[99] Steinhardt's account of his interrogation uncannily traces the key points of this interrogation scenario, leading from physical to psychological disorientation and all the way to defeating oneself. Compressing this trajectory, his obsessive "*mă pierd*" (I am getting lost; I lose my cool; I lose myself) comes as close as words can to capturing the moment when the subject's world and "his image of himself within that world are exploded."

As the *Kubark* notes, its interrogation techniques were often shared by

Soviet interrogators.[100] Contemporary CIA and Department of Defense studies on Soviet investigation techniques similarly detail the same basic steps of the interrogation scenario: breaking the suspect's ties with the outside world and creating disorientation and confusion so as to sap resistance and prompt confession.[101] Victims of Soviet interrogations often give the most vivid picture of the interrogation techniques of the GPU and their effects on the suspect. In his memoir, *My Century: The Odyssey of a Polish Intellectual*, Alexander Wat left us a striking description of the estranging effects of isolation techniques used in the GPU headquarters at the Lubianka in 1940: "The rule here was strict and permanent closure, a cutting off of ties with the outer world, the world of authentic reality and logic, in order to drive the prisoner, by the devastation of his mind and moral degradation, into a universe which was not an imaginary one, as people usually suppose, but fundamentally different, governed by laws unintelligible to the prisoner."[102] In *The Gulag Archipelago*, Alexander Solzhenitsyn describes interrogation methods aimed at inducing "extreme confusion" that closely recall the "Alice in Wonderland or confusion technique."[103] Thus "the psychological contrast" method was based on sudden reversals of the interrogator's tone and was often corroborated with "sound effects," "light effects," and imposed sleeplessness with the intent to "befog the reason, undermine the will" so that the "prisoner ceases to be himself, to be his own 'I.'"[104] To respond to this interrogation room estrangement of the self, Solzhenitsyn advises prisoners to take leave of life as they step into the interrogation room: "At the very threshold, you must say to yourself:

> 'My life is over, a little early to be sure, but there's nothing to be done about it. . . . For me those I love have died, and for them I have died. From today on, *my body* is useless and *alien to me* . . .' Confronted with such a prisoner, the interrogator will tremble. Only the man who has renounced everything can win that victory. But how can one turn one's body to stone? (my emphasis)[105]

The willful self-estrangement that aims to turn the body into stone is a direct response to the realization of the extreme vulnerability of the body. Solzhenitsyn's account of the interrogation is famous for compiling an appallingly comprehensive list of the physical and psychological tortures used during Soviet investigations. Having followed his own trajectory from a violent, traumatic estrangement of the self to defensive self-estrangement, Solzhenitsyn meets Shklovsky at the finish line. Their stories end with the same peculiar metaphor for the estranged self: the body turned to stone.

## Eulogy to the Lie:
## Self-Estrangement and Reeducation

Steinhardt refers to this paragraph from Solzhenitsyn in the preface to *Happiness Journal*, calling it one of the few viable responses to secret police interrogations.[106] However, the account of interrogation that opens the actual text of *Happiness Journal* is defined by a feverish search for his own personal solution. The interrogation revolved around a seemingly innocuous question: whether during a dinner party Steinhardt had broken a glass. At first, Steinhardt cannot answer the question, simply because he does not remember the facts; so the interrogator obligingly offers a solution: admit to breaking it; don't even bother to recall the actual events. The stakes of the question seem low; the pressure to answer it is enormous, and thus it appears tempting to acquiesce. However, as Steinhardt soon realizes, once he gives up the effort to remember and "makes the psychological gesture of relaxing" and giving in to the interrogator, he is well on the road to indiscriminate confession, and then he is "lost."[107]

Through an effort of memory and lucidity, he establishes to himself that in fact he had indeed broken the glass, and considers telling the truth and, he immediately adds, the objective truth: "If I acknowledge that I broke it, I tell the truth, (the *objective* truth) and once I've told the truth, I have to go ahead and acknowledge that Nego has spoken against the regime. (This is the whole goal of this nocturnal meeting)" (original emphasis).[108] The addition of this truth in parenthesis, "the *objective* truth," marks the very moment when telling the objective truth becomes questionable for Steinhardt. For from now on, truth can be categorized; there are different types, kinds, and degrees, and the possibility of telling a truth other than the objective one insinuates itself. For Steinhardt, telling the objective truth was the most basic moral law of the world outside. In the light of the interrogation room, however, this objective truth is redefined as factual truth, which appeared to be not only narrow and simplistic but also ethically compromised. For the interrogators want nothing but this factual truth: Steinhardt's exact memories of the dinner party. The friend turned collaborator is not telling lies but repeating the objective truth "with the precision of computer memory."[109] The problem is that once the interrogator entered the scene, this truth became an object of extrapolation that deeply politicized it and turned it into a proof of guilt. Steinhardt describes a typical exchange between a suspect and the investigator: "'Have you been in Gheorghe Florian's house?' 'Yes.'" But instead of this innocuous answer, the investigator writes down, "'Yes, I admit that I have

been in the conspiratorial house on street . . . , number . . . where I had criminal exchanges with the fascist Gheorghe Florian.'"[110] Similarly, Steinhardt's
objectively true answer—yes, he had broken a glass—would amount in the
investigator's tendentious logic to an incriminating proof against his friend
Nego: the broken glass would be taken as proof that the atmosphere during
the dinner was tense because Nego had spoken against the regime.

    Steinhardt thus refused to answer the question about the broken glass,
declining to simply confirm the interrogator's version or tell the objective
truth. Instead, he found a "third solution—unexpected and strange [stranie]:
the lie."[111] So as not to incriminate his friend Nego, he stubbornly claimed to
be unable to remember the broken glass episode, even though the shards of
glass had in fact become sharply defined in his memory. This simple lie presupposes the ability to grasp and anticipate the logic of the interrogator and
concoct an answer that the latter would deem innocent and nonincriminating.
At the same time, it requires that Steinhardt renounce his former values, such
as objective truth, in order to transmit a fundamental truth that he believed
in: his and Nego's innocence. This is a dangerous path to take, since as the
*Kubark* explains, pressuring the suspect to renounce his values is a critical aim
of interrogation: "As the sights and sounds of the outside world fade away,
its significance for the interrogatee tends to do likewise. The world is replaced
by the interrogation room, its two occupants [interrogator and suspect], and
the dynamic relationship between them. As interrogation goes on, the subject
tends increasingly to divulge or withhold in accordance with the values of the
interrogation world, rather than those of the outside world."[112] Steinhardt's
strange solution is based on the renunciation of the values of outside world:
but instead of latching on to the values of the interrogation room (here, indiscriminate confession), he redefines his value system and chooses to lie in order
to resist his interrogator's wish that he incriminate himself and his friend. By
so doing, he overcomes what American psychiatrists have called "an additional
vulnerability of highly moral people" to Soviet-style investigation, the fact
"that they find it difficult to tell a lie under any circumstances."[113] Steinhardt's
solution lies in the ability to distance himself from the values of both the outside world and the interrogation room. Steinhardt's eulogy to the "strange lie"
closely recalls Joseph Brodsky's famous lines: "The real history of consciousness starts with one's first lie. . . . My first lie had to do with my identity. Not
a bad start."[114] Brodsky's first lie strikingly resembles Steinhardt's—he refused
to admit a truth about himself, his Jewishness, that would have incriminated
him in the twisted logic of the regime. This lie becomes the foundation of
a liberating everyday art of estrangement from the self and from the world.
"Marx's dictum that 'existence conditions consciousness' was true only for as

long as it takes consciousness to acquire the art of estrangement; thereafter, consciousness is on its own and can both condition and ignore existence."[115]

Steinhardt's first lie also "had to do with his identity." Like Brodsky, Steinhardt also concocted his first lie at the moment when his very identity had become grounds for incrimination: "you are not accused for what you have done, but rather for what you are."[116] In the estranging light of the interrogation room, he realized that his former values, indeed his very identity, had been turned against him. According to the *Kubark*, this estrangement of the self or loss of autonomy saps resistance and induces the suspect to confess and divulge all the information she possesses. At this moment, interrogation can be considered successfully closed. But this was not true in the Soviet system, where the last stage of the interrogation was the conversion and "reeducation" of the suspect that was to culminate in the creation of a "new man," a lengthy process that often continued during imprisonment.[117] The Romanian secret police conducted some of the most extensive and savage experiments in reeducation. The Pitești prison was the most notorious and best-studied center of reeducation, and it provides a detailed if extreme reeducation scenario.[118] An informer chosen to match closely the profile of the prisoner was introduced into his cell with the aim of becoming "best friends." Once this goal was reached and the informer knew the prisoner intimately, he would abruptly turn against him. He would administer tortures that were the more horrible the more they were personalized. For example, religious people were asked to eat their feces and say thanks for "Communion." This grueling process was meant to induce the prisoner to renounce all her former values. Next she had to write a fictitious autobiography, made up of self-incriminating lies as well as trumped-up denunciations of others. The prisoner was finally considered reeducated when she was ready to turn torturer, and subject others to the same ordeals. As a consequence of this treatment, "the [reeducated] student would see the world as a god with two faces; the first, which he had thought was real, had now become unreal; the second, fantastic and ugly beyond any previous imaginings, had now become real . . . the lie was accepted as a biological necessity for survival."[119]

Steinhardt's lie also secured his survival. Like most reeducated prisoners, he renounced his former values, including objective truth. His lie appropriated the traumatic lesson of interrogation: the estrangement from a self that had been proved vulnerable to being taken apart and reassembled according to a new ideological mold. Steinhardt turned this lesson to his own advantage; renouncing his former self, he did not let himself be reforged into an informer. He lied about himself, but his lie manipulated rather than obeyed his interrogator's wishes. And rather than writing a fictitious biography and turning into a communist new man, he turned to writing a journal that recorded his transformation into a different kind of new man—the road to the religious faith he found in prison.

However, writing as the medium for self-fashioning seemed "risky" to Steinhardt, since he believed that language was tainted by the experience of prison and of totalitarianism in general. Thus, his literary criticism insisted on the theme "of the malefic power of words, usually less taken into consideration than the benefic one."[120] He prefaced his article "Everything About the Power of Words" with a quotation from Adrian Păunescu, the flashy poet of the Ceaușescu regime, who occasionally turned dissident: "It doesn't matter what was real, words make all they want out of the world." In response to this quotation, he argued, "Words are always capable of dissimulating an unpleasant or unwanted reality or to do violence to an indifferent one. . . . The paradox of the *strange* and constant Victory [of words over reality] has been proved and rendered banal by totalitarian and dogmatic regimes, where the accent has fallen without exception on writing and telling (corollary: the necessity of a ministry of propaganda)" (my emphasis).[121] Expressing what he perceives as his new self through words was always a challenge; thus, after his baptism in the prison cell, Steinhardt exclaimed, "new, I am a new man. . . . All that was old has passed, look, all things are new. . . . New, but unsayable. Words I cannot find, except banal, stale, the same ones I always use. I am in the middle of the chalk circle of known words and of ideals taken from daily scenery."[122] While directly referring to Brecht's *Caucasian Chalk Circle,* Steinhardt adds his own touch: the routine-laden chalk circle is made of words, and its prisoner is the self. The "malefic power" of words is rooted in a degradation, which he follows in detail: "There is a degradation. In the beginning there was the Word, the Logos. Humans are given the word. The word is degraded to empty chatter, which turns into automatisms, then to slogans."[123] In front of this degradation, "the contact with artistic chef-d'ouevres succeeds in breaking the charm, and as such establishes direct contact with God."[124] Steinhardt's description of the automatization of the world and the ability of artworks to break this spell almost literally recalls Shklovsky's description of artistic estrangement. However, for Steinhardt automatization was not simply routine but rather a religiously marked fall and a politically coercive device; and conversely, the estranging power of art became both a spiritual and a political weapon.

Let us return to the question that the imaginary tribunal asked Brecht, "'Now tell us, Mr. Brecht, are you really in earnest?'" and consider his answer, "I would have to admit that no, I'm not completely in earnest. I think too much about artistic problems, you know, about what is good for the theater, to be completely in earnest."[125] His sincere answer about not being sincere was at least partly determined by the fact that this is a polite imaginary tribunal. They address him as Mr. Brecht. The actual interrogators addressed Steinhardt much less politely, as he had never thought of himself—that is, as a criminal. Their estranging address questioned his whole value system, including such concepts as truth and sincerity. His answer to the interrogator's question was not at all in earnest; it was a lie that he proudly described as strange, well-concocted, and crafty. The eulogy to the "lie" that "has to do with one's identity" connects not only Brodsky and Steinhardt but also the advocates and victims of reeducation. Indeed, Steinhardt's and Brodsky's subversive autobiographical narratives surprisingly share a lot with the reeducation narrative. They are all conversion narratives, which tell the story of a "rebirth" seen as the "real birth." The "lie" is the fulcrum of these conversion narratives, the turning point between the incriminating estrangement of one's given identity and the creation of a new identity. The difference lies of course in the direction of the turn. In the reeducation scenario, the radical estrangement and breaking of the self was meant to lead to the adoption of the official mold of the communist new man. Steinhardt and Brodsky took private turns that required a double estrangement, both from the establishment and from their former identities. The lie translated the self for survival in a dangerous environment, both expressing and dissimulating it when needed.

Shklovsky also experienced estrangement of the self and flirted with self-estrangement as a subversive art of living. However, he soon relinquished it and turned to writing a memoir. While modeled on a trial deposition, his memoir was not a conversion narrative. As the trial depositions of the convicted SRs show, this was still possible in 1922, when the narrative of conversion and rebirth was not yet fully established. Unlike the victims of the Stalinist show trials of the 1930s, Shklovsky, as the accused in the SR trial, did not confess to his alleged crimes, nor did he undergo a rebirth. Rather than performing the miracle of reforging the self, Shklovsky's memoirs reveal the drama of an individual caught in the crossfire of his times. His art was based on juxtaposing irreconcilables rather than synthesizing them into a new set of values.

Studies of *ostranenie* often start with the thorny problem of terminology and translation. There is *estrangement* and *enstrangement* (making it strange), *defamiliarization*, and *deautomatization*. Benjamin Sher notes that "estrangement" is a good translation but "too negative and limited," whereas "making it strange" is "also good, but too positive."[126] And indeed, *ostranenie* is an ambiguous term, not just positive, not just negative. This ambiguity is instructive in itself. The many overlapping, contentious, and complicit terms for *ostranenie* suggest that there are many "different kinds" of estrangement that coexist in entangled relationships to one another. By adding terms like *revolutionary*, *secret police*, and *interrogation room* to *estrangement*, I have attempted not only to reveal a darker side of estrangement but also to draw attention to the constitutive mixtures between the artistic and political histories of this concept. In particular, estrangement appeared deeply involved in the politicized fashioning of the self and subject during Soviet times. The effects of estrangement on the self were certainly not limited to the therapeutic value ascribed to artistic estrangement; rather, they ranged widely between estrangement of the self—a key coercive device in interrogation and reeducation practices—and self-estrangement, an empowering device of survival and subversion. This story of many estrangements illustrates how even a famously "apolitical" literary concept was shaped by the influence of the secret police; it also shows how in dire times, even such a literary device as estrangement can be adapted to secure a vital distance from the most authoritarian discourses and actions of power.

# Concluding Thoughts

In 1959 five men and a woman, all young professionals of Jewish descent, as the secret police never tired of noting, were accused of robbing the Romanian National Bank. Within just a few months of the bank heist, they were caught, judged, and sentenced. All sentences were speedily carried out: the men were shot and the woman was shipped to a women's prison, but not before all six prisoners were made to participate in a feature-length film reconstructing their crime. The film, *Reconstruction (Reconstituirea*, 1960), called itself "a collaboration" between the secret police and the State Documentary Film Studio. The secret police provided the protagonists—the criminals and the investigators—as well as the extras: for one scene, a central part of the city was temporarily evacuated and filled with over a hundred secret police agents. The film studio then provided the equipment and the know-how, in the persons of some of its leading names. The film made a dramatic statement about the place of cinema in the new socialist society from the very opening sequence. The first shots reveal a collection of open history books, as an authoritative voice-over tells us that these chronicles recorded some of our past, while some is forever lost in the darkness of history. A shot of an open book gradually covered in darkness illustrates this meditation. We are cheerfully informed that today, for the first time, history is written by a chronicler—the film camera—"that offers a perfect living record that can be contested by nobody." As the book recedes into the darkness, the image of a film camera fills the screen.

Authoritatively spelling out the end of the written word and the secret police's embracement of cinema, this secret police cinematic *ars poetica* might appear as the denouement of the complicated relationships between the written word, film, and the secret police that we have followed in this book. We have seen those dangerous liaisons range widely. There were the complicities between words and images of different kinds at play in camp exotica films, inmate mug shots, and idealized drawings. And there were overblown

Parading the illegible secret police file. *Reconstruction,* 1960, frame enlargements.

disjunctures between names, photographs, and their human referents, dramatically sutured in a denouement cowritten by Stalin himself. Battles raged even within one image, between foreground and background and between the gazes that met on this visual battleground—such as empirical vision, vigilance, and clairvoyance. Just in time for this conclusion, a neat replacement of the word by the police-scripted image could put a dramatic end to a story whose vicissitudes resist quick summary. However, the movie that starts by loudly proclaiming the end of the written word and the reign of the cinematic image proceeds with an image of a collection of words—a secret police file. This file lies ceremoniously on a table in front of a military judge, who starts browsing through it in a tantalizing gesture for the audience positioned to look over his shoulder. But no matter how much the spectator strains her vision to focus on the out-of-focus letters, the text of the file remains illegible until, through a cinematic trick, the name of the movie, *Reconstituirea,* is superimposed on it in bold letters. The film is thus posited as the illustration of this authoritative text. Rather than presenting the results of a zero-sum game between word and image, *Reconstruction* allows us a carefully framed glimpse at the authoritative text that scripts the image. However, that text, the secret police file, is itself carefully framed as an illegible image.

As we have seen, this is a most common mode of representing the secret police file, initiated in Vertov's representation of the first show trial in 1924, and repeated in three different scenes in *Solovki.* The audience is shown the file covers, which are then opened to reveal the interior of the file. To increase the tease, file pages can even appear in extreme close-up. However, those browsing and filming the files made sure that the pages were turned quickly enough to become illegible, or that the resulting image was out of focus. The secret police file did not then simply revert the supremacy, loudly trumpeted in *Reconstruction*'s first sequence, of the cinematic image over words. Instead, the file built and preserved its power as a canny concoction of words, images, and above all particular practices of writing, copying, collating, reading, and exhibiting designed to capture the gaze of the audience while denying any

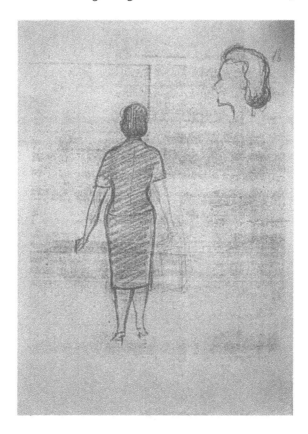

Police sketches of
Monica Sevianu.
Arhiva S.R.I., *Fond
Penal, Dosar nr.
40038/22*, 1959.

possibility of reading. The secret police file gained its power by its histrionic
framing "in the shadows," to paraphrase Stalin's stage directions, as an image
that is illegible to anyone but the secret police itself.

We are now finally in the position to read these files, and many others.
Copies of the bank heist file crowd my desk as I write.[1] Reading them confirms the film's not-so-subtle insinuations about the incontestable power of
the secret police file, which forcefully *scripted* the movie. The separate volume of the file dedicated to the movie reveals that the secret police literally
authored the first and last words of the script before the director of the film
was even selected. As such, the file exposes the actual terms of the advertised
"collaboration" between the secret police and the film industry, presenting
a particularly striking configuration of the relationship between culture and
policing that we have tracked in this book. Reading on, we also discover the
file's forceful narrative drive, predictably leading from a mysterious suspect to
a proven criminal. The first pages of the bank heist file offer a striking visual
representation of the mysterious figure of the suspect: a repeated portrait of
the female suspect, Monica Sevianu, shows her figure from the back, walking

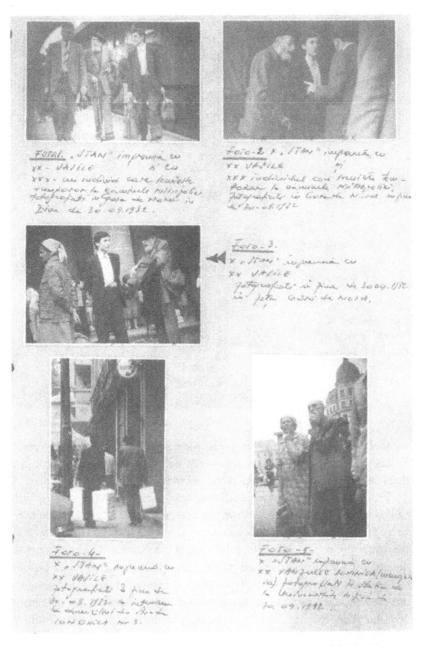

Surveillance photographs collated on a page from Nicolae Steinhardt's file. The "objective," Steinhardt, is designated by his codename, STAN, and marked with an X. *Dosar de urmărire informativă nr. 49342, I 207*, 30 September 1982, Fond Informativ (CNSAS), vol. VI, p. 29.

away as if on the point of getting lost in the distance. However, when the film's voice-over identified the figure of the enemy that does not deserve the title of human being, all I could see was Monica Sevianu's terrified face as she listened to her sentence. Like any text, yet more forcefully than most, the file guides toward certain readings. *Reconstruction* demonstratively performed such a reading for us, since we were not trusted with reading the file for ourselves.

The readings proposed, indeed often imposed, by the secret police file need to be well understood, if only so that they can be truly left behind. Most recent readings of the files, like those feeding the scandals around pivotal cultural figures such as Milan Kundera, István Szabó, and Constantin Noica are quick to tarnish reputations, especially the reputations of public figures famous for their resistance to the Soviet regime.[2] As such they are in fact rooted in the ways that the police devised for writing and reading these files—to assign guilt, to compromise individuals and break social networks, to turn art into incriminating evidence, and to pass quick judgment. Such readings mostly take secret police documents at their word, treating them as texts with the authority to tell us the truth about their subjects. I question that authority, showing some of the ways it was constructed. Instead, I believe that the verbal portrait of the subject painted in the files tells us much more about the police itself than about the subject. Hence, I chose to turn the bright light that shone on the suspect onto the words and images the police used to incriminate, compromise, exoticize, bully, or dazzle. And once that light was shifted onto these texts, I tried to devise ways to read them. Indeed, the first question that this book has tried to ask critically as much as to answer is how to go about reading these texts.

I recall the first day I spent with the files. Wondering where to start, I browsed a few volumes of Nicolae Steinhardt's file that were lying on the archive table. Then I took out for closer inspection the odd-sized pieces of paper that had not been sewed into the binders: identity card photographs next to photos of the suspect haggling over tomatoes—snapshots taken from the curiously low angles of surveillance cameras hidden in agents' perforated pockets. Letters still nested in their quaint envelopes or triangular postcards that came all the way from Soviet camps stood next to shiny Western postcards bringing a piece of Mediterranean sky into the defining grayness of the files. There were whole books presented as corpora delicti, photographs, copies of all kinds, the originals of literary manuscripts, graduation diplomas, and medical records such as a pocket-size x-ray of a prisoner's lungs, whose cloudy image haunted me for years.[3] They soon covered the desk and made it look like a surrealist collage. These objects had been taken out of their usual context and inserted into a radically different one—the file; a *détournement* had taken place. In the file, the knife does not kill but reveals the identity of the killer; the cup does not help quench thirst but provides latent fingerprints; the manuscript is not read for its literary interest but rather for its incriminatory value. As I read on, I came to see that the police file converts all other discourses into its (il)legal discourse, and all these sundry objects, texts, and images into evidence. The heterogeneity that had so struck me, the many voices recorded in the police file, are there, from the point of view of the file composers, faute de mieux. The file is not interested in creating a collage portrait of the subject, from various points of view, but rather in *collating*, that is, "bringing together and comparing," different documents with the aim "to ascertain *the* correct text," *the* correct version of the subject.[4] The ultimate goal is to erase all incongruities in a synthetic characterization, a characterization ideally reduced down to one incriminating sentence.

Steinhardt's file is certainly no surrealist collage. Why then compare it with one—why bring literature into this, making a collage on the archive table? I must have been inspired by Steinhardt himself, whose first impression on entering the interrogation room, we might recall, was, "See, *this* is surrealism. ... Now, yes, the teapot is also a woman, the stove is an elephant."[5] Steinhardt's strange pairings of unrelated objects recall Comte de Lautréament's famous definition of beauty, "the chance meeting on a dissection table of a sewing machine and an umbrella," which delighted and inspired the surrealists. However, in the interrogation room, the familiar turns more strange than any surrealist dreamscape, as the woman, a childhood friend, metamorphoses into something stranger than a teapot, a sewing machine, or an umbrella; she turns into the informer whose deposition seals your fate. Steinhardt soon realized the fundamental differences between surrealism and the interrogation room, where the explosion of familiar meanings and associations did not open up a field of possibilities but was instead designed to lose the subject so that she succumbed to the interrogator's version of words, events, people, and ultimately oneself.

And yet, "nor are books useless" in dealing with the secret police, affirms Steinhardt right after he realizes the dangers of conflating surrealism and the interrogation room. The estrangement of familiar objects and worldviews in surrealist art is as good a preparation as one can get for the interrogator's violent estrangement of the interrogatee's values. Well-read and thus well prepared, Steinhardt can even hope to resist the interrogator's estrangement. Inspired by Steinhardt, I would add, nor are books useless in dealing with the records of the secret police. The comparison with a surrealist collage foils the collation that actually defines the file, through similarities—as a collection whose extraordinarily diverse and clashing components defy previous categories—and through differences. In the case of the police file, this manic inclusiveness is rooted in a refusal to admit any limits in the pursuit of the subject. As a result, anything—from x-rays to papers listing the exact kinds of underwear, medications, toiletry items, and books received in a package from abroad—can be included in a file. A surrealist collage of the same materials could also explode the limits of previous representations of the subject, without quickly sweeping the fragments and traces of that subject into a criminal profile. Besides the mutual illuminations that occur when considering file confessions in the larger context of first-person narratives, interrogation room estrangement in relation to artistic estrangement, or literary characterization next to the *portrait parlé*, such triangulations through literature provide a critical distance and a vital breathing space when reading these "grisly archives."[6] This is crucial, as the files wrote the lives of others in ways that attempt to force any reading within narrow and ethically compromised confines. Can we even read the files and make sense of their language without somehow collaborating in the secret police's writing of its subjects? The question echoes Jacques Derrida's fundamental query, "Can one feign speaking a language," whether Greek or any other language of power?[7] Can one feign reading the files? Each time we take a file from its shelf, we run a great risk built into the simple act of reading: the risk of bringing to life once again the secret police's writing of its subject; the risk of becoming cocreators of this story by reading it on its own terms. Not taking the files off of their shelves, not reading, is no better solution; indeed, from the police's point of view, this is the ideal outcome, the end of reading that they staged so carefully. In the attempt to tackle this conundrum, reading particular works of literature—whether by Mandel'shtam, Shklovsky, Bulgakov, or Steinhardt—in relationship to the files provides invaluable inspiration. These writers developed *other* ways of reading and writing in often heated contact with the secret police and its textual practices. These other ways of reading and writing not only enriched literature but also worked as tactics of survival, camouflage, distancing, remembrance, or poetic justice. My juxtaposition of files and literature does not mean to conflate them but to profit from their differences. Indeed, files and literary works are different enough that when we bring them together, on a reading desk rather than a dissection table, their juxtaposition unsettles any one interpretation or one way of reading, including the reading scripted by the secret police.

Echoing Steinhardt's description of the interrogation room as surrealism, Hannah Arendt famously described twentieth-century police states as sites where the limits of what had been thought of as "the real" and of "the possible" were transgressed and a fictional world was set in their place.[8] A

The collage effect produced by the files, various years. On top, a list of personal items, including "cotton pajamas," "Lux soap," and "Gillette shaving blades," contained in a package received from abroad. The crossed-out page numbers testify to the many alterations undergone by the file during the archiving process. *Dosar nr. 118 988, P336*, Fond Penal (CNSAS), vol. 4, pp. 240, 241, 243, 248.

key challenge of this study was to identify the genres and particular devices of this "fiction" in the Soviet context. Previously, scholars interested in this question have focused mainly on the official textual production of the state—propaganda. However, the world of the police state was not produced only through propaganda: an army of words and images occupying thousands of miles of archives supported and documented the activity of the secret police. I started my exploration with the basic unit of the secret police archives, the personal file. Closely reading one file at a time might seem like a self-defeating approach to texts measured in kilometers, but in fact, since files followed standard composition rules at any given time, understanding one personal file takes us quite far in the study of the archives. Each personal file records the ways in which the secret police tracked, investigated, wrote, edited, and archived a life. Therefore, I tried to use each file like Ariadne's thread, guiding us through the archives and further, through the whole network of practices that defined the activity of the secret police, practices such as surveillance, interrogation, reeducation, misinformation, and secrecy. If these secret police texts all belong to the most powerful and ubiquitous biographical genre of the Soviet period, the personal file, the films featured in this study span a variety of genres, such as newsreel, ostensibly "unplayed" documentary, camp exotica, and melodrama. They come together as representatives of a kino police that was meant to identify the changing portrait of the Soviet negative hero and secret police agent on-screen and to manipulatively mold the audience's response.

Despite the close standardization of secret police practices at any given time, what never stopped surprising me was the extreme dynamism and elasticity of secret police aesthetics through time. Inexplicably at first, a film that the secret police had endorsed in 1928 could be viciously attacked and banned in 1930. The search for an explanation for such censure is unlikely to unearth one definitive answer, but it sometimes offers new perspectives on the interplay of forces shaping a secret police aesthetics constantly in the making. Thus, in the case of a 1928 film like *Solovki*, the explanation for its censure might be traceable to internal purges in the secret police: if the film happened to be linked to anyone recently fallen out of grace, that could be a good enough reason to have the film banned. Beyond scapegoating, a film's fate could also be symptomatic of major changes in criminological or even psychological dogma, which repeatedly condemned yesterday's portrayal of the Soviet criminal as an aberration. The impetus of the censure could even be rooted outside of the secret police, in the audience. The immediate cause of *Solovki*'s undoing seems to have been the indignation of factory workers who complained that their own living standards were lower than those of *Solovki*'s prisoners.[9] Since the most vertiginous changes in the relationship between aesthetics and policing happened in the foundational decades of the secret police, my analysis often privileges this early period, while at the same time attempting to describe the overarching transition from the histrionic spectacle of Stalinist secrecy and terror to the drab hyperrealism epitomized by 1970s surveillance.

Just as Mandel'shtam's "police aesthetics" shaped not only the coiffed moustache of a marine but also the sensibility of his young admirer and the very different, even inimical, aesthetics of the adult writer, secret police aesthetics overflowed the Lubianka and haunted, sometimes in full regalia and often incognito, the culture of its times. On close inspection, police aesthetics appears to have cast shadows where we might least expect: in Mikhail Bulgakov's *The Master and Margarita*, a novel that both artfully appropriates and parodies a personal file; in Viktor Shklovsky's *Sentimental Journey*, a collection of memoirs that echoes a trial deposition; in the politicized development of the notion of estrangement, a cornerstone concept in modern literary theory; in early Soviet cinema's penchant for "life caught unawares" and direct audience interpellation techniques; and in the constantly changing relationship between authority and authorship, writer and reader, filmed subjects and closely watched audiences.

Tracing these instances when secret police aesthetics casts shadows and sometimes bleeds into literature or cinema no doubt challenges the traditional dichotomy between subversive artists and the repressive state. The artists presented in this study sometimes subvert and sometimes participate in the constant reforging of police aesthetics, but more often they prefigure, expose, mock, echo, and refract it. However, just because the demarcations between subversion and repression are not always clear-cut does not mean that we should paint over the distinctions. The more ubiquitous and insidious the shadow of the secret police turns out to be, the more deserving of recognition any instances of independence, dissent, distancing, and subversion. As Primo Levi has movingly shown, survival in a police state was predicated on compromises, and not even on one grand compromise, like Pilate's betrayal of Jesus in *The Master and Margarita*, but on everyday, conscience-eroding compromises.[10] Nicolae Steinhardt, whose behavior during interrogation and in prison was nothing short of heroic, describes himself in his memoir as "soiled, failed, aging in concessions and acquiescence . . . isn't my natural place among dirt, among the lukewarm, in the soothing cesspool of surrender and obeisance?"[11] It is of course an indictment of life in the police state, rather than of Steinhardt, that not even heroism was enough to preserve one's basic human dignity. The fact that subversion and complicity are so thoroughly entangled does not mean that we should renounce these distinctions but that we should look closer and sharpen our discernment. Thus, we can nuance these distinctions and create others, opening to the possibility that besides subversion and complicity there were many other nodal points in this entangled relationship between the police and art, points such as mimicry, parody, appropriation, and estrangements of many shades.

# Notes

## Acknowledgments

1. Vladimir Nabokov, *Lectures on Russian Literature* (New York: Harcourt Brace Jovanovich, 1981), 58.

## Introduction

*A note on the transliteration of Russian characters:* Throughout the book, I used the Library of Congress transliteration system, omitting, as is common practice, most diacritical marks and tie bars. However, the traditional transliteration of certain proper names (e,g.,Tolstoy, Shklovsky, Trotsky) has been retained.

1. Vladimir Nabokov, *Speak, Memory* (New York: Vintage, 1989), 263.

2. As I will discuss in more detail, the Soviet secret police underwent many name changes (Cheka, GPU, OGPU, NKVD, NKGB, MGB, MVD, KGB), thus the different acronyms that appear in my writing and in various quotations that refer to particular moments of its history. Vitalii Shentalinskii, *Les surprises de la Loubianka: retour dans les archives littéraires du K.G.B.* (Paris: R. Laffont, 1996), 24. Both stories were supposed to be published in the journal *30 dnei*, but for unknown reasons they did not make it into print. Instead, they were preserved in the Cheka archives.

3. Ibid.

4. Ibid., 25–26; Mikhail Bulgakov, *Zoikina kvartira* (Ann Arbor: Ardis, 1971).

5. Shentalinskii, *Les surprises de la Loubianka*, 24.

6. Marietta Chudakova, "Conversation with Viktor Borisovich Shklovsky, January 9, 1981," *Poetics Today* 27, no. 1 (2006): 241.

7. J. Arch Getty, *Origins of the Great Purges: The Soviet Communist Party Reconsidered, 1933–1938* (Cambridge: Cambridge University Press, 1985), 182. The film shot on the occasion of the great anniversary gala of the NKVD in the Bol'shoi Theater was called *The Glorious Twenty* (*Slavnoe dvadtsatiletie VChK-OGPU-NKVD*) and is preserved in the Krasnogorsk Archive. In his report on the former KGB archives, Nikita Petrov notes that he found eleven didactic and documentary films for the anniversary dates of the KGB and its predecessors. Nikita Petrov, "'Politika rukovodstva KGB v otnoshenii arkhivnogo dela byla prestupnoi . . .'" *Karta (Riazan)* 1 (1993): 4–5.

8. Maxim Gorky et al., *Belomorsko-Baltiiskii kanal imeni Stalina: istoriia stroitel'stva* (Moscow: Gos. izd-vo "Istoriia fabrik i zavodov," 1934).

9. Besides the actual "prisoners' files (prosecuting verdicts, investigation material, testimonies, orders of the GPU collegium)," the bibliography lists numerous GPU orders, the camp journal *Reeducation (Perekovka)*, "thousands of prisoners' letters," and "hundreds of prisoner autobiographies" (ibid., 407).

10. For a full list of the Securitate's name changes and their lack of relation to actual changes in the practices of this institution see Cristina Anisescu, "'Partiturile' agenturii," in Cristina Anisescu et al., eds., *"Partiturile" Securităţii: Directive, ordine, instrucţiuni (1947–1987)* (Bucharest: Nemira, 2007), 16–17.

11. A comprehensive review of the literature was published under the title "The Secret Police and State Socialism—From Cheka to Stasi," *Kritika* 5, no. 2 (2004), while a special issue of *Cahiers du Monde Russe* was titled "La police politique en Union soviétique, 1918–1953," *Cahiers du monde russe* 42, 2–3–4 (2001), 205–715. Arguably the most influential Russian book-length study on the topic, V. S. Izmozik's *Glaza i ushi rezhima*, demonstrates the institution's early interest in population surveillance and uses both "political police" *(politicheskaia politsiia)* and "secret police" *(tainaia politsiia)*. V. S. Izmozik, *Glaza i ushi rezhima: gosudarstvennyi politicheskii kontrol' za naseleniem Sovetskoi Rossii v 1918-1928 godakh* (Sankt-Peterburg: Izd-vo SPbUEF, 1995).

12. Egon Bittner has influentially argued that the police should be defined by its means, in particular by the capacity to use force, rather than by its goals. Egon Bittner, *The Functions of the Police in Modern Society* (Chevy Chase: National Institute of Mental Health, 1970).

13. José Ortega y Gasset, "The Dehumanization of Art," in *The Dehumanization of Art and Other Essays on Art, Culture, and Literature* (Princeton: Princeton University Press, 1968).

14. Departamentul Securităţii Statului, "Instrucţiuni N. D-00180–1987," in Anisescu et al., *"Partiturile" Securităţii*, 653.

15. CNSAS, "Termeni si abrevieri in documentele Securitatii," http://www.cnsas.ro/documente/arhiva/Dictionar%20termeni.pdf. A similar, if less thorough, attempt for Russian terms is "Terminologiia i sleng spetssludzb," http://www.agentura.ru/library/vocabulair/.

16. CNSAS, "Termeni si abrevieri."

17. "Terminologiia i sleng spetssludzb."

18. Hannah Arendt, *The Origins of Totalitarianism* (New York: Meridian Books, 1958), 351–73.

19. Ibid., 434.

20. Stephen Brockmann, "Literature and the Stasi," in *Literature and German Reunification* (Cambridge: Cambridge University Press, 1999), 82.

21. Cristina Anisescu, "Evidenţele şi arhivele Securităţii," in Anisescu et al., *"Partiturile" Securităţii*, 52. This registry *(cartoteca generală)* included suspects, informers, as well as third parties mentioned in the files.

22. "O politicheskikh techeniiakh v moskovskom obshchestve" cited in V. S. Izmozik, *Glaza i ushi rezhima*, 62–63.

23. Vitaly Shentalinskii, *Arrested Voices: Resurrecting the Disappeared Writers of the Soviet Regime*, trans. John Crowfoot (New York: Free Press, 1996), 226.

24. Alexandru Andrieş, "Ingerul meu," *Verde-n faţă* (1998), http://alexandries.free. fr/andries/documente/discografie/discografie.html.

25. There are a few literary critics who have shown some interest in the files, but they constitute exceptions. For example, Stephen Brockmann's article "Literature and the Stasi" offers rich factual information on the relationship between German writers and Stasi agents. Brockmann, "Literature and the Stasi."

26. Boris Tomashevskii, "Literatura i biografiia," *Kniga i revoliutsiia* 4 (1923): 9.

27. Shentalinskii, *Les surprises de la Loubianka*, 196.

28. Ibid., 197.

29. Dariusz Tolczyk summarizes the condition of the novel in postrevolutionary Russia: "The crisis of the novel is a crisis of authority. With the absence of one acknowledged, authoritative presentation of the universe, each point of view, being questionable and relative, becomes an object of potential irony. . . . Consequently, the rhetorical universe implied by the direction of the structural evolution of the modern novel is entirely opposite to the rhetorical universe inherent in the Bolshevik world view" (Dariusz Tolczyk, *See No Evil: Literary Cover-Ups and Discoveries of the Soviet Camp Experience* [New Haven: Yale University Press, 1999], 40).

30. Boris Eikhenbaum, *Moi vremennik* (Leningrad: 1929), 49. Quoted in Victor Erlich, *Russian Formalism. History—Doctrine* (London: Mouton, 1965), 127.

31. Iurii Tynianov, "Literaturnoe segodnia," *Russkii sovremennik* I (1924): 292. Quoted in Erlich, *Russian Formalism*, 149.

32. Erlich, *Russian Formalism*, 148.

33. Nikolai Evreinov, *Teatr kak takovoi* (St. Petersburg: Sklad Izd. Sovremennoe Iskusstvo, 1912), 12. Cited in Julie Cassiday, *The Enemy on Trial: Early Soviet Courts on Stage and Screen* (DeKalb: Northern Illinois University Press, 2000), 15.

34. Nikolai Evreinov, "Teatral'noe iskusstvo na sluzhbe u obshchestvennoi bezopasnosti," *Zhizn' iskusstva* 4 (1921). Cassiday also notes that "Evreinov began his career in the theater after completing a legal education and publishing a thesis devoted to the history of corporal punishment and the theatrical aspects of execution in Russia" (Cassiday, *Enemy on Trial*, 15).

35. Erlich, *Russian Formalism*, 120.

36. Iurii Tynianov, "Literaturnyi fakt," in *Arkhaisty i novatory* (Leningrad: Priboi, 1929), 9, 15. Quoted in Erlich, *Russian Formalism*, 121.

37. An early critic of the Formalist movement, Mikhail Bakhtin concurred however in emphasizing the porosity of the boundaries between artistic and extra-artistic genres: "After all, the boundaries between fiction and non-fiction, between literature and nonliterature and so forth are not laid up in heaven. Every specific situation is historical. And the growth of literature is not merely development and change within the fixed boundaries of any fixed definition; the boundaries themselves are constantly changing" (Mikhail Bakhtin, *The Dialogic Imagination*, trans. Mikhail Holquist and Caryl Emerson [Austin: University of Texas Press, 1981], 33).

38. Ibid., 321, 428, 338.

39. Jochen Hellbeck has influentially argued that the received wisdom about "pervasive and uniform repression of personal narratives is countered now by a flood of personal documents from the first decades of Soviet power—diaries, letters, autobi-

ographies, poems—which have emerged from the recently opened Soviet archives. Diaries in fact appear to have been a popular genre of the period, especially during Stalin's reign" (Jochen Hellbeck, *Revolution on My Mind: Writing a Diary Under Stalin* [Cambridge: Harvard University Press, 2006], 4). See also Irina Paperno's fascinating body of work on diaries. Igal Halfin's work on autobiography similarly documents the proliferation of personal narratives at this time. Igal Halfin, *Terror in My Soul: Communist Autobiographies on Trial* (Cambridge: Harvard University Press, 2003).

40. Alexander Solzhenitsyn, *The First Circle*, trans. Thomas Whitney (New York: Harper and Row, 1968), 358.

41. Denise J. Youngblood, *Movies for the Masses: Popular Cinema and Soviet Society in the 1920s* (Cambridge: Cambridge University Press, 1992), 26.

42. Robert Conquest, *The Soviet Police System* (London: Bodley Head, 1968), 61. RSFSR Laws, 1923, 27: 310. The secret police's presence in cinemas was anything but short lived. A month before Nicolae Ceaușescu's fall in December 1989, writer Stelian Tănase wrote in his journal, "In cinemas, plain clothes Securitate agents attend all the shows, on the prowl to snatch those who make comments against [the regime]" (Stelian Tănase, *Acasă se vorbește in șoaptă: Dosar & Jurnal din anii târzii ai dictaturii* [Bucharest: Compania, 2002], 173).

43. *Chekist* is a common appellation for a Soviet secret police agent.

44. This paragraph's account of Ermler's early career relies mostly on Fridrikh Ermler, "Kak ia stal rezhisserom," *Iskusstvo kino* 9 (1927); Denise J. Youngblood, "Fridrikh Ermler and the Social Problem Film," in Youngblood, *Movies for the Masses*, 100–101, 151.

45. Ermler's wife witnessed that her husband spoke a lot and with great pride of his work in the Cheka. Fridrikh Ermler, *Dokumenty, stat'i, vospominaniia* (Leningrad: "Iskusstvo" Leningradskoe otd-nie, 1974), 327.

46. Ibid., 328.

47. Youngblood, "Fridrikh Ermler and the Social Problem Film," 151.

48. V. Fomin, *Kino i vlast': sovetskoe kino 1965–1985 gody* (Moscow: "Materik," 1996), 95.

49. Ermler, *Dokumenty, stat'i, vospominaniia*, 328.

50. Since Hungary falls outside the focus of this work on the Soviet Union and Romania, I analyze these films in a separate essay. The Interior Ministry films dealing specifically with the training of state security agents are the subject of Zsigmond Gábor Papp's documentary film *La vie d'un espion* (2004).

51. Boris Groys, *The Total Art of Stalinism: Avant-Garde, Aesthetic Dictatorship, and Beyond* (Princeton: Princeton University Press, 1992).

52. Mark Sanders, "Reading Lessons," *Diacritics* 29, no. 3 (1999): 4. For more on the potential and trappings of such rhetorical readings, see also Thomas Keenan, *Fables of Responsibility* (Stanford: Stanford University Press, 1997), Gayatri Spivak, "The Rani of Sirmur: An Essay in Reading the Archives," *History and Theory* 24, no. 3 (1985).

53. Robert Darnton, "A Police Inspector Sorts His Files: The Anatomy of the Republic of Letters," in *The Great Cat Massacre and Other Episodes in French Cultural History* (New York: Vintage Books, 1985), 157.

54. For a recent introduction to and bibliography on the uses of police documents in historical research and beyond, see Amy Gilman Srebnick, "Does the Repre-

sentation Fit the Crime?" in *Culture and Crime: An Historical Perspective*, ed. Amy Gilman Srebnick and René Lévy (Aldershot: Ashgate, 2005). For a pioneering study on the relationship of law to literature in nineteenth and twentieth century Russia see Harriet Murav, *Russia's Legal Fictions* (Ann Arbor: University of Michigan Press, 1998).

55. The most cited model of communal authorship is probably Maxim Gorky et al., *Belomor: An Account of the Construction of the New Canal Between the White Sea and the Baltic Sea* (New York: H. Smith and R. Haas, 1935). As I will later argue in my analysis of this text, it is no accident that this official "example of 'group composition' tells of the fate of the political prisoner" (ibid., 5).

56. Shentalinskii, *Les surprises de la Loubianka*, 15–16.

57. Ibid., 100.

58. Christopher Andrew and Vasili Mitrokhin, *The Sword and the Shield: The Mitrokhin Archive and the Secret History of the KGB* (New York: Basic Books, 1999).

59. A number of instructions exclusively devoted to the registration and archive department were written in 1951 when the Securitate found this department to be in need of improvement. Direcţiunea Generală a Siguranţei Statului, "Instrucţiuni asupra înfiinţării cartotecii pentru urmărirea executării lucrărilor, 30.III.1951," in Anisescu et al., *"Partiturile" Securităţii*; Ministerul Afacerilor Interne, "Instrucţiuni pentru organizarea si funcţionarea Birourilor si Secţiilor de Evidenţă din cadrul Regiunilor de Securitate, 1951," in Anisescu et al., *"Partiturile" Securităţii*; D.G.S.S. Evidenţa, "Completare la instrucţiuni pentru organizarea si funcţionarea Birourilor si Secţiilor de Evidenţă din cadrul Regiunilor de Securitate, 1951," in Anisescu et al., *"Partiturile" Securităţii*. After that, instructions regarding registration and archiving were often organized as separate chapters within larger documents. Ministerul Afacerilor Interne, "Ordinul Ministrului Afacerilor Interne al RPR nr. 85 si Instrucţiunile privind supravegherea operativă a organelor MAI, 1957," in Anisescu et al., *"Partiturile" Securităţii*, 425; Ministerul Afacerilor Interne, "Instrucţiuni nr. 144 privind munca organelor Ministerului Afacerilor Interne pentru asigurarea păstrării secretului de stat, 1959," in Anisescu et al., *"Partiturile" Securităţii*, 433–34; Ministerul de Interne, "Sistemul informaţional al Departamentului Securităţii Statului, 1984," in Anisescu et al., *"Partiturile" Securităţii*; Departamentul Securităţii Statului, "Instrucţiuni N. D-00180–1987," 652–64.

60. Ministerul Afacerilor Interne, "Instrucţiuni pentru organizarea," 255–65.

61. Ministerul Afacerilor Interne, "Directiva asupra organizării evidenţei operative de către organele Securităţii Statului, a elementelor duşmănoase din Republica Populară Română," in Anisescu et al., *"Partiturile" Securităţii*, 257–58, 266.

62. Ministerul Afacerilor Interne, "Instrucţiuni pentru organizarea," 255.

63. Ministerul Afacerilor Interne, "Directiva asupra organizării evidenţei," 248. An addition to this document is largely concerned precisely with the archivists' signaling of materials unexploited or incompletely exploited and thus of overlooked subjects new files. While quoting the six pages on which these recommendations had been made in the previous document, it adds two more pages of detailed instructions on the topic. D.G.S.S. Evidenţa, "Completare la instrucţiuni," 288–89.

64. Ministerul Afacerilor Interne, "Directiva asupra organizării evidenţei," 239.

65. Walter Benjamin, "The Work of Art in the Age of Mechanical Reproduction," in *Illuminations* (New York: Schocken Books, 1988), 242.

66. Shentalinskii, *Les surprises de la Loubianka*, 27.

67. Ibid., 111.

68. Evgeniia Ginzburg, *Journey into the Whirlwind*, trans. Paul Stevenson and Max Hayward (New York: Harcourt Brace Jovanovich, 1995), 68.

69. Benjamin, "Work of Art in the Age of Mechanical Reproduction," 242.

70. For a thorough study and critique of the pervasive accusation of theatricality in the reception of show trials see Cassiday, *Enemy on Trial*. For another excellent study of agitation trials see Elizabeth A. Wood, *Performing Justice: Agitation Trials in Early Soviet Russia* (Ithaca: Cornell University Press, 2005).

71. Walter Benjamin, *Moscow Diary*, trans. Richard Sieburth (Cambridge: Harvard University Press, 1986), 49–50.

72. Benjamin, "Work of Art in the Age of Mechanical Reproduction," 242.

73. Ginzburg, *Journey into the Whirlwind*, 68.

74. Jacques Rossi, *The Gulag Handbook* [*Spravochnik po Gulagu*] (London: Overseas Publications, 1987), 100.

75. Carmen Bragaru, *Dinu Pillat: un destin implinit* (Bucharest: Style, 2000), 205. Pillat's biographer heeds his example and indeed convincingly uncovers the traces of torture in Pillat's own file. Ibid., 205–7, 212–13.

76. Arnold Mesches, "The FBI Files," MOMA affiliate, *P.S. 1 Contemporary Art Center*, Long Island City, Queens, New York, September 2002–February 2003. I thank Amy Powell for drawing my attention to Mesches's work.

77. Arnold Mesches, "The FBI Files," http://www.artistsnetwork.org/news6/news252.html#NYTimes.

78. James Osterburg and Richard Ward, *Criminal Investigation: A Method for Reconstructing the Past* (Cincinnati: Anderson, 2000), 370.

79. Mesches, "FBI Files."

80. For more information on the exhibition see the catalogue: Thomas E. Levin et al., eds., *Ctrl (space): Rhetorics of Surveillance from Bentham to Big Brother* (Cambridge: MIT Press, 2002); Eleanor Heartney, "Big Brother Is Being Watched, by Artists," *New York Times*, January 6, 2003, 37–38.

81. Heartney, "Big Brother Is Being Watched," 38.

82. Svetlana Boym, "Poetics and Politics of Estrangement: Victor Shklovsky and Hannah Arendt," *Poetics Today* 26, no. 4 (2005): 587; Boym, *Another Freedom* (Chicago: University of Chicago Press, 2010).

83. Boym, "Poetics and Politics of Estrangement," 605, 583.

84. Shentalinskii, *Arrested Voices*, 28.

85. Osip Mandel'shtam, "Shum vremeni," in *Sobranie sochinenii* (Moscow: Art-Biznes, 1993), 352.

86. Osip Mandel'shtam, *The Noise of Time: The Prose of Osip Mandelstam*, trans. Clarence Brown (New York: Penguin, 1986), 73.

87. Ibid., 74.

88. Terry Eagleton, *The Ideology of the Aesthetic* (Oxford: Oxford University Press, 1990), 13.

89. Ibid., 27. Eagleton's critique here revisits Max Horkheimer's view of aesthetic as a form of "internalized repression," which "insert[s] social power more deeply into

the very bodies of those it subjugates, and so operating as a supremely effective mode of political hegemony" (Eagleton, *Ideology of the Aesthetic*, 28).

90. "The aesthetic ... exemplify[ies] new forms of autonomy and self-determination, transforming the relations between law and desire, morality and knowledge, recasting the links between individual and totality, and revising social relations on the basis of custom, affection, and sympathy.... If the aesthetic is a dangerous, ambiguous affair, it is because ... there is something in the body which can revolt against the power which inscribes it; and that impulse could only be eradicated by extirpating along with it the capacity to authenticate power itself" (Eagleton, *Ideology of the Aesthetic*, 28).

91. Caygill argues that even though Baumgarten considered himself a close follower of Christian Wolff, whose system provided the philosophical justification for the German police state, Baumgarten's "aesthetics pointed beyond Wolff." Indeed once the revolutionary implications of Baumgarten's aesthetics were developed in the work of Herder and Kant, aesthetics proved to be the stumbling block upon which Wolff's philosophical justification of the police state collapsed. Howard Caygill, "Aesthetic and the Police-State," in *The Art of Judgement* (London: Blackwell, 1989), 141–48.

92. Mandel'shtam, *Noise of Time*, 109–10.

93. Ibid., 74.

94. Osip Mandel'shtam, "My zhivem, pod soboiu ne chuia strany," in *Strofy veka* (Minsk: Poligraf, 1995).

95. D. A. Miller, *The Novel and the Police* (Berkeley: California University Press, 1988), 1. The phrase "the most free, the most lawless" belongs to André Gide, and is quoted by D. A. Miller as the dominant conception of the novel that he sets out to question.

96. For elaborations of the concept of "distribution of the sensible" see Jacques Rancière, *Politique de la littérature* (Paris: Galilée, 2007), 12, 23; Rancière, *The Politics of Aesthetics: The Distribution of the Sensible* (London: Continuum, 2004), 12–13. While Rancière's concept of "the (re)distribution of the sensible" has been of great inspiration to my work, my understanding of aesthetics in Soviet times is quite independent of his notion of "the aesthetic regime," which he sees as "the true name for what is designated by the incoherent label 'modernity,'" and defines in opposition to "the poetic regime," which the aesthetic regime started to challenge in the eighteenth century. Rancière, *Politics of Aesthetics*, 20–24; Jacques Rancière, "What Aesthetics Can Mean," in *From an Aesthetic Point of View: Philosophy, Art, and the Senses*, ed. Peter Osborne (London: Serpent's Tail, 2000), 20–23.

97. For an illuminating discussion of the importance of the distinction between words and cries of pain in the (re)distribution of the sensible see Rancière's thesis that "In a sense, all political activity is a conflict for deciding what is a word and a cry, for retracing the frontiers of the sensible through which political capacity is attested" (Rancière, *Politique de la littérature*, 12).

98. Dennis Deletant, *Ceauşescu and the Securitate: Coercion and Dissent in Romania, 1965–1989* (London: Hurst, 1995), 20, 54–56.

99. See Mariia Shneerson, "Sila mastera i bessilie vlastelina: Bulgakov i Stalin," *Grani* 167 (1993).

## Chapter 1

An early version of this chapter has been published as Cristina Vatulescu, "Arresting Biographies: The Secret Police File in the Soviet Union and Romania," *Comparative Literature* 56, no. 3 (2004). The current version has been expanded and extensively revised.

1. Jacques Derrida, *Archive Fever: A Freudian Impression* (Chicago: University of Chicago Press, 1996), 4.

2. Ibid., 2–4; Michel Foucault, *The Archaeology of Knowledge* (New York: Pantheon Books, 1972), 128–31.

3. For those fighting for the opening of the archives, the German Gauck commission became a coveted ideal impossible to attain without the popular, governmental, and material support available in Germany.

4. The power struggles around the archives and the different articulation and implementation of lustration laws in Hungary, the Czech Republic, and Poland are documented in Monika Nalepa, "The Power of Secret Information: Transitional Justice After Communism" (Ph.D. diss., Columbia University, 2005).

5. For country by country accounts of the history of lustration in Easter Europe and Russia, see Lavinia Stan, ed., *Transitional Justice in Eastern Europe and the Former Soviet Union: Reckoning with the Communist Past* (London: Routledge, 2009), and Mark S. Ellis, "Purging the Past: The Current State of Lustration Laws in the Former Communist Bloc," *Law and Contemporary Problems* 59, no. 4 (1996). For a comprehensive collection of documents pertaining to lustration law, see Neil Kritz, ed., "Transitional Justice: How Emerging Democracies Reckon with Former Regimes" (Washington: U.S. Institute of Peace Press, 1995).

6. Law no. 187, December 7, 1999, http://www.CNSAS.ro/main.html.

7. For a thorough critique of CNSAS's shortcomings see Lavinia Stan, "Spies, Files and Lies: Explaining the Failure of Access to Securitate Files," *Communist and Post-Communist Studies* 37, no. 3 (2004).

8. Cristina Anisescu et al., eds., *"Partiturile" Securității: Directive, ordine, instrucțiuni (1947–1987)* (Bucharest: Nemira, 2007 Other valuable collections of documents are Constantin Aioanei et al., *Cartea albă a Securității: istorii literare si artistice, 1969–1989* (Bucharest: Editura Presa Româneasca, 1996); Dan Catanus et al., eds., *Intelectuali români in arhivele comunismului* (Bucharest: Nemira, 2006). See also Cristian Troncotă, *Istoria serviciilor secrete românești: De la Cuza la Ceaușescu* (Bucharest: Editura Ion Cristoiu, 1999). This study illustrates SRI's position toward the past in its attempt to minimize the abuses of the secret police as temporary missteps in an overall meritorious story of the Romanian secret services.

9. Ellis, "Purging the Past," 195.

10. Decree on the Activities of the Communist Party of the Soviet Union and the Communist Party of the Russian Soviet Federated Republic. (No. 169) (Nov. 6, 1991), reprinted in Kritz, "Transitional Justice," 434.

11. Nikita Petrov, "'Politika rukovodstva KGB v otnoshenii arkhivnogo dela byla prestupnoi . . .'" *Karta (Riazan)* 1 (1993).

12. Arsenii Roginskii and Nikita Okhotin, "Die KGB Archive ein Jahr nach dem

Putsch von August 1991," in *Russland heute: von innen gesehen. Politik, Recht, Kultur*, ed. Arsenii Roginskii (Bremen: Temmen,1993).

13.  Vitalii Shentalinskii, *Raby svobody: v literaturnykh arkhivakh KGB* (Moscow: Parus, 1995); Shentalinskii, *Donos na Sokrata* (Moscow: "Formika-S," 2001).

14.  The full text of the law is available in Kritz, "Transitional Justice," 797–807.

15.  Sergei Eremeev, "Chto khranit'sia v arkhivakh FSB?" *Novosti razvedki i kontrrazvedki*, October 1, 2003, 10.

16.  For example, the collaboration between Andrei Sakharov's widow, Elena Bonner, and Yale University Press has resulted in the publication of selections from the late dissident's files: Joshua Rubenstein and Alexander Gribanov, *The KGB File of Andrei Sakharov* (New Haven: Yale University Press, 2005).

17.  See for example the remarkable series from Yale University: *Annals of Communism*. A fascinating collection of reports of the secret police to the Kremlin leadership about attitudes among intellectuals was published in Katerina Clark et al., eds., *Soviet Power and Culture, 1917–1953* (New Haven: Yale University Press, 2007). For important secret police materials relating to the great terror see Arch Getty and Oleg Naumov, *The Road to Terror: Stalin and the Self-Destruction of the Bolsheviks, 1932–1939* (New Haven: Yale University Press, 1999). The Hoover Institution also features invaluable documents originated by the secret police, such as its Fond R-393, a collection of mostly administrative NKVD documents dealing with the early activity of the secret police. Fond R-393 (People's Commissariat for Internal Affairs of the RSFSR, 1917–1930). Of similar interest is Fond R-4042 (Main Administration of the Places of Confinement of the People's Commissariat of Internal Affairs of the RSFSR [NKVD RSFSR], 1922–1930).

18.  V. V. Doroshenko and V. M. Chebrikov, *Istoriia sovetskikh organov gosudarstvennoi bezopasnosti: uchebnik* (Moscow: Vyshaia krasnoznamennaia shkola KGB, 1977). The entire text is available at http://www.fas.harvard.edu/%7Ehpcws/istoriaı.pdf.

19.  Peter Holquist, "Constructing a New Past: The Soviet Experience in Post-Soviet Historiography" (paper presented at "Russia at the End of the Twentieth Century" conference, Stanford University, 1998).

20.  It is common knowledge that the current administration is extensively staffed by Vladimir Putin's former colleagues from the Leningrad office of the KGB.

21.  For a deconstruction of the myriad fantasies surrounding the archive see Derrida, *Archive Fever*.

22.  Thus, about a third of the short history of the Securitate archives available on the SRI website is dedicated to the destruction or absence of files. Serviciul Român de Informaţii, "Istoricul arhivelor fostei Securităţi," http://www.sri.ro.

23.  Walter Benjamin, *Charles Baudelaire: A Lyric Poet in the Era of High Capitalism* (London: Verso, 1983), 43.

24.  Bertillon is often considered the father of anthropometrics and of judicial photography. See his studies: Alphonse Bertillon, *Identification anthropométrique: instructions signalétiques* (Melun: Typographie-lithographie administrative, 1885); *La photographie judiciaire: avec un appendice sur la classification et l'identification anthropométriques* (Paris: Gauthier-Villars, 1890).

25.  Russia appears in line with these world developments. A rogues gallery (a

record of criminals' photographs) already existed in Moscow by 1867, preceded only by the Danzig collection of 1864. Hans Gross, *Handbuch für Untersuchungsrichter als System der Kriminalistik* (Munich: J. Schweitzer, 1914), 459.

26. Quoted in Dariusz Tolczyk, *See No Evil: Literary Cover-Ups and Discoveries of the Soviet Camp Experience* (New Haven: Yale University Press, 1999), 19.

27. Nicolae Steinhardt, *Jurnalul Fericirii* (Cluj: Dacia, 1997), 240.

28. Anthony Olcott, *Russian Pulp: The Detektiv and the Russian Way of Crime* (Oxford: Rowman and Littlefield, 2001), 44.

29. Jochen Hellbeck, *Revolution on My Mind: Writing a Diary Under Stalin* (Cambridge: Harvard University Press, 2006), 30.

30. Katerina Clark, *The Soviet Novel: History as Ritual* (Chicago: University of Chicago Press, 1981), 45.

31. Ibid.

32. John Bender, *Imagining the Penitentiary* (Chicago: University of Chicago Press, 1987), 22–23.

33. Michel Foucault, *Discipline and Punish: The Birth of the Prison* (New York: Vintage Books, 1979), 252.

34. Peter Becker argues that in nineteenth century Germany criminologists used biography to describe the *Gauner*, the professional criminal and volitional wrongdoer, and genealogies to describe the degenerate or inborn criminal. Peter Becker, "Criminological Language and Prose from Late Eighteenth to the Early Twentieth Century," in *Crime and Culture: An Historical Perspective*, ed. Amy Gilman Srebnick and René Lévy (Aldershot: Ashgate, 2005), 32–33. Elsewhere in Europe, there seems to have been quite a mix of these narratives in criminological attempts to describe criminals. While theories of inborn criminality were ultimately superseded by more sociological approaches to crime, in practice there seemed to have been significant mixtures and dialogues between various criminological approaches. Thus, Cesare Lombroso, the most famous proponent of the inborn criminality theory, confessed admiration for Alphonse Bertillon, the father of modern policing. Christian Phéline, "L'image accusatrice," *Les Cahiers de la Photographie* 17 (1985): 72. In some cases, one person could represent very different criminological trends, as in the famous case of Francis Galton, who was an early proponent of eugenics and also the inventor of the fingerprint. Allan Sekula, "The Body and the Archive," *October* 39, no. 4 (1986): 34–50.

35. Sekula, "Body and the Archive," 30, 33–35.

36. For a history of the fingerprint see Simon A. Cole, *Suspect Identities: A History of Fingerprinting and Criminal Identification* (Cambridge: Harvard University Press, 2001).

37. Sekula, "Body and the Archive," 10.

38. A. Grigoriev argued that the most common starting point for a file was a denunciation. A. Grigoriev, "Investigative Methods of the Secret Police," in *The Soviet Secret Police*, ed. Simon Wolin and Robert Slusser (New York: Frederock A. Praeger, 1957), 229. Sheila Fitzpatrick cites more recent research that shows that "most denunciations in investigation files are statements obtained by the police in the process of investigation, and only a few are voluntary 'signals' from members of the public" (Sheila Fitzpatrick, "Signals from Below: Soviet Letters of Denunciations of the 1930s," in *Accusatory Practices: Denunciation in Modern European History*, ed. Sheila Fitzpat-

rick and Robert Gellately [Chicago: University of Chicago Press, 1997], 88). Fitzpatrick also writes that in the late 1920s the regime decided to punish "whole categories of enemies, notably kulaks (prosperous peasants) and Nepmen" (ibid., 87).

39. Igal Halfin, *Terror in My Soul: Communist Autobiographies on Trial* (Cambridge: Harvard University Press, 2003), 246.

40. Ministerul Afacerilor Interne, "Directiva asupra organizării evidenței operative de către organele Securiţătii Statului, a elementelor duşmănoase din Republica Populară Română" in Anisescu et al., *"Partiturile" Securităţii*, 238–41.

41. Ibid., 239.

42. Ibid., 238–41. It is likely that while in the beginning of its existence the Securitate relied mainly on lists of whole categories of people to be endowed with files and often arrested; as these lists were "processed," the Securitate started relying more on its investigation and archival material as well as on its growing network of informers as sources for the opening of the files. In both cases, identification was a minor part of the police's processing of its suspects.

43. It is significant that Securitate internal memos detail identification procedures only for one type of (hardly common) file, the country-wide search file (*dosar de urmărire pe ţară*), which dealt with "state criminals who had disappeared" from the Securitate's radar and "who were attempting to flee arrest or have escaped from prison." In the instructions concerning the writing of regular suspect or informer files, identification procedures such as peculiar characteristics are not mentioned, and instead there is a strong emphasis on detailed characterization. Ibid., 236–46.

44. Ibid., 241.

45. Ibid., 239–41.

46. Ibid., 244.

47. Cristina Anisescu, "Evidenţele şi arhivele Securităţii," in Anisescu et al., *"Partiturile" Securităţii*, 44.

48. "Terminologiia i sleng spetssludzb," http://www.agentura.ru/library/vocabulair/.

49. Ibid. A brief description of the "transformation" of the *delo-formuliar* into *sledstvennoe delo* is available in L. Belkovets, "Sudby spetsposelentsev v arkhivnykh dokumentakh," Memorial Foundation, http://www.memo.ru/HISTORY/nem/Chapter4.htm. The ruling that investigation files (*dosare de anchetă*) should be kept under separate binders appears in Ministerul Afacerilor Interne, "Instrucţiuni pentru organizarea si funcţionarea Birourilor si Secţiilor de Evidenţă din cadrul Regiunilor de Securitate, 1951," in Anisescu et al., *"Partiturile" Securităţii*, 259. The files sometimes continue after the investigation was finished, with records of trial proceedings and camp records. Since I have just recently started getting access to such files, my present account does not include them.

50. A list of the typical contents of a surveillance file was detailed in Ministerul Afacerilor Interne, "Directiva asupra organizării evidenţei," 242–43. The files of Romanian writers Lucian Blaga, Stelian Tănase, and Nicolae Steinhardt contain the most instructive examples of surveillance records partially published to date. Dorli Blaga and Ion Balu, *Blaga supravegheat de Securitate* (Cluj: Biblioteca Apostrof, 1999); Stelian Tănase, *Acasă se vorbeşte in şoaptă: Dosar & Jurnal din anii târzii ai dictaturii* (Bucha-

rest: Compania, 2002); Silviu Moldovan et al., eds., *Nicu Steinhardt în dosarele Securității 1959–1989* (Bucharest: Nemira, 2005).

51. Cristina Anisescu, "'Partiturile' agenturii," in Anisescu et al., *"Partiturile" Securității*, 19.

52. Ibid., 18–19.

53. Direcțiunea Regională a Securității Poporului, "Ordin Circular nr. 399 din 23 Decembrie 1948," in Anisescu et al., *"Partiturile" Securității*, 191. This early Securitate document is especially revealing as it offers a table of contents for the informer file and for the DUI. A lengthy 1987 document describes in more detail the categories of informers, the table of contents of the informers' files, and provides blank forms for informer's and supportive person's agreements. Departamentul Securității Statului, "Instrucțiuni N. D-00180–1987," in Anisescu et al., *"Partiturile" Securității*.

54. Direcțiunea Generală a Siguranței Statului, "Organizarea, încadrarea si funcționarea Direcțiunii Generale a Siguranței Statului (1947)," in Anisescu et al., *"Partiturile" Securității*, 168.

55. Ibid.

56. Direcțiunea Regională a Securității Poporului, "Ordin Circular," 192.

57. Ibid.

58. *Dosar de urmărire informativă nr. 49342, I 207*, Fond Informativ (ACNSAS), 11:34.

59. Vitalii Shentalinskii, *Les surprises de la Loubianka: retour dans les archives littéraires du K.G.B.* (Paris: R. Laffont, 1996), 50.

60. Mikhail Bulgakov, *Master i Margarita* (Moscow: ACT, 1999), 10.

61. Direcțiunea Regională a Securității Poporului, "Ordin Circular," 191.

62. N. Ezhov, "Operativnyi prikaz narodnogo komissara vnutrennix del S.S.S.R No. 00447 ob operatsii po repressirovaniiu byvshikh kulakov, ugolovnikov i dr. antisovetskikh elementov," Krasnoiarskoe Obshchestvo Memorial, http://www.memorial.krsk.ru/DOKUMENT/USSR/370730.htm.

63. Grigoriev, "Investigative Methods of the Secret Police," 229.

64. Shentalinskii, *Les surprises de la Loubianka*, 23; Shentalinskii, *Raby svobody*, 28.

65. For a fascinating analysis of the process through which "one woman's life was constructed and reconstructed (by herself) and deconstructed by the NKVD," based on a reading of her workplace *avtobiografiia* and investigation file, see Sheila Fitzpatrick, "The Two Faces of Anastasia: Narratives and Counter-Narratives of Identity in Stalinist Everyday Life," in *Everyday Life in Early Soviet Russia*, ed. Christina Kiaer and Eric Naiman (Bloomington: Indiana University Press, 2005).

66. Shentalinskii, *Les surprises de la Loubianka*, 53.

67. David T. Hawkings, *Criminal Ancestors* (Stroud: Sutton 1996), i–ii.

68. This section refers to the Stalinist period in the Soviet Union and Romania. Stalinist-type files survived in Romania until 1962, when political prisoners started to be amnestied and arrests were drastically curbed.

69. For an interesting study of the beginnings of the surveillance apparatus in the Soviet Union (1918–24), see Izmozik, *Glaza i ushi rezhima*, particularly parts 4 and 6. Izmozik focuses mostly on population mood reports filled by the Cheka on large categories of people such as members of political parties, the intelligentsia, or army personnel.

70. Ezhov, "Operativnyi prikaz."

71. Most of Babel's secret police investigation file 419, later reclassified as P-1252, is published in Sergei Povartsov, *Prichina smerti—rasstrel: khronika poslednikh dnei Isaaka Babelia* (Moscow: Terra, 1996). The record of the first interrogation cited throughout this paragraph is reproduced on pages 49–50.

72. Mikhail Bakhtin, *The Dialogic Imagination*, trans. Mikhail Holquist and Caryl Emerson (Austin: University of Texas Press, 1981), 350.

73. Ibid.

74. Povartsov, *Prichina smerti*, 106.

75. Shentalinskii, *Raby svobody*, 43–52.

76. Shentalinskii, *Les surprises de la Loubianka*, 119; Shentalinskii, *Raby svobody*, 162.

77. Shentalinskii, *Les surprises de la Loubianka*, 229; Shentalinskii, *Raby svobody*, 307.

78. Halfin, *Terror in My Soul*, 231.

79. Benjamin, *Charles Baudelaire*, 43; Michel Foucault, *Surveiller et punir: naissance de la prison* (Paris: Gallimard, 1975).

80. Bender, *Imagining the Penitentiary*, 1–2, 210–13, and passim; Foucault, *Discipline and Punish*, 144.

81. Halfin, *Terror in My Soul*, 240.

82. Ibid., 262.

83. Ibid., 254. It is no accident that millions of prisoners in the Stalinist camps fell under one article in the Penal Code, the infamous Article 58 that covered "counter-revolutionary crimes," inclusive enough to cover both Babel and Ezhov. Otto Pohl, *The Stalinist Penal System. A Statistical Study of Soviet Repression and Terror, 1930–1953* (London: McFarland, 1997), 19.

84. The amnesty of political prisoners took place between 1962 and 1964. Ceaușescu came to power in 1965, and the first years of his regime brought "a relaxation of terror" as well as a critique of the repressive excesses of the past. Dennis Deletant, *Ceaușescu and the Securitate: Coercion and Dissent in Romania, 1965–1989* (London: Hurst, 1995), 53, 70–82.

85. As mentioned in the introduction, Denis Deletant has documented the development of the Romanian Securitate on the Soviet model. Deletant furthermore argues that even after 1964 when the Romanian leadership became interested in demonstrating some independence from Moscow—as showcased in the removal of the Soviet councilors in 1964 and in Ceaușescu's condemnation of the Soviet invasion of Czechoslovakia in 1968—the Romanian secret police did not reform the model inherited from the Soviets, and the relationships between the two secret services remained strong. Ibid., 20, 54–56. Given the similarity between the structure and development of the two secret services, it is likely that the changes that I describe concerning post-Stalinist Romanian files also took place in the Soviet Union. Indeed, the published fragments of Soviet files from the 1960s and 1970s support these conclusions. See for example the fragments from the Solzhenitsyn files published in Michael Scammell, *The Solzhenitsyn Files: Secret Soviet Documents Reveal One Man's Fight Against the Monolith*, trans. Catherine A. Fitzpatrick (Chicago: Edition Q 1995). However, given the paucity of post-Stalinist Soviet secret police personal files available in their complete version to researchers, we cannot rush to conclusions until the archives become more accessible.

86. *Dosar de urmărire informativă nr. 49342, I 207, Dosar penal nr. 118988, P 336*, vol. III (ACNSAS).

87. For more information on the Noica-Pillat case, complete with fragments from the relevant secret police files and interviews with the participants in the events, see Stelian Tănase, *Anatomia mistificării* (Bucharest: Humanitas, 2003).

88. *Dosar de urmărire informativă nr. 49342, I 207* XI: 03.30.1989. Not all files have coherent pagination. In case a page number was not available, I will note the date of the document.

89. Julie Petersen argues that "In the early 1970s, Government and press disclosures made it seem as though everyone was bugging everyone else and this may have been true. . . . As soon as the miniature technology [bugging] became widely available, it appears to have become widely used" (Julie Petersen, *Understanding Surveillance Technologies: Spy Devices, Their Origins and Applications* [New York: CRC Press, 2001], 2–38, 2–39).]

90. *Dosar de urmărire informativă nr. 226083* (Paul Goma's Securitate File) (ACNSAS).

91. *Dosar de urmărire informativă nr. 49342, I 207* VII: 11.30.1972–12.10.72.

92. Ibid., vols. X, XI.

93. Ibid., XI: 21.10.88.

94. Ministerul de Interne, "Extras din proiectul Ordinului privind munca cu rețeaua informativă, 30.xi.1972," in Anisescu et al., *"Partiturile" Securității*, 66.

95. The results of these first months of research on Preda are then summarized in a far-reaching biography: *Dosar de urmărire informativă nr. 761423* (Marin Preda's Securitate File) (ACNSAS), I:48–49.

96. Ibid., II: 61.

97. Ibid., I: 71.

98. Roland Barthes, "The Reality Effect," in *The Rustle of Language* (Berkeley: University of California Press, 1989), 141–46.

99. Peter Holquist has convincingly argued that from the beginning of the Soviet regime, "surveillance was not a passive, observational endeavor; it was an active, constructivist one." "[I]t's whole purpose was to act on people, to change them." Holquist's study focuses on the early Soviet regime's intense interest in large-scale population surveillance rather than individual policing. Peter Holquist, "'Information Is the Alpha and Omega of Our Work': Bolshevik Surveillance in Its Pan-European Context," *Journal of Modern History* 69, no. 3 (1997): 449, 17, 20.

100. Ministerul de Interne, "Instrucțiuni, 20.I.1973," in Anisescu et al., *"Partiturile" Securității*, 588–90. The privileging of prevention and the description of the above-mentioned preventive measures was reiterated in 1987 in Departamentul Securității Statului, "Instrucțiuni N. D-00190–1987," in Anisescu et al., *"Partiturile" Securității*, 675–78.

101. Ministerul de Interne, "Instrucțiuni, 20.I.1973," 589.

102. Departamentul Securității Statului, "Instrucțiuni N. D-00180–1987," 651; Cristina Anisescu, "Glosar de termeni utilizați de Securitate," in Anisescu et al., *"Partiturile" Securității*, 684. For example, isolation was among the chief stated goals of Steinhardt's surveillance file. *Dosar de urmărire informativă nr. 49342, I 207*, VII: 2.

103.  Nicu Steinhardt, "Declarație" (Statement), 14 Decembrie 1972, IV:290–91.

104.  Ibid., IV:293–94.

105.  Nicu Steinhardt, "Declarație" (Statement), 16 December 1972, IV:296–97.

106.  Ibid., IV:300.

107.  Ministerul Afacerilor Interne, "Directiva asupra organizării evidenței," 242.

108.  Laura Engelstein, "Combined Underdevelopment: Discipline and the Law in Imperial and Soviet Russia," in *Foucault and the Writing of History*, ed. Jan Goldstein (Oxford: Blackwell, 1994), 224. Engelstein's article provides a different, and extremely thorough, criticism of Foucault through an analysis of the relationship between law, discipline, and state power in Tsarist Russia and in the Soviet Union.

## Chapter 2

1.  For excellent general overviews of criticism tracing various influences on the novel see Laura Weeks, "Introduction: 'What I Have Written, I Have Written,'" in *The Master and Margarita: A Critical Companion*, ed. Laura Weeks (Evanston: Northwestern University Press, 1996); Andrew Barratt, "*The Master and Margarita* in Recent Criticism," *The Master and Margarita*, ed. Laura D. Weeks.

2.  "influence" in *Collins Essential Thesaurus* (New York: HarperCollins, 2006).

3.  Boris Gasparov, "Iz nabliudenii nad motivnoi strukturoi romana M. A. Bulgakova *Master i Margarita*," *Slavica Hierosolymitana* 3 (1978): 203.

4.  Mikhail Bulgakov, *Master i Margarita* (Moscow: ACT, 1999), 7.

5.  Ivan whispers to Berlioz: "He is no tourist, he's a spy. He's a Russian émigré, who has wormed his way back here. Ask to see his documents before he gets away . . ." Bulgakov, *Master and Margarita*, trans. Mirra Ginzburg (New York: Grove Press, 1996), 14. Throughout this chapter, I use Ginzburg's translations with slight modifications; for longer or otherwise important citations, I also provide references to the Russian ACT edition.

6.  Ibid., 7. Bulgakov, *Master i Margarita*, 7.

7.  James Osterburg and Richard Ward, *Criminal Investigation: A Method for Reconstructing the Past* (Cincinnati: Anderson, 2000), 201.

8.  Sheila Fitzpatrick, *Tear Off the Masks! Identity and Imposture in Twentieth-Century Russia* (Princeton: Princeton University Press, 2005), 24.

9.  The standard rubrics of the "*slovesnyi portret*" are reproduced in the file of the major Yiddish writer Der Nister. Peter B. Maggs, *The Mandelstam and "Der Nister" Files: An Introduction to Stalin-Era Prison and Labor Camp Records* (Armonk: M. E. Sharpe, 1996), K-4/5.

10.  Christian Phéline, "L'image accusatrice," *Les Cahiers de la Photographie* 17 (1985): 119.

11.  Bulgakov, *Master and Margarita* 348; Bulgakov, *Master i Margarita*, 376.

12.  Bulgakov, *Master i Margarita*, 378.

13.  For a brilliant discussion of graphomania and graphomaniacs in the Russian context see Svetlana Boym, *Common Places: Mythologies of Everyday Life in Russia* (Cambridge: Harvard University Press, 1994), 168–75.

14.  The model socialist realist book at the time when Bulgakov was writing *The*

*Master and Margarita, Belomor Canal,* was authored by such a hybrid composed of the secret police agent and camp commander Semen Firin and the leading Soviet writers Maxim Gorky and Leopold Averbakh. For this heavy tome, 120 writers representing the elite of Soviet literature were asked to (re)write the life stories of camp inmates that had been first drafted by secret police investigators in personal files. Bulgakov was well aware of the Belomor project, as he had been asked to participate in it and declined. He claimed that he was tired, but maybe it was just that he knew better than most the challenges of working over the prose of secret police agents. Cynthia Ann Ruder, *Making History for Stalin: The Story of the Belomor Canal* (Gainesville: University Press of Florida, 1998), 52.

15. The lesson was certainly assimilated by Sheinin, whose short autobiography written at age fifty is framed by a first sentence that emphasizes precisely the roots of his writing in criminal investigation: "Many are the paths which lead a writer to literature. Mine began in the Criminal Investigation Department" (Lev Sheinin, *Diary of a Criminologist* [Honolulu: University Press of the Pacific, 2004], 5, 10).

16. Ibid., 12.

17. Boris Ershov, "Mozaika sud'by sledovatelia Sheinina," *Sait kluba vypusknikovMGU,* http://www.moscowuniversityclub.com/home.asp?artId=4375.

18. Boris Efimov, "Literaturno-prokuraturnyi sintez," *Lekhaim* 84, no. 4 (1999).

19. Ibid. According to A. N. Pirozhkova, Babel's wife, Sheinin was on intimate visiting terms with Babel until the latter's arrest, when Sheinin tried his best to distance himself from the fallen writer. L. I. Slavin et al., *Vospominaniia o Babele* (Moscow: Izd-vo Knizhnaia palata, 1989).

20. Vitalii Shentalinskii, *Les surprises de la Loubianka: retour dans les archives littéraires du K.G.B.* (Paris: R. Laffont, 1996), 25–26.

21. "cachet" in *The Oxford English Dictionary* (Oxford: Oxford University Press, 2008).

22. Ibid.

23. Laura Weeks documents how the puzzling patchwork quality of the novel, "not cut from whole cloth but pieced together from a variety of familiar genres," has preoccupied critics from the novel's appearance to these days. Weeks, "Introduction," 18.

24. Weeks also gives a comprehensive overview of the various critical attempts to come to terms with the problem of the narrative voice(s). Ibid., 27–33.

25. Edward E. Ericson, *The Apocalyptic Vision of Mikhail Bulgakov's The Master and Margarita* (Lewiston: E. Mellen, 1991), 11.

26. Thus, both Riitta Pittman and Judith Mills ingeniously account for the discordance of the narrative voices by reading the whole novel as the schizophrenic dream or hallucination of the poet Ivan Bezdomnyi. For a comprehensive introduction to the debates on the riddle of the narrative voices, see Barratt, "*Master and Margarita* in Recent Criticism," 93–96.

27. J. A. E. Curtis, "Mikhail Bulgakov and the Red Army's Polo Instructor: Political Satire in *The Master and Margarita,*" in *The Master and Margarita* ed. Laura D. Weeks.

28. Ibid., 222–23.

29. Ibid., 222. On the same page, Curtis cites a good example of such a lightly

veiled euphemism: "'Take the telegrams personally. Let them sort it out,' Rimsky tells Varenukha (525). Varenukha needs no further instructions as to where to go, and when he does not return, Rimsky's only question is, 'What on earth for?' (i.e., 'Why have they arrested him?')." Curtis, "Mikhail Bulgakov and the Red Army's Polo Instructor," 222.

30. Curtis, "Mikhail Bulgakov and the Red Army's Polo Instructor," 223.

31. D. G. B. Piper, "An Approach to *The Master and Margarita*," *Forum for Modern Language Studies* 7, no. 2 (1971): 146; M. P. Lamperini, "Glosse al 23ismo capitolo del Maestro e Margherita di M. A. Bulgakov," in *Atti del Convegno "Michail Bulgakov"* (Milan: 1986), 281–86. Cited in Curtis, "Mikhail Bulgakov and the Red Army's Polo Instructor," 218.

32. Curtis, "Mikhail Bulgakov and the Red Army's Polo Instructor," 223. Unfortunately, Curtis seems to regard this insight as an inconsequential curiosity, and immediately turns his attention away from the traces that the secret police leaves on the novel's form to those it leaves on its content—the actual topic of his analysis.

33. Bulgakov, *Master and Margarita*, 5; Bulgakov, *Master i Margarita*, 5–6. For the comparison between censored and uncensored versions of the novel, I used the excellent Posev edition, where the formerly censored passages are italicized. Mikhail Bulgakov, *Master i Margarita* (Frankfurt: Posev, 1969).

34. Bulgakov, *Master and Margarita*, 5; Bulgakov, *Master i Margarita*, 5–6.

35. Bulgakov, *Master and Margarita*, 132.

36. Stelian Tănase, *Acasă se vorbește in șoaptă: Dosar & Jurnal din anii târzii ai dictaturii* (Bucharest: Compania, 2002), 158–59.

37. Bulgakov, *Master and Margarita*, 6.

38. Bulgakov, *Master i Margarita*, 47.

39. Bulgakov, *Master and Margarita*, 247.

40. Ibid., 372.

41. Michael Holquist, "Corrupt Originals: The Paradox of Censorship," *PMLA* 109, no. 1 (1994): 15.

42. Bulgakov, *Master and Margarita*, 160.

43. Ibid., 161.

44. Ibid., 162.

45. Ibid., 21–22; Bulgakov, *Master i Margarita*, 22.

46. Marietta Chudakova and Edward Ericson agree that Bulgakov showed a sustained interest in biblical apocrypha, of which he made extensive use in *The Master and Margarita*. See Ericson, *Apocalyptic Vision*, 24–43.

47. Bulgakov, *Master and Margarita*, 16.

48. Fedor Dostoevsky, "Brat'ia Karamazovy," in *Sobranie sochinenii* (Moscow: Gosudarstvennoe izdatel'stvo khudozhestvennoi literatury, 1958), 10:162, 169.

49. Ivan more coarsely describes this "special method" as lying: "You are lying, your aim is to convince me you exist apart and are not my nightmare, and now you are asserting you are a dream" (ibid., 166).

50. Ibid., 10:151.

51. Catharine Theimer Nepomnyashchy, "Interview with Andrei Siniavskii," *Formations* 6, no. 1 (1991): 9, 20.

52.   T. R. N. Edwards, *Three Russian Writers and the Irrational: Zamyatin, Pil'nyak, and Bulgakov* (Cambridge: Cambridge University Press, 1982), 138.

53.   Tzvetan Todorov, *The Fantastic: A Structural Approach to a Literary Genre*, trans. Richard Howard (Ithaca: Cornell University Press, 1975), 34.

54.   The circumstances of the diary's unearthing in the former KGB archives and of its publication in 1990 are described in Viktor Losev, "Bessmertie—Tikhii svetlyi breg," in *Dnevnik Mastera i Margarity* (Moscow: Vagrius, 2001), 10–12; Vitalii Shentalinskii, *Arrested Voices: Resurrecting the Disappeared Writers of the Soviet Regime*, trans. John Crowfoot (New York: Free Press, 1996), 15–16. Bulgakov's letter to the OGPU, the copy of his letter to the government underlined by Iagoda, and an informer's account of the "great deal of talk" that the letter provoked "in literary and intelligentsia circles," are available in Shentalinskii, "The File on Mikhail Bulgakov," in *Arrested Voices*.

55.   Shentalinskii, "Under the Heel," in *Arrested Voices*, 73, 83.

56.   A famous illustration of the dangers of first-person narratives is to be found in the trial of Andrei Siniavskii. The prosecutor disregarded the painstakingly crafted ambiguity of the narrative voice in Siniavskii's text "What Is Socialist Realism?" and stubbornly conflated the author and narrator, taking the author to task for all the inflammatory comments made in the text. Siniavskii's fate depended on his ability to convey a point most often made in introductory literature classes: the difference between the author and narrator. As a consequence, he went to pains to draw attention to the complex, indeed obfuscating play of narrative voices in the text. But the judge did not (want to) get the point, and Siniavskii was condemned to five years in a labor camp. For a detailed account of the Siniavskii/Daniel trial see Aleksandr Ginzburg and Russian S.F.S.R. Verkhovnyi Sud, *Belaia kniga po delu A. Siniavskogo i Iu. Danielia* (Frankfurt: Posev, 1967).

57.   Edythe C. Haber, *Mikhail Bulgakov: The Early Years* (Cambridge: Harvard University Press, 1998), 5–7.

58.   Shentalinskii, "Under the Heel," 121.

59.   Ibid., 121.

60.   Ibid., 93.

61.   Bulgakov, *Master and Margarita*, 3; Bulgakov, *Master i Margarita*, 3.

62.   Bulgakov, *Master and Margarita*, 3.

63.   Ibid., 5.

64.   Ibid., 186.

65.   Bulgakov, *Master i Margarita*, 376–78.

66.   Bulgakov, *Master and Margarita*, 181.

67.   Ibid., 182.

68.   Ibid., 311.

69.   Bulgakov, *Master i Margarita*, 377.

70.   Mikhail Bulgakov, *Sobach'e serdtse* (Moscow: EKSMO-PRESS, 2000), 377.

71.   Curtis, "Mikhail Bulgakov and the Red Army's Polo Instructor," 223.

72.   Bulgakov, *Sobach'e serdtse*, 334.

73.   Ibid.

74.   Nicolae Steinhardt, *Jurnalul Fericirii* (Cluj: Dacia, 1997), 3.

75.   Vitalii Shentalinskii, *Raby svobody: v literaturnykh arkhivakh KGB* (Moscow: Parus, 1995), 113.

76. The first, still incomplete, version was published in *Teatr* 2 (1990); an updated version is available in Mikhail Bulgakov and Elena Bulgakova, *Dnevnik Mastera i Margarity* (Moscow: Vagrius, 2001), 15–127.

## Chapter 3

1. Natalia Nussinova, "The Soviet Union and the Russian Émigrés," in *The Oxford History of World Cinema*, ed. Geoffrey Nowell-Smith (Oxford: Oxford University Press, 1996), 167.

2. Dziga Vertov, "Kiev 1 Sept. 28g. chelovek s kinoapparatom," in *Dziga Vertov: die Vertov-Sammlung im Österreichischen Filmmuseum*, ed. Thomas Tode et al. (Vienna: Synema, 2006), 72. I am grateful to Yuri Tsivian for this reference.

3. Lilya Kaganovsky, "Visual Pleasure in Stalinist Cinema: Ivan Pyr'ev's *The Party Card*," in *Everyday Life in Soviet Russia*, ed. Eric Naiman and Christina Kiaer (Bloomington: Indiana University Press, 2005), 53.

4. A contemporary critic recorded what he called "Vertov's striking comparison" of the movie camera and the GPU agent. Alexander Belenson, "Kino-Eye by Dziga Vertov (2)," in *Lines of Resistance: Dziga Vertov and the Twenties*, ed. Yuri Tsivian (Gemona: Le Giornate del Cinema Muto, 2004), 107.

5. Ibid.; Dziga Vertov, "The Artistic Drama and Kino-Eye," in Tsivian, *Lines of Resistance*, 106–7; Vertov, "The Council of Three," in *Kino-Eye: The Writings of Dziga Vertov*, ed. Annette Michelson (Berkeley: University of California Press, 1984), 14.

6. Dziga Vertov, "An Answer to Five Questions," in Tsivian, *Lines of Resistance*, 95; Vertov, "An Introductory Speech Before a Showing of the First Part of Kino-Eye," in Tsivian, *Lines of Resistance*, 103.

7. Dziga Vertov, "On the Significance of Newsreel," in *Kino-Eye: The Writings of Dziga Vertov*, ed. Annette Michelson (Berkeley: University of California Press, 1984), 32.

8. Nikolai Bukharin, "Krasnyi Pinkerton," *Zrelishcha* 12 (1922): 9.

9. Ibid.

10. Dziga Vertov, "Kino-Eye," in Tsivian, *Lines of Resistance*, 120.

11. Tsivian, *Lines of Resistance*, 282.

12. Dziga Vertov, "Ruki, étude," in Tsivian, *Lines of Resistance*, 282–85. Tsivian notes that "the exact date and purpose of this manuscript is unclear," but that a reference to *Kino-Pravda 19* dates it "no earlier than 1924." He adds that it is tempting to assume that Vertov jotted down this list of "shots" in response to Rodchenko's idea, but he could have conceivably written this any time after 1924. Tsivian, *Lines of Resistance*, 287. It could also be that the line of influence goes the other way, or both ways, as Rodchenko's 1927 sketch of the ten rouble note being exchanged by various hands shot in close-up could well describe the speculators' sequence in *Kino-Eye* (1924).

13. Yuri Tsivian, "Audio Essay," in *The Man with the Movie Camera* (Chatsworth: Image Entertainment, 1998).

14. In the Soviet Union of the early twenties, hands were also dramatically used as markers of identity. Richard Stites notes that "when the Revolution deepened it became a 'visible revolution' wherein personal appearance became a political statement. In the Civil War, citizens with clean fingernails and smooth hands were shot

in Sevastopol by the incoming Reds. In the Omsk region, a White commander surrounded a factory, examined the hands of the employees, and shot those with calloused hands." Richard Stites, *Revolutionary Dreams: Utopian Vision and Experimental Life in the Russian Revolution* (New York: Oxford University Press, 1989), 132.

15. Simon A. Cole, *Suspect Identities: A History of Fingerprinting and Criminal Identification* (Cambridge: Harvard University Press, 2001), 118.

16. Ibid., 177–89. Cole provides a fascinating analysis of the ways in which dactyloscopy proponents in the late teens made use of contemporary as well as earlier cases to prove their point. He argues that even though fingerprinting was used already in the nineteenth century, "only slowly, over the course of the 1920s, did fingerprinting become the preferred criminal identification technique in the United States" (140–43, 163).

17. A. I. Bastrykin, *Znaki ruki* (St. Petersburg: Oreol, 2004), 175–248.

18. The first case solved through fingerprinting in Russia concerned the 1912 murder of a Saint Petersburg pharmacist, and it was an immediate press "sensation." Ibid., 198–218. The 1923 case of the sons accused of killing their mother was solved when the victim was shown through fingerprinting to not actually be the mother but a different woman, who the sons had no motive to kill. The 1924 case concerned two Mongolian women disputing their maternity of a boy returning from boarding school. Having reached the Mongolian Supreme Court, the case was referred to the anthropologist Teplukhov. On the basis of the study of fingerprints, the boy was taken away from the woman who had claimed him first and given to the second claimant. Bastrykin, *Znaki ruki*, 231–32, 241. A serious full-length monograph on fingerprinting was published in 1923: P. S. Semenovskii, *Daktiloskopiia kak metod registratsii* (Moscow: Izd. tsentropozyska respubliki, 1923).

19. "fingerprint" in *Encyclopædia Britannica Online* (2009).

20. This understanding of the index, as differentiated from the icon and the sign, is rooted in C. S. Pierce's semiotic system. Laura Mulvey, *Death 24x a Second* (London: Reaktion Books, 2006), 9.

21. André Bazin, *What Is Cinema?*, trans. Hugh Gray, vol. 1 (Berkeley: University of California Press, 1967), 15.

22. Mulvey, *Death 24x a Second*, 9.

23. Ibid.

24. Lev Manovich, "What Is Digital Cinema?" in *The Digital Dialectic: New Essays on New Media*, ed. Peter Lunenfeld (Cambridge: MIT Press, 1999), 176.

25. First adopted by the police around the world as a means of criminal identification, fingerprinting was at various points extended to other sectors of the population. In the United States, even though persistent calls for universal fingerprinting have been resisted for decades, the categories of people subject to fingerprinting have continued to expand, including American Indians, military personnel, state employees, and more recently all foreigners and resident aliens entering the country. In 1956, "of the total 141,231,713 fingerprint sheets on file with the FBI, no less than 112,096,777 were not those of criminals, but of respectable permanent or temporary residents of the United States who never had any brushes with the law" (Jurgen Thorwald, *The Century of the Detective* [New York: Harcourt, Brace & World, 1956], 110). Simon Cole

provides a fascinating account of the use and abuse of fingerprinting for colonial purposes. Cole, *Suspect Identities*, 60–97.

26. Dziga Vertov, "The Birth of Kino-Eye," in Michelson, *Kino-Eye*, 41.

27. Tsivian provides a whole catalogue of hidden camera techniques used by Vertov and Kaufman in Tsivian, "Audio Essay."

28. Izmail Urazov, "A Sixth Part of the World," in Tsivian, *Lines of Resistance*, 186.

29. Mikhail Kaufman, "An Interview with Mikhail Kaufman," *October* 11, Winter (1979): 64.

30. Ibid.

31. Ibid.

32. Dziga Vertov, "From the Kinoks' Field Manual," in Michelson, *Kino-Eye*, 162.

33. Urazov, "Sixth Part of the World," 186, emphasis mine.

34. Vertov, "Kiev 1 Sept. 28g. chelovek s kinoapparatom," 72.

35. Ibid.

36. Vertov, "Kino-Eye," 120.

37. Walter Benjamin, "The Work of Art in the Age of Mechanical Reproduction," in *Illuminations* (New York: Schocken Books, 1988), 232.

38. Ibid., 231.

39. Annette Michelson, "The Wings of Hypothesis: On Montage and the Theory of the Interval," in *Montage and Modern Life: 1919–1924*, ed. Matthew Teiltelbaum (Cambridge: MIT Press, 1992), 80–81.

40. Julie Cassiday, *The Enemy on Trial: Early Soviet Courts on Stage and Screen* (DeKalb: Northern Illinois University Press, 2000), 113.

41. Graham Roberts, *Forward Soviet!: History and Non-fiction Film in the USSR* (London: I. B. Tauris, 1999), 21.

42. The film covers the trial of Mironov and his codefendants for insubordination in the army. Just like in the SR trial, the defendants were condemned to be shot, but their sentence was commuted. *The Trial of Mironov* even prefigures some of the original devices used in the *Kino-Pravda* coverage, such as the identification of the key players at the courthouse entrance at the time their papers are checked by the guards.

43. Mironov's codefendant Bulatkin gives the defiant performance.

44. On the theatrical staging of the courtroom in the Colonnade Hall, see Cassiday, *Enemy on Trial*, 44.

45. Ibid., 46.

46. Ibid., 46.

47. A. Z., "At an Evening of *Kino-Pravda*," in Tsivian, *Lines of Resistance*, 41.

48. Cassiday, *Enemy on Trial*, 47.

49. In a 1923 manifesto, Vertov advocated the forceful manipulation of the viewer's experience in no uncertain terms: "I *make* the viewer see in the manner best suited to my presentation. The eye submits to the will of the camera. . . ." "One cannot present" "a series of scattered perceptions, *different for each spectator*, to the viewer" (Vertov, "Council of Three," 16). Instead, the director, cameramen, and editor work together towards "the forceful transfer of the viewer's eye to the successive details that *must* be seen" (ibid., emphasis mine).

50. Carol J. Clover, "Judging Audiences: The Case of the Trial Movie," in *Reinvent-*

*ing Film Studies*, ed. Christina Gledhill and Linda Williams (Oxford: Oxford University Press, 2000).

51.   Alexander Medvedkin, "Interview with Alexander Medvedkin," in *Inside the Film Factory: New Approaches to Russian and Soviet Cinema*, ed. Richard Taylor and Jan Christie (London: Routledge, 1991), 171.

52.   For informative accounts of the film-train, see Richard Taylor, *The Politics of the Soviet Cinema, 1917–1929* (Cambridge: Cambridge University Press, 1979), 52–63, and Emma Widdis, *Alexander Medvedkin* (London: I. B. Tauris, 2005), 22–34.

53.   Named after Lenin, the first military agitation train "left Moscow for a trial run to Kazan on 13 August 1918" (Ibid., 53).

54.   Krupskaia published her recollections of *Krasnaia zvezda*'s journey in Nadezhda Krupskaia, "Po gradam i vesyam sovetskoi respubliki," *Novyi mir* 11, no. 113–130 (1960).

55.   Peter Kenez, *The Birth of the Propaganda State: Soviet Methods of Mass Mobilization, 1917–1929* (Cambridge: Cambridge University Press, 1985), 58–63. Taylor cites evidence showing that already by the end of 1920, the film train "*Oktiabr'skaia revoliutsiia* alone had provided over 430 film shows which drew an audience in excess of 620,000 people" (58). Taylor bases these figures on the work of L. V. Maksakova, *Agitpoezd Oktiabr'skaia revoliutsiia (1919–1920gg)* (Moscow: Akad. nauk, 1956), 27–33.

56.   Alexander Medvedkin, "294 dnia na kolesakh," in *Iz istorii kino*, ed. Institut istorii iskusstv (Moscow: Iskusstvo, 1977), 39.

57.   Medvedkin, "Interview with Alexander Medvedkin," 169.

58.   Medvedkin, "294 dnia na kolesakh," 39.

59.   Ibid.

60.   Ibid., 36–37.

61.   Ibid., 37.

62.   Medvedkin, "Interview with Alexander Medvedkin," 169.

63.   Medvedkin, "294 dnia na kolesakh," 40–41.

64.   Ibid., 43.

65.   Ibid., 37.

66.   Ibid.

67.   For more on the "factory-gate" films see Simon Popple and Joe Kember, *Early Cinema: From Factory Gate to Dream Factory* (London: Wallflower Press, 2004), 36–37.

68.   Medvedkin, "294 dnia na kolesakh," 37.

69.   Medvedkin, "Interview with Alexander Medvedkin," 166.

70.   Ibid., 169.

71.   Quoted in *Forward Soviet!* from interview transcript provided by Richard Taylor. Roberts, *Forward Soviet!*, 119.

72.   Vladimir Il'ich Lenin, "Sistema Teilora-Poraboshchenie cheloveka mashinoi," in *Polnoe sobranie sochinenii* (Moscow: Gos. izd-vo polit. lit-ry, 1958), 24:369–70. Quoted in Taylor, *Politics of the Soviet Cinema*, 29.

73.   Taylor, *Politics of the Soviet Cinema*, 152.

74.   Roberts, *Forward Soviet!*, 111.

75.   Medvedkin, "Interview with Alexander Medvedkin," 169.

76.   Ibid.

77. Medvedkin, "294 dnia na kolesakh," 44.

78. Medvedkin, "Interview with Alexander Medvedkin," 169.

79. Ibid., 165.

80. Ibid., 169.

81. Alexander Medvedkin, "Chto takoe kinopoezd," in *Iz istorii kino*, ed. Institut istorii iskusstv (Moscow: Iskusstvo, 1985), 60.

82. The letter was published in *La Nature* no. 291 (December 28, 1878): 54, and is cited in Martha Braun, *Picturing Time: The Work of Etienne-Jules Marey (1830–1904)* (Chicago: University of Chicago Press, 1992), 47. Marey's detailed description of his camera-gun can be found in Etienne-Jules Marey, "Le fusil photographique," *La Nature* no. 444 (1881).

83. Marey's letter to his mother is also cited in Braun, *Picturing Time*, 57.

84. Susan Sontag, *On Photography* (New York: Farrar, Straus and Giroux, 1990), 15.

85. Paul Virilio, *War and Cinema: The Logistics of Perception* (London: Verso, 1989).

86. Ibid., 1.

87. Terry Gordon, the owner of 2002 patent no. 6,363,223 for a digital camera-gun, explained its appeal for hunters: "The pictures could be another way for hunters to display their successes," if the hunter had "a simple, straightforward way to photograph his or her prey or target just before, during, and/or after the kill." Comparing the picture with antlers, skins, and other trophies, Gordon makes it easy to imagine the moment when the hunter does not just use the picture to document the killing, but instead kills for the picture. Gordon also "envisions a use for his device when the targets are human" and touts his invention's potential for the police and military. Sabra Chartrand, "Patents; A New Camera Attachment for Guns Automatically Photographs the Target as the Trigger Is Pulled," *New York Times*, August 26, 2002. Of course, both the police and the military have long been aware of the uses of camera-guns, as is made graphically clear by a photograph, taken at the National Academy of Sciences in Washington, D.C. in 1939, of a camera machine gun used for the training of aerial gunners.

88. Cassiday, *Enemy on Trial*, 182; Peter Kenez, "Soviet Cinema in the Age of Stalin," in *Stalinism and Soviet Cinema*, ed. Richard Taylor and Derek Spring (London: Routledge, 1993), 57.

89. Maxim Gorky et al., *Belomorsko-Baltiiskii kanal imeni Stalina: istoriia stroitel'stva* (Moscow: Gos. izd-vo "Istoriia fabrik i zavodov," 1934), 47.

90. Ibid.

91. Ibid.

92. Ibid.

93. Iegudiil Khlamida (pseud. Maxim Gorky), "Mezhdu prochim," *Samarskaia Gazeta*, January 23, 1896. Cited in Yuri Tsivian, "Media Fantasies and Penetrating Vision: Some Links Between X-Rays, the Microscope, and Film," in *Laboratory of Dreams: The Russian Avant-Garde and Cultural Experiment*, ed. John E. Bowlt and Olga Matich (Stanford: Stanford University Press, 1996), 92.

94. Gorky et al., *Belomorsko*, 47.

95. Ibid., 47–48.

96. I am grateful to Julie Cassiday for sharing her copy of *The Party Card* with me.

97. Ivan Pyr'ev, "Pomnit' o nashem zritele," *Iskusstvo kino* 5 (1936): 7.

98. Christian Phéline, "L'image accusatrice," *Les Cahiers de la Photographie* 17 (1985): 59.

99. Ibid.

100. National Library of Medicine, "'Visible Proofs: Forensic Views of the Body,' New Exhibition at NLM," http://www.nlm.nih.gov/news/press_releases/visibleproofs_pro6.html.

101. Amanda Schaffer, "Solving Puzzles with Body Parts as the Pieces," *New York Times*, February 28, 2006.

102. Ibid.

103. My account of the State Institute for the Study of Crime and the Criminal is based on Sharon Kowalsky, "Making Crime and Sex Soviet: Women, Deviance, and the Development of Criminology in Soviet Russia" (Chapel Hill: University of North Carolina, 2004), 107–9, 300–307.

104. Regarding the foundation of the institute, Kowalsky notes, "Although the State Institute was conceived as an interdepartmental organization equally represented by four commissariats, the NKVD took the lead, establishing the institute by its Order No. 97, on 1 July 1925. In turn, the State Institute fell under the auspices of the NKVD, obtained its primary funding from the NKVD, and was held accountable to it" (ibid., 107). Kowalsky locates NKVD Order no. 97 in GARF, f. R-4042, op. 10, d. 7, 1.55.

105. Ibid., 306–7.

106. My account of the verification and party card exchange campaign is based on the thorough study of these events found in J. Arch Getty, *Origins of the Great Purges: The Soviet Communist Party Reconsidered, 1933–1938* (Cambridge: Cambridge University Press, 1985), 33–91.

107. Ibid., 48.

108. Ibid., 34.

109. Ibid., 33.

110. Sheila Fitzpatrick, *Tear Off the Masks! Identity and Imposture in Twentieth-Century Russia* (Princeton: Princeton University Press, 2005), 270–72.

111. Golfo Alexopoulos, "Portrait of a Con Artist as a Soviet Man," *Slavic Review* 57, no. 4 (1998): 778.

112. Getty, *Origins of the Great Purges*, 34.

113. Ibid., 88. Getty bases his account on the detailed instructions concerning the exchange of party cards sent to local party organizations: "Instruktsiia o poriadke i tekhnike obmena partiinykh biletov i drugikh partiinykh dokumentov," in *WKP 54* (Smolensk Archive).

114. For a fascinating historical account of postrevolutionary preoccupations with identity and imposture see Fitzpatrick, *Tear Off the Masks!*

115. Pyr'ev, "Pomnit' o nashem zritele," 7.

116. Getty, *Origins of the Great Purges*, 41.

117. Fitzpatrick, *Tear Off the Masks!*, 3.

118. Otto Iul'evich Shmidt, ed., *Bol'shaia sovetskaia entsiklopediia* (Moscow: Sovetskaia entsiklopediia, 1926), V:146; S. I. Babilov, ed., *Bol'shaia sovetskaia entsiklopediia*, 2nd ed. (Moscow: Bol'shaia sovetskaia entsiklopediia, 1949), IV:365–67.

119. Babilov, *Bol'shaia sovetskaia entsiklopediia*, 366. The speech that the encyclopedia quotes has been published as I. V. Stalin, *O nedostatkakh partiinoi raboty i merakh likvidatsii trotskistskikh i inykh dvurushnikov. Doklad i zakliuchitel'noe slovo na plenume TSK VKP(b) 3–5 marta 1937 g* (Moscow: Gospolitizat, 1954).

120. A. M. Prokhorov, ed., *Bol'shaia sovetskaia entsiklopediia*, 3rd ed. (Moscow: Sovetskaia entsiklopediia, 1970), III:71–72.

121. Indeed, as Lilya Kagonovsky noticed, the parallels between the circumstances of Kirov's 1934 assassination and *The Party Card* plot can hardly be accidental. Kaganovsky, "Visual Pleasure in Stalinist Cinema," 41.

122. Hannah Arendt, *The Origins of Totalitarianism* (New York: Meridian Books, 1958), 351.

123. For more audience responses in this vein, as well as an interesting reading of the gender politics of *The Party Card*, see Kaganovsky, "Visual Pleasure in Stalinist Cinema," 53–54.

124. Leonid Trauberg, "Kakim on byl . . . ," in *Ivan Pyr'ev v zhizni i na ekrane*, ed. Grigorii Mar'iamov (Moscow: Kinotsentr, 1994), 117.

125. Pyr'ev, "Pomnit' o nashem zritele," 7.

126. Ibid., 7–11.

127. Ibid., 11.

128. Ibid., 7.

129. Osaf Litovskii, "Fil'm o bditel'nosti," *Kino-gazeta*, March 30, 1936, 729.

130. Pyr'ev, "Pomnit' o nashem zritele," 7.

131. Ibid., 8.

132. David Bordwell, *Narration in the Fiction Film* (Madison: University of Wisconsin Press, 1985), 269, 238.

133. Pyr'ev, "Pomnit' o nashem zritele," 8.

134. David Bordwell, "Eisenstein, Socialist Realism, and the Charms of Mizanstsena," in *Eisenstein at 100*, ed. Al La Valley and Barry P. Scherr (New Brunswick: Routledge, 2001), 23.

135. Ibid., 21.

136. Ibid., 21–22.

137. For more on the difficulties encountered by the film from scenario to final version, see Kaganovsky, "Visual Pleasure in Stalinist Cinema," 38–40.

138. B. Z. Shumiatskii, "Moia kratkaia zapis' ukazanii i otsenki chernogo montazha fil'ma 'Anna' (pokazannogo bez kontsa, kotorogo eshche net). 28.II.36 g.," *Kinovedcheskie zapiski* 62 (2003): 163.

139. Peter Brooks, *The Melodramatic Imagination: Balzac, Henry James, Melodrama, and the Mode of Excess* (New York: Columbia University Press, 1985), 2.

140. Cited in ibid., 1.

141. Tom Gunning, "The Horror of Opacity: The Melodrama of Sensation in the Plays of André de Lorde," in *Melodrama: Stage, Picture, Screen*, ed. Jacky Bratton et al. (London: BFI, 1994), 54.

142. Ibid.

143. Shumiatskii, "Moia kratkaia zapis'," 163.

144. Allan Sekula, "The Body and the Archive," *October* 39, no. 4 (1986): 4.

145. Jonathan Crary, *Techniques of the Observer: On Vision and Modernity in the Nineteenth Century* (Cambridge: MIT Press, 1990), 13.

146. Tom Gunning, "Tracing the Individual Body," in *Cinema and the Invention of Modern Life*, ed. Leo Charney and Vanessa Schwartz (Berkeley: University of California Press, 1995), 19.

147. Sekula, "Body and the Archive," 7; Gunning, "Tracing the Individual Body," 19.

148. Sekula, "Body and the Archive," 27.

149. Stephen Kotkin, *Magnetic Mountain: Stalinism as a Civilization* (Berkeley: University of California Press, 1997), 100.

150. Getty, *Origins of the Great Purges*, 88.

151. Vitalii Shentalinskii, *Les surprises de la Loubianka: retour dans les archives littéraires du K.G.B.* (Paris: R. Laffont, 1996), 21. Sheila Fitzpatrick also attests that "impersonation of OGPU/NKVD personnel was a flourishing line of fraud" (Fitzpatrick, *Tear Off the Masks!*, 277). For a fascinating study of one particular case of such an impersonation see Alexopoulos, "Portrait of a Con Artist as a Soviet Man."

## Chapter 4

1. The polemic was published in *Pravda*, September 7, 1923, and October 2, 1923. Quoted in Richard Taylor, *The Politics of the Soviet Cinema, 1917–1929* (Cambridge: Cambridge University Press, 1979), 84.

2. Ibid., 84.

3. Quoted in ibid., 98.

4. Quoted in ibid.

5. "O politicheskikh techeniiakh v moskovskom obshchestve" cited in Izmozik, *Glaza i ushi rezhima*, 64.

6. Alexander Lemberg, "Iz vospominaniia starogo operatora," in *Iz istorii kino: materialy i dokumenty*, ed. S. S. Ginzburg (Moscow: Izdatel'stvo akademii nauk SSSR, 1959), 119.

7. The secret police was already in charge of a partial nationalization drive in January 1918 when they published a decree that granted "Soviets of Workers and Soldiers' Deputies . . . the right to requisition on behalf of the general public cinemas and their stock, together with the right of exhibition thereof" (quoted in Taylor, *Politics of the Soviet Cinema*, 44).

8. Graham Roberts, *Forward Soviet!: History and Non-fiction Film in the USSR* (London: I. B. Tauris, 1999), 16.

9. Taylor, *Politics of the Soviet Cinema*, 99–100.

10. Quoted in ibid., 99.

11. Ibid., 101, 175.

12. Denise J. Youngblood, *Movies for the Masses: Popular Cinema and Soviet Society in the 1920s* (Cambridge: Cambridge University Press, 1992), 26.

13. Taylor, *Politics of the Soviet Cinema*, 100.

14. A. A. Cherkasov, *Solovki* (Moscow: Sovkino, 1927–28).

15. B. Solonevich, *Molodezh' i G.P.U.* (Sofia: Golos Rossii 1937), 312; cited in Natalia

Kuziakina, *Theatre in the Solovki Prison Camp*, trans. Boris M. Meerovich (Luxembourg: Harwood Academic, 1995), 20.

16.  Sergei A. Malsagov, *An Island Hell: A Soviet Prison in the Far North* (London: A. M. Philpot, 1926). For more on the campaign prompted by Malsagov's memoir see Dariusz Tolczyk, *See No Evil: Literary Cover-Ups and Discoveries of the Soviet Camp Experience* (New Haven: Yale University Press, 1999), 118.

17.  The most well-known description of Solovki can be found in Alexander Solzhenitsyn, *The Gulag Archipelago: An Experiment in Literary Investigation*, vol. 2 (New York: Harper and Row, 1975), 36–63. Another classic memoir devoted to life in Solovki and Belomor is Ivan Luk'ianovich Solonevich, *Rossiia v kontslagere* (Moscow: Redaktsiia zhurnala "Moskva," 1999). A courageous, and fascinating, documentary filmed during *glasnost'* is Marina Goldovskaya, *Vlast' solovetskaia/Solovky Power* (Moscow-San Francisco: Kinostudiia "Mosfil'm," The Video project, 1989).

18.  The typhus epidemic on Solovki had two peaks, in the winter of 1928 and 1929–30. Kuziakina, *Theatre in the Solovki Prison Camp*, 21, 88.

19.  The reports of the OGPU-appointed Shanin commission, which investigated the performance of supervisory staff in 1928–29 and gave horrifying details on prisoner abuse, are available in Vsesoiuznoe istoriko-prosvetitel'skoe obshchestvo "Memorial," *Zven'ia*, 2 vols., vol. 1 (Moscow: Progress, 1991), 357–88.

20.  Berman's reminiscences were published in Maxim Gorky et al., *Belomorsko-Baltiiskii kanal imeni Stalina: istoriia stroitel'stva* (Moscow: Gos. izd-vo "Istoriia fabrik i zavodov," 1934), 69, 78.

21.  This summary of the history of the criminology museum is based on an interview with Rostislav Liubvin, researcher at the Saint Petersburg Museum of the Militia (the present-day name of the museum), published in Oleg Syromiatnikov, "Kastet byl—Kastet ostalsia," Kollektsiia N.G., http://dlib.eastview.com/sources/article.jsp?id=3218639.

22.  Viktor Bobykin, "Kartina dnia. Nashlas' golova Len'ki Panteleeva!," Komsomol'skaia pravda, http://dlib.eastview.com/sources/article.jsp?id=3231565.

23.  Maxim Gorky, "V. Solovki," in *Sobranie sochinenii v tridtsati tomakh* (Moscow: Gosudarstvennoe izdatel'stvo, 1952).

24.  Sergei Eisenstein et al., "Bezhin Meadow (Reconstruction)," in *Alexander Nevsky* (Irvington, NY: Criterion Collection, 2001).

25.  Sergei Eisenstein, "Montage and Architecture," *Assemblage* 10 (1989).

26.  On playing cards and postcards see Kuziakina, *Theatre in the Solovki Prison Camp*, 149.

27.  Ibid., 91.

28.  On cinema as a "spectatorial means of transportation" see Giuliana Bruno, *Atlas of Emotion: Journeys in Art, Architecture, and Film* (New York: Verso, 2002), 20.

29.  Maxim Gorky et al., *Belomor: An Account of the Construction of the New Canal Between the White Sea and the Baltic Sea* (New York: H. Smith and R. Haas, 1935), 18–21.

30.  Some of the activities of this map division are revealed in declassified NKVD documents, Fond R-6890 in the Archives of the Soviet Communist Party and Soviet State in Moscow. The informative finding aid to this Fond is available in the United States: *Opis', Fond r-6890, RSFSR NKVD: Map publishing*, Archives of the Soviet Com-

munist Party and Soviet State: Microfilm Collection, Box no. 3.314, Hoover Institution Archives.

31. For a concise account of the introduction of internal passports see Sheila Fitzpatrick, *Everyday Stalinism: Ordinary Life in Extraordinary Times: Soviet Russia in the 1930s* (New York: Oxford University Press, 1999), 120–22.

32. Gilles Deleuze, *Cinema 1: The Movement-Image* (Minneapolis: University of Minnesota Press, 1986), 22.

33. The following short account of the history of Solovki theater is based on Kuziakina, *Theatre in the Solovki Prison Camp*.

34. Ibid., 63.

35. Ibid., 69.

36. Ibid., 91.

37. Gorky, "V. Solovki," 225–26.

38. Tolczyk, *See No Evil*, 118.

39. Gorky, "V. Solovki," 226.

40. Gorky, *Literaturnoe nasledstvo*, no. 70, pp. 33–34, quoted in Tolczyk, *See No Evil*, 149.

41. Given that Gorky spent three days on Solovki (June 20–23, 1929), he hardly had time to attend all the shows and tours that his OGPU guides had organized for him (Gorky, "V. Solovki," 226). As a result there are few spontaneous scenes of camp life described in the travelogue; the few there are, he carefully notes as confirmation of the overall picture of the camp. But from the very first page of the travelogue, Gorky appears more interested in panoramic views of Solovki and in compiling written sources on its history than in detailed empirical observation (201). A telling example is Gorky's account of his trip to Sekirnaia Gora, the mountain where the feared punishment cells on Solovki were located. Gorky glosses over the immediate sight of the punishment cells, and instead turns his gaze to the beauty of the distant panorama offered by the mountain's elevation (201).

42. Ibid., 225.

43. Solonevich, *Molodezh i G.P.U*, 312; cited in Kuziakina, *Theatre in the Solovki Prison Camp*, 20.

44. Tolczyk gives various examples of the Soviet practice of constructing "entire Potemkin villages" to cover up the reality of the camps, including the disguise of OGPU officers' wives as prisoners. Tolczyk, *See No Evil*, 114.

45. Dziga Vertov started *The Man with a Movie Camera* in 1926, and showed parts of it first in 1927–28. The first showing of the complete film took place in Kiev in January 1929. Roberts, *Forward Soviet!*, 171.

46. Edgar Morin, "Chronicle of a Film," *Studies in Visual Communication* 11, no. 1 (1985): 4.

47. One such moment of life-caught-unawares is movingly documented in Marina Goldovskaya's *Solovky Power*, where one of the camp's survivors recognizes himself in *Solovki* as a young man reading a newspaper while unwittingly captured by camera.

48. Roberts, *Forward Soviet!*, 163.

49. Gorky, "V. Solovki," 201.

50. Maya Turovskaya, "The 1930s and 1940s: Cinema in Context," in *Stalinism and*

*Soviet Cinema*, ed. Richard Taylor (London: Routledge, 1993), 45. According to Denise J. Youngblood, *"A Start in Life* earned 15 million rubles, far exceeding the previous record, *Miss Mend*'s 3.1 million" (Youngblood, *Movies for the Masses*, 173).

51. This reminiscence belongs to Lidiia Lubedinskaia and is recorded in the transcript of a *Radio Svoboda* round table about *Putevka v zhizn'* moderated by Sergei Iur'enen, "Putevka v zhizn'," http://www.svoboda.org/programs/cicles/cinema/russian/RoadToLife.asp.

52. The French Communist Party (PCF) censured the surrealists' criticism of the film as expressed in Ferdinand Alquié, letter to André Breton of March 7, 1933, published in *Le surréalisme au service de la révolution 5* (Paris), May 15, 1933, 43. As a result, the Surrealists broke their allegiance to the Association des Écrivains et Artistes Révolutionnaires (AEAR), the PCF's cultural front organization. For more on this conflict see Paul Hammond, "Bunuel Bows Out," *Rouge* 1, no. 3 (2004), http://www.rouge.com.au/3/bunuel.html.

53. Ekk was singularly fitted for this task. His career was marked by a fascination for experiments: he was the director not only of the first major Soviet sound feature film but also of the first color film, the first adaptation of Shakespeare, and the first stereoscopic film that dispensed with special glasses. Iur'enen, "Putevka v zhizn'," 2.

54. Jay Leyda, *Kino: A History of the Russian and Soviet Film* (Princeton: Princeton University Press, 1983), 284.

55. Lidiia Lebedinskaia, who watched the film upon its release in 1931, comments, "I must say that the homeless children were a very sensitive problem in Moscow; there was such a scourge, that you could practically not go out into the streets. Everybody denigrated them . . . except I think my grandmother, who said that you should not judge them, since they are the victims of the world cataclysm" (Iur'enen, "Putevka v zhizn'").

56. Makarenko published his *Pedagogicheskaia poema,* literally translated as *The Peda-gogical Poem* but more commonly translated into English as *Road to Life,* in 1934–35, after the release of Ekk's *Road to Life* (1931). It is likely that the translation of the title was trying to capitalize on the film's success in the West. Both the film and the book cover roughly the same founding period of the juvenile detention colonies, i.e. the early 1920s. Anton Semenovich Makarenko, *Pedagogicheskaia poema* (Moscow: Gos. izd-vo khudozh. literaturu, 1952); Makarenko, *Road to Life,* trans. Stephen Garry (London: Stanley Nott, 1936).

57. Makarenko, *Road to Life,* 19.

58. Ibid., 20.

59. Ibid., 161.

60. Oscar Fricke, "The Dzerzhinsky Commune: Birth of the Soviet 35mm Camera Industry," *History of Photography* 3, no. 2 (1979): 7. My page references are based on the web edition, http://www.fedka.com/Useful_info/Commune_by_Fricke/commune_A.htm.

61. Ibid., 8.

62. Ibid., 13.

63. *Sovkinozhurnal No.14* (1939).

64. "The announcement [of the Cheka's intervention] caused quite a stir, it seems,

and even the *Narkompros* journal carried an article largely devoted to calming its readers" (Fricke, "Dzerzhinsky Commune," 34).

65. The very setting of the commune in a remote and impressive old monastery strongly resembles Solovki. We are never told where exactly the commune is located, but its connection to the rest of the country is fragile enough that when the spring floods come, the communards are completely cut off. Through labor, however, the children build their way back to the Soviet society; their "road to life" is literally embodied in their grand construction project, a train line that (re)connects them to the rest of the country.

66. Interview with Edgar Morin, cited in "Mémoire de cinéphiles," Fiches Cinéma Spécial 70 ans, http://www.crdp.ac-nice.fr/cannes2004/cinephilie. htm.

67. Peter Cowie, *Revolution!: The Explosion of World Cinema in the Sixties* (London: Faber and Faber, 2004), 2.

68. Iur'enen, "Putevka v zhizn'."

69. Ibid., Maya Turovskaya interview. This theatrical dedication to Dzerzhinsky, originally superimposed over an image of his bust, was cut in the version of the film distributed in the United States.

70. In his groundbreaking analysis of realist conventions, Roland Barthes singled out details that neither advance the narrative nor easily lend themselves to symbolic interpretation as a key ingredient of what he termed *l'effet de réel* [realist effect]. Roland Barthes, "L'effet de réel," in *Le bruissement de la langue: Essais critiques IV* (Paris: Seuil, 1984), 141–46.

71. As we have seen in the first chapter, the elusiveness of the criminal's identity in growing urban centers is also at the origin of modern criminology.

72. As Hannah Arendt famously argued, in totalitarian societies the spectacle of secrecy was necessary to camouflage the absence of a real secret. Hannah Arendt, *The Origins of Totalitarianism* (New York: Meridian Books, 1958), 351–73.

73. Another key moment structured around this ambiguity is the children's march to the special commission. An impressive number of heavily armed policemen precipitately appear ready to violently oppose the crowd of marching children. When a social worker informs them that the children are marching to voluntarily join the commune, the expression of the policemen dramatically shifts to gleeful kindness.

74. *Belomor* proudly documents this divide-and-conquer tactic in action. In his inaugural speech to the whole camp, commander Berman divides the camp population into common and political prisoners, and asks the common prisoners to "help us to take care of and reeducate the counterrevolutionaries" (Gorky et al., *Belomorsko*, 116–21).

75. Edgar Allan Poe, "Philosophical Composition," in *The Complete Poems and Stories of Edgar Allan Poe, with Selections from His Critical Writings* (New York: Alfred A. Knopf, 1958), 982.

76. Tolczyk, *See No Evil*, 121.

77. An English edition was promptly prepared in Moscow, but it often diverges from the original text. Therefore, unless otherwise noted, all translations from the Russian are mine. Gorky et al., *Belomor*. In the following, I will refer to the Russian edition as *Belomorsko*, and to the English edition as *Belomor*.

78. The third editor was Leopold Averbakh, leader of the Russian Association of Proletarian Writers (RAPP).

79. Gorky et al., *Belomorsko*, 407.

80. Cynthia Ann Ruder, *Making History for Stalin: The Story of the Belomor Canal* (Gainesville: University Press of Florida, 1998), 47–52.

81. Rodchenko also published a selection of these photographs in a special issue of the oversize, lavishly illustrated journal *SSSR na stroike*, a journal that was simultaneously produced in Russian, English, and German. G. Piatakov, *USSR in Construction*, English ed., vol. 12 (Moscow: State Publishing House of the RSFSR, 1933). For more about Rodchenko's work on Belomorstroi, see Margarita Tupitsyn, *The Soviet Photograph, 1924–1937* (New Haven: Yale University Press, 1996), 136–38.

82. Iu. Poliakov and S. Drobashenko, *Sovetskaia kinokhronika: 1918–1925*, vol. 1 (Moscow: Tsentral'nyi arkhiv fotodokumentov, 1965), 42–43; Alexander Lemberg, *Port piati morei* [Port to Five Seas], Vostokfil'm, 1932–33; *Belomorstroi raportuet* [Belomor reports]. Leningradskaia studiia Soiuzkinokhroniki, 1933; *Belomorsko-Baltiiskii vodnyi put'* [Belomor-Baltic Canal], Vostokfil'm, 1935.(?).

83. Cynthia Ruder has dedicated a thorough monograph to the construction of the Belomor canal, including detailed analysis and informative literary history of *Belomorsko;* see Ruder, *Making History for Stalin*. Dariusz Tolczyk also provides an excellent analysis of Belomor; see Dariusz Tolczyk, "The Glory of the Gulag: Stalin's Camps as Social Medicine," in Tolczyk, *See No Evil*. However, no critic has paid sustained attention to the visual aspect of the Belomor project.

84. Gorky et al., *Belomor*, vi–vii.

85. Quoted in Tolczyk, *See No Evil*, 152.

86. Ibid., 153.

87. Ruder, *Making History for Stalin*, 79.

88. Mikhail Zoshchenko, "Istoriia odnoi perekovki," in *Belomorsko-Baltiiskii kanal imeni Stalina: istoriia stroitel'stva*, ed. Maxim Gorky et al. (Moscow: Gos. izd-vo "Istoriia fabrik i zavodov," 1934), 323.

89. Ibid., 323.

90. Ibid.

91. Alexander Rodchenko, "Perestroika khudozhnika," *Sovetskoe foto* 5–6 (1936). This paragraph's translation comes from Tupitsyn, *The Soviet Photograph*, 136–37.

92. Ibid., 342.

93. Ibid.

94. A. Zorich, "From Volkhovstroi," in *Dnieprostroi: The Biggest Dam in the World*, ed. D. Saslavskii (Moscow: International Press, 1932).

95. Ibid., 16.

96. Ibid., 21.

97. Ibid.

98. Gorky et al., *Belomor*, 20.

99. Tolczyk, *See No Evil*, xix.

100. The story of one such prisoner begins, "Not everyone worked conscientiously. There were among the prisoners incorrigible idlers who refused to work, and skirted for months. . . . And there were wreckers" (Gorky et al., *Belomor*, 176).

101. Gorky et al., *Belomorsko*, 275.

102. Gorky, "V. Solovki," 229–32.
103. Gorky et al., *Belomorsko*, 23.
104. Gorky et al., *Belomor* 236–37.
105. Gorky et al., *Belomorsko*, 466.
106. Ibid., 467.
107. Gorky et al., *Belomor*, 467.
108. Gorky et al., *Belomorsko*, 387.

109. Alphonse Bertillon, *Identification anthropométrique: instructions signalétiques* (Melun: Typographie-lithographie administrative, 1885), 99. Cited in Christian Phéline, "L'image accusatrice," *Les Cahiers de la Photographie* 17 (1985): 101.

110. Gorky et al., *Belomor*, 237.
111. Gorky et al., *Belomorsko*, 384.

112. The 1935 English translation is even more telling than the original: "But if we look attentively for *the impress of their biographies, which has eaten into their skin and muscle . . ."* (Gorky et al., *Belomor*, 325, emphasis mine).

113. Gorky et al., *Belomorsko*, 383–84.
114. Ibid., 324.
115. Zoshchenko, "Istoriia odnoi perekovki," 324.
116. Ibid., 341.
117. Gorky et al., *Belomor*, vi–vii.

118. Katerina Clark, *The Soviet Novel: History as Ritual* (Chicago: University of Chicago Press, 1981), 46.

## Chapter 5

An earlier version of this chapter was published as Cristina Vatulescu, "The Politics of Estrangement: Tracking Shklovsky's Device Through Literary and Policing Practices," *Poetics Today* 27, no. 1 (2006).

1. Walter Benjamin, "Conversations with Brecht," in *Aesthetics and Politics*, ed. Ronald Taylor (London: Verso NLB, 1977), 87.

2. Viktor Shklovsky, *A Sentimental Journey: Memoirs, 1917–1922*, trans. Richard Sheldon (Ithaca: Cornell University Press, 1970), 245; Shklovsky, *Sentimental'noe puteshestvie: vospominaniia, 1917–1922* (Moscow-Berlin: Gelikon, 1923), 345. Throughout this chapter, I use Richard Sheldon's and Benjamin Sher's translations with slight modifications.

3. Benjamin, "Conversations with Brecht," 88.

4. Brecht coined his famous term *Verfremdung* [estrangement] during his visit to Moscow in 1935. Before that, and thus at the time of his conversation with Benjamin in 1934, "he had used Entfremdung (distancing) for the defamiliarization necessary to stop an event from seeming natural, readily acceptable: in his native dialect, entfremden and verfremden are synonymous" (Ronald Hayman, *Brecht: A Biography* [Oxford: Oxford University Press, 1983], 189). After 1935, Brecht used *Entfremdung* specifically for estrangement in the Marxist-informed sense of alienation, a negative phenomenon that artistic estrangement (*Verfremdung*) was designed to expose and resist. By changing the prefix of the existing noun *Entfremdung* to *Verfremdung,* Brecht emphasized the difference between his new term and Marx's negative term; but by choosing to keep the

same root, he reminded us of their fundamental connection. As a result, *Entfremdung*'s "deformation" into the artistic *Verfremdung* does not break its ties to its former political past; rather, it makes it better fit to expose the negative effects of the political term. In Brecht's work after 1935, estrangement [*Verfremdung*] works as a vaccine against alienation [*Entfremdung*] developed by using the elements of that alienation as antibodies.

5. Fredric Jameson, *The Prison-House of Language: A Critical Account of Structuralism and Russian Formalism* (Princeton: Princeton University Press, 1974), 58.

6. Ibid., 71. For Jameson's account of Shklovsky's estrangement, see "The Formalist Projection," especially pages 50–75.

7. G. Gorbachev, "My eshche ne nachinali drat'sia," *Zvezda*, 1930. Quoted in Viktor Erlich, *Russian Formalism. History—Doctrine* (London: Mouton, 1965), 138. For a detailed account of the relationship between Marxist and Formalist critics see "Marxism Versus Formalism," in Erlich, *Russian Formalism,* 99–117.

8. As William Mills Todd III showed, this recognition was the exception rather than the rule: "Certainly [the Formalists'] early polemical opposition to sociological and ideological analyses of art made them an inviting target for such powerful opponents as Trotsky (1924) and Bakhtin (1928), both of whose works, however, drew exclusively on the early Formalist statements and could not take fully into account the sociologically significant Formalist studies that began to appear during the middle and late 1920s, such as Tynianov's "The Literary Fact" (1924) . . . and Shklovsky's "In Defense of the Sociological Method" (1927). . . . With few exceptions, the Western reception of Formalism has likewise focused upon their early activities" (William Mills Todd III, "Literature as an Institution: Fragments of a Formalist Theory," in *Russian Formalism: A Retrospective Glance*, ed. Robert Louis Jackson and Stephen Rudy [New Haven: Yale Center for International and Area Studies, 1985], 16).

9. Mikhail Bakhtin and Pavel Medvedev, *The Formal Method in Literary Scholarship: A Critical Introduction to Sociological Poetics*, trans. Albert J. Wehle (Cambridge: Harvard University Press, 1985), 69.

10. Erlich, *Russian Formalism,* 179.

11. Jurij Striedter, *Literary Structure, Evolution, and Value: Russian Formalism and Czech Structuralism Reconsidered* (Cambridge: Harvard University Press, 1989), 24.

12. Ibid., 23.

13. Svetlana Boym, "Estrangement as a Lifestyle: Shklovsky and Brodsky," in *Exile and Creativity*, ed. Susan Suleiman (Durham: Duke University Press, 1998), 243.

14. Galin Tikhanov, "Politics of Estrangement: The Case of the Early Shklovsky," *Poetics Today* 26, no. 4 (2005).

15. Viktor Shklovsky, *Theory of Prose*, trans. Benjamin Sher (Elmwood Park, IL: Dalkey Archive Press, 1990), 5–6.

16. Ibid., 5.

17. Benjamin Sher, "Translator's Introduction: Shklovsky and the Revolution," in Shklovsky, *Theory of Prose*, xix.

18. Shklovsky, *Theory of Prose*, 6.

19. Ibid., 3.

20. Ibid., 6.

21. Ibid., 14.

22. Ibid., 6.

23. Ibid., 6, 17.

24. Ibid., 13.

25. Ibid., 61–63. "Stroenie rasskaza i romana" was first published in *Zhizn' iskusstva*, January 11, 1920, 348; my references are to its reprint in Viktor Shklovsky, *O teorii prozy* (Moscow: Federatsiia, 1929), 61.

26. Shklovsky, *Sentimental Journey*, 134; Shklovsky, *Sentimental'noe puteshestvie*, 188.

27. Shklovsky, *Sentimental Journey*, 184; Shklovsky, *Sentimental'noe puteshestvie*, 259.

28. Shklovsky, *Sentimental Journey*, 271.

29. Ibid.; Shklovsky, *Sentimental'noe puteshestvie*, 383.

30. Viktor Shklovsky, *Khod konia: sbornik statei* (Moscow-Berlin: Gelikon, 1923), 201.

31. Shklovsky, *Sentimental Journey*, 126.

32. Ibid., 216–19.

33. Ibid., 134; Shklovsky, *Sentimental'noe puteshestvie*, 188.

34. Shklovsky, *Sentimental Journey*, 142.

35. Richard Sheldon, "Introduction to *A Sentimental Journey*," in *Sentimental Journey* (Ithaca: Cornell, 1970), xiii. For a history of the strained relationship between the Socialist Revolutionaries and the Bolsheviks see Mark Jansen, "The Socialist Revolutionaries and the Soviet Regime," in *A Show Trial Under Lenin* (The Hague: Martinus Hijhoff, 1982).

36. Shklovsky, *Sentimental Journey*, 184.

37. Ibid., 153.

38. Ibid., 141.

39. Ibid., 151. Shklovsky, *Sentimental'noe puteshestvie*, 212–13.

40. Shklovsky, *Sentimental Journey*, 24; Shklovsky, *Sentimental'noe puteshestvie*, 34.

41. "How Don Quixote Is Made" [Kak sdelan "Don Kikhot"] is the title of Shklovsky's famous Formalist reading of Cervantes' novel, included in Shklovsky, *Theory of Prose*, 72–101.

42. Shklovsky, *Sentimental Journey*, 133.

43. Ibid., 188.

44. Ibid., 133; Shklovsky, *Sentimental'noe puteshestvie*, 188.

45. One of the many contemporary examples of such accusations is Georgii Gorbachev's assessment of the darling of Formalist narrative studies, *skaz*: "The most important thing in the "skaz" style is the possibility to hide one's authorial face from the public, to express some of one's authorial ideas, while not taking responsibility for them personally" (quoted in Boris Eikhenbaum, "V ozhidanii literatury," in *Literatura. Teoriia. Kritika. Polemika* [Leningrad: Priboi, 1927], 288).

46. Sidney Monas, "Driving Nails with a Samovar: A Historical Introduction," in *Sentimental Journey* (Ithaca: Cornell University Press, 1970), xxxvii.

47. Ibid.

48. Shklovsky, *Sentimental Journey*, 184–85.

49. Julie Cassiday, *The Enemy on Trial: Early Soviet Courts on Stage and Screen* (DeKalb: Northern Illinois University Press, 2000), 44.

50. Monas, "Driving Nails with a Samovar," xxix.

51.  Quoted in Cassiday, *Enemy on Trial*, 115. Indeed, in the 1920s, autobiography emerged as a privileged genre of the new Soviet regime. Thus many communications between the citizen and the state, whether denunciations, letters to the editor, or party membership applications were routinely prefaced by the autobiography of the writer. For a thorough account of autobiography in party membership applications, see Igal Halfin, *Terror in My Soul: Communist Autobiographies on Trial* (Cambridge: Harvard University Press, 2003).

52.  In "Investigative Methods of the Secret Police," A. Grigoriev accurately asserts that "[In] its 'classic' form an interrogation begins by having the prisoner fill out a detailed questionnaire and write his autobiography and a list of his acquaintances" (New York: Frederick A. Praeger, 1957], 229).

53.  Shklovsky, *Sentimental Journey*, 151.

54.  Jean-Jacques Rousseau, *Les confessions* (Paris: Garnier-Flammarion, 1968), 43.

55.  Mikhail Bakhtin, *The Dialogic Imagination*, trans. Mikhail Holquist and Caryl Emerson (Austin: University of Texas Press, 1981), 350.

56.  Althusser's illustration of interpellation is the policeman's address to the passerby: "'Hey, you there!' . . . the hailed individual will turn round. By this mere one-hundred-and-eighty-degree physical conversion, he becomes a *subject*" (Louis Althusser, "Ideology and Ideological State Apparatuses," in *Lenin and Philosophy and Other Essays* [New York: Monthly Review Press, 1972], 174).

57.  I am here in agreement with Eric Naiman's assessment of Igal Halfin's and Jochen Hellbeck's fascinating work on Soviet subjectivity as expressed in Eric Naiman, "On Soviet Subjects and the Scholars Who Make Them," *Russian Review* 60, no. July (2001). In their programmatic attempt to read the Soviet text rather than read between the lines, these scholars too often take that text at face value, ignoring the subjects' possible distancing and manipulations of the text.

58.  While the scenario of these later trials was established in the 1930s in Moscow, its influence spread throughout the Soviet bloc for decades after. For a fascinating study of the poetics of these later show trials, see Peter Steiner, "Justice in Prague, Political and Poetic: Some Reflections on the Slánský Trial (with Constant Reference to Franz Kafka and Milan Kundera)," *Poetics Today* 21, no. 4 (2000): 653–79.

59.  Cassiday, *Enemy on Trial*, 47.

60.  Viktor Shklovsky, *Zoo, or, Letters Not About Love* (Ithaca: Cornell University Press, 1971), 103–4.

61.  Quoted in Richard Sheldon, "Introduction: Viktor Shklovsky and the Device of Ostensible Surrender," in Viktor Shklovsky, *Third Factory* (Ann Arbor: Ardis, 1977), xi.

62.  Ibid., x.

63.  Halfin, *Terror in My Soul*, 236.

64.  Ibid., 162.

65.  Ibid., 180.

66.  Ibid., 231.

67.  Shklovsky, *Sentimental Journey*, 141; Shklovsky, *Sentimental'noe puteshestvie*, 198.

68.  Shklovsky, *Third Factory*, 22.

69.  Ibid., 8; Viktor Shklovsky, *Tret'ia fabrika* (Moscow: Krug, 1926), 16.

70. Karl Marx, *Capital: A Critique of Political Economy* (New York: International Publishers, 1967), 83.

71. Stelian Tănase, *Anatomia mistificării* (Bucharest: Humanitas, 2003), 371–72. The legal indictment was "plotting against the social order" [*uneltire împotriva ordinii sociale*]. One of the defendants asked at the end of the trial "what fighting against the social order meant. The president of the tribunal answered: 'It could mean a gesture, a smile'" (ibid., 367). Tănase's *Anatomia mistificării* is an excellent source for the study of this case, bringing together investigation and trial documents, as well as letters, memoirs, and interviews with survivors.

72. This account is based on my reading of Steinhardt's secret police file, *Dosar de urmărire informativă nr. 49342, I 207* Fond Informativ (ACNSAS). The summary of the investigation regarding *Happiness Journal* is found in "Notă-Raport privind lucrarea intitulată 'Jurnalul fericirii' redactată de Steinhardt Nicu," 103/A/CI/ 21 December 1972 [Report concerning the work titled "Happiness Journal" written by Steinhardt Nicu].

73. The denunciation is found in ibid., IV:276. The admission that this denunciation was fabricated by the secret police appears in ibid, V:85. During the first week of Steinhardt's interrogation in January 1960, the secret police had already managed to pressure him into admitting to having been charged with homosexuality in 1949: "Proces verbal de interogator, 8.01.1960," *Dosar penal nr. 118988, P 336*, vol. III (ACNSAS), III:292. The secret police commonly blackmailed homosexuals and threatened them with exposure through public trials. Charges of homosexuality previously initiated the legal action against one of Steinhardt's codefendants, Mihai Rădulescu. After the trial that condemned him to prison for homosexuality, Rădulescu was taken directly to the secret police headquarters, where he was charged with participating in the same subversive group as Steinhardt. Rădulescu died during this investigation after being severely tortured. It is still unclear whether he died as the immediate result of this abuse or whether he committed suicide. Tănase, *Anatomia mistificării*, 281–82.

74. Ibid.

75. Nicolae Steinhardt, *Jurnalul Fericirii* (Cluj: Dacia, 1997), 12. All translations from Romanian to English are mine.

76. Roland Barthes famously unmasked realism's attempt to hide its devices and pass itself off as unmediated reality. Bender traced his understanding of realism to Barthes's definition: "[n]ot only do signifier and signified seem to unite, but in this confusion, the signifier seems to be erased or to become transparent so as to let the concept present itself just as if it were referring to nothing but its own presence" (quoted in John Bender, *Imagining the Penitentiary* [Chicago: University of Chicago Press, 1987], 210).

77. Quoted in Erlich, *Russian Formalism*, 11.

78. Ibid., 179–80.

79. Steinhardt, *Jurnalul Fericirii*, 13.

80. Ibid., 12.

81. Ibid., 17.

82. Ibid., 15.

83. Ibid., 12.

84. Ibid., 13.

85.   Central Intelligence Agency, *Human Resource Exploitation Training Manual* (1983). This manual was largely based on its predecessor, Central Intelligence Agency, *Kubark Counterintelligence Interrogation* (1963). Many changes are written in by hand over still legible deleted phrases, so that it is relatively easy to monitor them. The changes are mostly directed against the use of radical coercive techniques such as severe physical torture and narcosis. Both manuals were declassified in 1997 in response to a Freedom of Information Act request filed by the *Baltimore Sun* in 1994. (*Kubark* is a CIA code name for itself.)

86.   Central Intelligence Agency, *Kubark*, 86.

87.   Ibid., 46.

88.   Ibid., 89.

89.   Ibid., 86.

90.   Ibid., 53.

91.   Ibid., 86.

92.   Ibid., 87.

93.   Ibid., 76.

94.   Central Intelligence Agency, *Human Resource*, L-17.

95.   Central Intelligence Agency, *Kubark*, 66.

96.   Ibid., 31.

97.   Ibid., 50.

98.   Ibid., 85, 40.

99.   Ibid., 52.

100.   Ibid., 75.

101.   Lawrence Hinkle and Harold Wolff, "Communist Interrogation and Indoctrination of 'Enemies of State': Analysis of Methods Used by the Communist Secret Police (A Special Report)," *A.M.A. Archives of Neurology and Psychiatry* 76, no. 2 (1956): 125–30. Leonard Hilden, "Conditioned Reflex, Drugs and Hypnosis in Communist Interrogations," *Studies in Intelligence* 2 (Spring 1958): 61–62. The most thorough of these studies is "Communist Interrogation and Indoctrination of 'Enemies of State'," written by two men who "played central roles in setting up the Society for the Investigation of Human Ecology, perhaps the most important academic cover organization for the mind-control programs of the CIA. . . . Wolff was president of the New York Neurological Association; later on he became president of the American Neurological Association. Hinkle was a professor at Cornell University" (István Rév, "The Suggestion," *Representations* 80 [Fall 2002]: 86–87). These studies point out that the Soviet "doctrine was developed and organized by the police officials themselves" ("Conditioned Reflex," Hilden, 59) and "developed through trial and error" ("Communist Interrogation," Hinkle and Wolff, 150), in contrast to American investigation manuals, like the *Kubark*, which relied heavily on psychological research (Central Intelligence Agency, *Kubark*, 2).

102.   Aleksander Wat, *Mój wiek: pamiętnik mówiony* (London: Polonia Books Fund, 1977), 2:38–39, quoted in Tomas Venclova, *Aleksander Wat: Life and Art of an Iconoclast* (New Haven: Yale University Press, 1996), 142.

103.   Alexander Solzhenitsyn, *The Gulag Archipelago: An Experiment in Literary Investigation*, vol. 2 (New York: Harper and Row, 1975), 46.

104.   Ibid., 51.

105.  Ibid., 63–64.

106.  Steinhardt, *Jurnalul Fericirii*, 6.

107.  Ibid., 13.

108.  Ibid., 12–13.

109.  Ibid., 12.

110.  Ibid., 169.

111.  Ibid., 14.

112.  Central Intelligence Agency, *Kubark*, 58.

113.  Hinkle and Wolff, "Communist Interrogation," 141.

114.  Joseph Brodsky, *Less Than One* (New York: Farrar, Strauss and Giroux, 1985), 7–8.

115.  Ibid., 3.

116.  Steinhardt, *Jurnalul Fericirii*, 240.

117.  The *Kubark* ends by drawing this distinction: unlike Western services, whose ultimate goal is to collect information, "the last step in an interrogation conducted by a Communist service is the attempted conversion" (103).

118.  My account of reeducation draws on the authoritative history of the Romanian secret service by Dennis Deletant, *Ceaușescu and the Securitate: Coercion and Dissent in Romania, 1965–1989* (London: Hurst, 1995), 29–51.

119.  D. Bacu, quoted in ibid., 38.

120.  Nicolae Steinhardt, *Monologul polifonic* (Cluj: Dacia, 1991), 61.

121.  Ibid., 62.

122.  Steinhardt, *Jurnalul Fericirii*, 84.

123.  Ibid., 51.

124.  Ibid., 52.

125.  Benjamin, "Conversations with Brecht," 87.

126.  Sher, "Translator's Introduction," xix.

## Concluding Thoughts

1.  Arhiva S.R.I., Fond Penal, *Dosar nr. 40038/22* (1959). I am grateful to the filmmaker Irene Lusztig, Monica Sevianu's granddaughter, for sharing her copies of the files and of *Reconstruction* with me.

2.  The Kundera scandal is summarized in Rachel Donadio, "Report Says Acclaimed Czech Writer Informed on a Supposed Spy," *New York Times*, October 16, 2008. The original Czech police document and its English translation are available at http://www.ustrcr.cz/en/recollections-of-anti-communist-fighters-and-resistants-miroslav-dvoracek. For a thoughtful close reading of the Kundera scandal, see Jonathan Bolton and Karel Hvížďala, "O úskalích překladu i 'kauze Kundera' s bohemistou z Harvardu," *Mladá fronta DNES*, September 19 2009. I thank Jonathan Bolton for sharing with me the English translation of his article and for enlightening exchanges about this case. The István Szabó scandal, together with other intensely debated Hungarian informer cases is covered in István Deák, "Scandal in Budapest," *New York Review of Books* 53, no. 16 (2006). The Constantin Noica scandal is analyzed in the prefaces to his published secret police files, Dora Mezdrea, ed., *Constantin Noica in arhiva Securității* (Bucharest: Humanitas, 2009).

3. A good example of a file is *Dosar penal nr. 118988, P 336*, vol. III (ACNSAS). For example, vol. VIII, dedicated to *corpora delicti*, contains a photographic reproduction of Emil Cioran's "Lettre à un ami lointain," and the original edition of Mircea Eliade's *Forêt interdite*, the reading of which constituted one of the main accusations against Steinhardt's group, as well as motley original manuscripts and reproductions. The x-ray is lodged in vol. XIV:54.

4. "collate" in *The Oxford English Dictionary* (Oxford: Oxford University Press, 2008), my emphasis.

5. Nicolae Steinhardt, *Jurnalul Fericirii* (Cluj: Dacia, 1997), 12.

6. The phrase is taken from Nadezhda Mandel'shtam's memoirs, where she poignantly wonders: "Who is likely to search through these grisly archives for the sake of Mandel'shtam?" Nadezhda Mandel'shtam, *Hope Against Hope: A Memoir*, trans. Max Hayward (New York: Modern Library, 1983), 401.

7. Jacques Derrida, *Writing and Difference*, trans. Alan Bass (London: Routledge, 2001), 110.

8. Hannah Arendt, *The Origins of Totalitarianism* (New York: Meridian Books, 1958), 443.

9. Marina Goldovskaya, *Zhenshchina s kinoapparatom* (Moscow: Materik, 2002), 152.

10. Primo Levi, *Survival in Auschwitz*, trans. Stuart Woolf (New York: Collier Books, 1987).

11. Steinhardt, *Jurnalul Fericirii*, 13.

# Index